Maternal Failure

a memoir

Barb Baltrinic

Dedicated to my husband, Michael Baltrinic,
who stood by me throughout this journey
and offered insurmountable support;

and to my siblings:
Emily, Susan, Dorothy Ann, Gladys
Mike, Rick
and Fran.
We are family!

Preface

I had longed to understand just why my mother could not love me. Throughout my childhood and adult life there was a rift that I could never understand. Everything I did was to make my mother proud of me, yet she was never able to show it, or express it to me. It was not until her death that I began to peel away the layers that made my mother who she was, and why she was unable to bond with her children, especially me. As I first uncovered the layers, I was left feeling embarrassed, mostly because of the Puritanical bias that had been passed down throughout the generations, as well as the religious ramifications of shame for those who broke the socially acceptable norms. My mother had sinned. I was born without benefit of marriage. Even today, we have relatives who will not celebrate the birth of a child born "out of wedlock." It is so unfair to the child. Some of these children may grow up feeling they have done something wrong because of the way people identify them as a product of a relationship not sanctioned by marriage. I believe future generations will disregard this bias, but for my mother who became a young woman in the 1940's, it became the backdrop of her relationships, her reputation, and her own happiness, and eventually the foundation of the relationship she had with me.

I want to document her story as well as the story of so many young women who fell into the disreputable category of "unwed mother." I also want to look at the reality of their "bastard" children. Perhaps this story will open the eyes of prejudice long held, and is still held even today. Therefore, Part One will focus on my mother's life. Since my mother took her secrets with her to her grave, I can only speculate as to what happened prior to my birth. To best understand her, one must know about her childhood and upbringing and the times in which she lived. The story is a blend of what I know of my mother and her past, stories shared by a couple of her friends and several relatives, and research I have done on such women during this time period. It is also colored by my discovery of the intake papers done by social workers when I became part of the adoption process in Cleveland, Ohio. Part Two will be biographical as it will describe the relationship I had with my mother. Part Three is about my uncovering the many secrets my mother held to her grave, and the secrets our society allowed others to keep, forever holding hostage information from illegitimate children who were never to learn their roots. Part Four consists of two research papers and several creative writing assignments I did dealing with my first blush of trying to better understand why my mother was unable to love me.

As to my book cover, it was a photograph which long fascinated me as a child. I had asked my mother who had ripped it and she told me she had done it herself. I could not understand why she would do that. It is significant that it was torn in four parts as that became the structure of her life: Her childhood and upbringing, her choices during her young adulthood, her challenges in parenting, and her firm grip on the secrets she kept throughout her life. As to the title, I slipped in and out of several titles. At first I wanted to use, "Why Can't My Mother Love Me?" Of course, I realized that as I researched and began writing the book I knew the answer to that question. I then considered, "Why My Mother Couldn't Love Me." It was only when my book was being edited that the suggestion came to use "Maternal Failings," or "Maternal Failure." It is a term used for women with personality disorders who cannot meet the typical expectations of motherhood, including bonding and showing affection.

I was asked by someone if I had written this book as revenge on my mother and how she treated me. The answer is *absolutely not!* I had only wanted her to love me, and the research I had done in the Adult Psychology course I took in 2000, and the reflective writing I did in the National Writing Project allowed me to truly understand why my mother behaved the way she did. It was writing this book that cemented my acceptance that she was "who she was" because of her upbringing and the choices she made. I do believe that she loved me, in her own way, but was incapable of showing that affection. It saddens me that any mother would experience such inability. I wrote this book to share my experiences, and hopefully help others who find themselves in dysfunctional relationships with their parent. I also hope that my sharing my experience in uncovering the secrets my mother kept will help others uncover their own family secrets. I will forever sing the praises of DNA testing, and this was the stone I uncovered which provided illuminating answers I had sought for decades as well as answers to questions I had never sought. I warn the reader that sometimes DNA answers are unsettling, but I truly believe knowing is better than not knowing, especially if you are seeking answers which will bring peace to your soul.

A friend recently said that I was brave to open myself up to the public and share my story, especially since some of my former colleagues and students may read the book and find out about my past. I have come to terms with my past, and if my experiences can help others in some way deal with questions they have, then sharing my story is well worth it. I learned I have a resilient personality and that my crutches in life were the networked relationships I had with teachers, colleagues, family, friends, and acquaintances, but most especially God as I believe my faith grounded me and provided me hope for a positive life. I do have a positive life and I openly tell people to not feel badly for my past as it is what made me who I am today.

Part One
Three Strikes

Chapter 1: 1917-1943

Some children have their destiny determined even before they are born. Such was the case for Hiram Clark. Hiram had come from a large family with very strong military roots. The family often spoke of being direct descendants to one of the founding fathers and signer of the Declaration of Independence. Growing up in the Clark household, Hiram was continually surrounded with the stories of military service the Clark family had done throughout the generations. Hiram's father had fought in the Civil War and he carried a bullet in his lung as a keepsake of his bravery. One of Hiram's older brothers, William, fought in the Spanish American War. Another brother, John, was a Marine and was in the first expeditionary force to enter China. It was only natural that Hiram would also become part of the military. World events certainly made that choice a reality.

In June of 1914, after the assassination of Archduke Franz Ferdinand of Austria, the heir to the throne of Austria-Hungary, the stage was set for a world war. Hiram Clark joined the Army when the United States entered the war. For Hiram, he was ready to show his commitment to his country. The news carried daily reports of deaths in the trenches caused by either attacks from the enemies, snipers' bullets aimed at those who peered over the parapets, as well being buried alive when the dugouts caved in from shell bursts. The horrors the soldiers in the trenches faced were overwhelming. Lice flourished in soiled clothing and even when the clothing was deloused, the eggs remained within the seams, hatching with the body heat of the soldier and forever tormenting him with itching and disease-carrying side effects. Hiram was sickened by the stories of soldiers being attacked by the brown rats in the trenches which often attacked the soldiers, or gorged on the dead, specifically the eyes and livers of the dead, making their bodies too gruesome to view. The rats could produce up to nine hundred offspring a year, making their elimination nearly impossible. If the lice, rats, and attacks were not bad enough, many of the soldiers suffered trench foot, and fungal infections caused by the unsanitary conditions of the trenches. Mentally the soldiers were given relief when they did their "morning hate" which was shelling the enemy and screaming at them across the abyss between the American trenches and the trenches of their enemy. A part of the everyday life of a soldier was the constant reeking of decomposing bodies, overflowing latrines, and the personal body odor of the soldiers themselves. Hiram felt like many soldiers, that his work in the military was necessary, despite the many hardships he endured as well as those suffered by his cousins, friends, and neighbors.

Hiram enlisted in the Ohio National Guard on August 1, 1917, and four days later they were drafted to the Federal service. By August 15th Hiram was given the rank of Sergeant of Co. K5 Infantry, and on September 14th he was promoted to First Sergeant, the highest non-commissioned rank in the army. Their regiment became part of the 145th Infantry and in June of 1918 they were deployed to Europe. Hiram fought in the Baccarat Sector in France from October 4-September 18, 1918; Meuse-Argonne, France September 26-October 3, 1918; St Michiel, France October 7-16, 1918; and Ypres-Lys, Belgium October 31-November 4, 1918. During this time he also served in the Supply Company, as a first class machinist, was in the defensive sector, and from June 15-September 11, 1918 was in the AEF, the American Expeditionary Forces.

After serving four tours of duty, Hiram received his honorable discharge February 20, 1919. It was not a difficult decision to remain a part of the National Guard when the war ended in November of 1918. He eventually worked his way to the rank of Captain in the Army.

Hiram was able to secure a job in the Post Office, and eventually became a postal inspector. His three youngest sisters, Helen, Sophia and Gertrude, had married prior to the war and moved to Canton, Ohio, thus the Clark home was quiet and lonely upon his return from war. Hiram felt it was time to settle down and find his own home and start his own family. Friends introduced Hiram to a young woman named Anna Louise Hahner.

When Anna left school many of the men her age were already off to war. Like many young women during this time, Anna was encouraged by her parents to become a nun. Anna entered the Sisters of Charity of St. Augustine. The nuns worked with the Diocese of Cleveland since 1851. Anna had completed her Canonical Novitiate, and second year of Novitiate. She was considered an Apostolic Novitiate. The convent was very strict; Anna was not allowed visits from anyone, including family. Once Anna became part of the convent, ties were broken with family, although she would be allowed home visits if chaperoned by another nun. Anna's family felt that the Catholic Church did not want to invest training if the girls were to change their minds.

Anna was dedicated to her work and became involved in the first public hospital in Cleveland. Some of the nuns also served in St. Ann Hospital for mothers and babies. She spent a good amount of time working at St. Ann's with the babies born of unwed mothers. As the war came to an end, Anna became more and more distraught at the number of women who surrendered their children to adoption because of the shame and scandal of their sins. Anna worked in the nursery and witnessed not only the painful separation of what they called "sinner" and child, but would hear of the happiness of those who eventually selected a surrendered child to raise. Catholic Charities arranged the adoptions and the unwanted babies were quickly taken by those who wanted children. There were also babies who were not quickly adopted. They were left behind to be raised in the orphanages which were also run by the nuns. The reality was that some of the nuns had referred to the babies as "bastard children" which further distraught Anna. She couldn't bear to be around such harsh attitudes toward innocent babies.

When the war ended, Anna decided to withdraw from the convent, a decision that was frowned upon by the nuns. With her parents' assistance, Anna insisted on resigning from the Sisters of Charity, and returned home. It was not long before family and friends were introducing Anna to some of the soldiers returning home. One was Hiram Clark.

Initially, Hiram found Anna to have a comfortable appearance, and although she was a bit shy, she warmed quickly to conversation, especially if it was about family. Hiram was caught when he looked into Anna's crystal blue eyes. They were kind and knowing, as if she had seen much of the reality of this world. For Anna, she knew her life had been very sheltered, but she was ready to meet someone and settle down. She knew she would never subject herself to the possibility of being an unwed mother. Although she was initially shy about meeting Hiram, his charm and good looks won her attention. In Hiram she found a man who was family oriented and hard working. She also knew that he was already past the age of carousing and was ready to settle down. After having worked at St. Ann's, she had witnessed the result of many young men who did not feel the need to share responsibility in raising a family and she wanted no part of that kind of relationship.

There was not much romance in the relationship between Hiram and Anna. The two married on November 26, 1919, less than a year after the war had ended. Hiram was age 29, and Anna was 26, both much older than the typical newlyweds. For Hiram, Anna represented a good Catholic girl from a good family, and someone who was rooted in strong family values. For Anna, she felt Hiram would protect her and provide her a good home. Both wanted a family of their own.

The two made their home in Cleveland until Hiram found a small house in Bedford, Ohio, a small community outside the city, which appeared to be a good place to raise a family away from all the potential problems of living in a large city. Hiram's job as a Postal Inspector often times had him traveling throughout Northeast Ohio. He felt a home in Bedford would afford Anna a safe place to live and raise their family. Their home was on Archer Road, and it was a small cottage-styled house. It was half concrete block, half clapboard painted white. There was a privy in the back yard and a chicken coup. The house was set back from the road and the large empty lot next door made the property appear to be more rural than suburban.

The couple soon had a daughter, Agnes, at the end of 1920, followed by another daughter, Emma in 1922. Henry, or Hank as he was called by family, was born in 1924. The small family lived frugally, yet was very happy. Anna raised chickens in the back yard, and had a small vegetable garden. Hiram was a good husband, and expected the children to be respectful and behave at all times. Life seemed rather ideal for everyone, until tragedy visited itself in the small Clark family.

In August, 1925, Anna was heavy with child when Emma contracted typhoid fever and died within weeks. Anna was inconsolable, and when William was born just a month later, she had great difficulty functioning. Within days of the death of Emma, Hiram noticed his wife's once beautiful dark hair began to fade in color. Her vibrant eyes were dull and darkly shadowed. She barely spoke to anyone. The couple's oldest daughter, Agnes, only being five years old, was expected to help with both her brother, Hank, and the newborn, William. Hiram tried to help as much as he could, but it took Anna months to finally begin functioning again. Just as it seemed Anna had turned the corner and was coming out of her depression, in March of 1926, baby William also developed typhoid fever and died.

The neighbors quickly became concerned after the second case of typhoid at the Clark household and the township sent out contractors who tested the well to find that it was contaminated. The decision to deepen the well may have solved the contaminated water; however, things were not well in the Clark household.

Anna walked as if in a stupor. The activity around the household, the digging of a new well, and the two active children who expected their mother to be attentive to them went unnoticed by Anna as she once again slipped into a deep depression. Her once joyful nature of raising a family was demolished by her overwhelming feeling of loss. Hiram was often away from home doing work for the Postal Service, or at his monthly National Guard meetings and training, leaving his wife alone to deal with her state of despair. When Anna found out she was once again with child, she was not at all happy. Her hair very quickly grew snow white in color and she was only thirty-four years old.

Dorothy was born in 1927, and her youngest brother, Joseph, was born in 1928. Agnes was once again quickly given the additional task of taking care of her younger siblings. Anna had changed. She became absorbed with her own survival and failed to take an interest in her home or her children. The once tidy house soon became one with unmade beds, dishes piled high in the sink, unwashed laundry, and floors that needed a good scrubbing, especially with the four children and family pets trailing dirt into the house. Anna also became absorbed with buying things which Hiram found unnecessary, like new coats when the old ones were still serviceable, or buying toys which Hiram felt were unnecessary. Hiram had always been very frugal, and Anna's new spending sprees often left the family in dire financial situations, struggling to pay the basic bills. Anna was good natured; however, she put her own siblings ahead of her own family and often gave food and money to her brothers and sisters rather than using her resources for her own family.

As these behaviors continued, Hiram became more and more saddened, and he spent more time volunteering to do extra duty and training with the National Guard and doing more Postal inspections for his work in an effort to escape the home life which was less than acceptable. When home, he expected his children behave in a both a militaristic and Puritanical manner, but without Anna's active intervention, the younger children were left to their own devices. Only when Hiram was in attendance in the small Bedford home did the younger children comply with the household rules. Although he was very strict, little Dorothy could charm her father and he could sometimes be persuaded to go easy on her when she misbehaved. Dorothy quickly learned that she could manipulate her father, and her mother stood by watching, rarely intervening. Dorothy worked this to her advantage.

Agnes had no chance at a childhood. Being eight years older than Dorothy built a distance between the two sisters. Perhaps losing Emma caused Agnes to subconsciously keep a minimal attachment to her younger sister. Instead, Agnes put her efforts into school. Her grades reflected that work in straight A's and B+'s. Her extra-curricular activities became her escape. She graduated 12th out of 113 students at Bedford High School. At home the responsibility of raising her younger siblings proved too much for her. She quickly took advantage of the opportunity to go to Bowling Green College where she majored in music. This gave her the satisfaction and recognition she found lacking at home. After two years of college she married, thus allowing her to never return to living at home again.

Hank was not as dedicated to school as his sister was. Outside of school he took on as many jobs as he could in an effort to save his money so he could one day move on. Because his father was absent from the home every month, Hank had to take care of many of the household chores and repairs. He became very handy and found that he could make money doing odd jobs for neighbors. Once he left school, he took a job in construction. This left Dorothy and Joe at home with Anna who offered no structure to her two youngest children. Anna felt she needed to reward herself for the hard life she had and she continued to spend money foolishly. Hiram was none too pleased with his wife as she never stayed on budget, nor did she try to keep their home maintained, and she had nearly dismissed her duties in parenting. Being Catholic, Hiram knew he had to somehow make his marriage work.

By the end of the 1930's the state of the world was once again in flux. War was already on everyone's minds, although the United States had not yet joined into the fray. In anticipation that things would change, 269,023 men enlisted in the Army in 1940. Hank was one of them, enlisting in the 112th Engineers. For the first time in a long time, Anna seemed to snap out of her lethargy when she realized her son would be going off to fight in the war. She sobbed uncontrollably and prayed that the United States would be able to stay out of the conflict which was escalating daily.

Because Hiram was in the National Guard, he was called into active duty in September of 1941. Hiram was trained in Military Intelligence, as because of this background he was sent to Texas to train officers. By December of 1941, the United States entered into the war. In Hiram's absence, Anna was left at home, alone, to take care of the household and the two younger Clark children. The harsh reality that Hiram would not be coming home for a very long time meant that Anna could not count on him taking care of the "business" of finances and everyday household needs. With Hank in the service and Agnes married and on her own, Anna knew she only had herself to take responsibility in raising her two youngest children. She would now have to face the consequences of her not having disciplined her children more closely as they were growing up.

The war was brutal both for the soldiers, and for those at home trying to survive. Joe was not obedient to his mother, and without his father's discipline or presence, he became more and more resistant to attending school or following rules. The thirteen year old got into trouble repeatedly and Anna was continually called upon to rescue him. Anna devoted much of her time trying to make a difference with Joseph, hoping her sudden interest and care for him would change his behavior. With her father's absence from the home, and her mother's constant attention on her brother's behavior, Dorothy felt ignored and lonely. Her sister had left, and now her brother and father were away from home and she was left in a household with a mother who she felt had never been attentive, and a younger brother who was constantly misbehaving and getting into trouble. It was not unusual for the police officers to stop by the Clark household to inform Anna that Joe was once again in trouble or being held in Juvenile Hall. Meanwhile, Dorothy was developing her own bad habits. Dorothy was only attentive to band and art classes at school, and her grades ranged from C's to F's causing her to have to repeat classes.

Perhaps it was hormones, or perhaps it was rebellion since her father was not home being attentive to her, but Dorothy bickered constantly with her mother. She was jealous of the attention her mother gave Joe. She was tired of her mother wanting her to clean house and do the chores which she, herself, was not doing. Dorothy was tired of the loneliness of the Clark home. She was tired of the war, the boredom, the loneliness, and being ignored. She spent as much time as possible visiting with her school friends and avoiding being home. She pestered her mother for the change it would take to buy a ticket to the movies, and Dorothy spent every moment she could enjoying the life of the movie stars she saw on the big screen. It was her favorite escape from her desperate reality.

The Clark family became a point of interest with the Cleveland newspaper when they realized Hiram, a World War I veteran, had been called back to active duty, and his son was also in active duty. A reporter came to the small Bedford home and interviewed Anna about her husband and son, as well as her Hahner nephews who were all part of the war effort. Anna called upon her sisters-in-law to share information about her father-in-law, Hiram Sr., a Civil War veteran, and stories of Hiram's brothers, who were also veterans. A series of articles appeared in the newspaper which were called, "The Fighting Clarks." The articles visited the military history of the family and several updates to the series were made with news coming from the war front about the father, son, and cousins all doing their part for this nation.

Two years into the war, life for the Clarks was forever changed. May 23rd, 1943, two Army officers pulled up in a car outside the Clark house. Anna's first thought was that her son had been injured or killed. Instead she was told that her husband had died of a heart attack in Texas. A telegraph was handed to her by the Army personnel along with condolences for her loss. Anna stood in the doorway, holding the telegraph, unable to talk, unable to cry, and unable to speak. She did not respond to the officers who attempted to talk with her. It was not possible, she thought, as Hiram was up for promotion to Major in just two weeks, and had his overseas orders. She reeled in disbelief as Hiram had plans in place. How could his life be over? Finally, the officers bid their goodbye, and Anna closed the door and stood still, in shock, unable to think of how her life would proceed from this point on. Not certain if her shock was in loss of this man, her husband, the father of her children, or for her now unfortunate situation which was just complicated as she was now a war widow and would have to make survival her full time responsibility with no hope of relief.

Dorothy was returning home when she saw the car leaving the driveway outside her house, and when she saw that soldiers were inside she at first hoped that her brother, or even her father, had returned home from the service. She rushed into the house eager to be greeted by her family, but instead found her mother standing in the middle of the room holding the telegram. Dorothy's heart beat quickly as she pulled the telegram from her mother's hands. Joe had entered through the back door and saw his mother, still standing facing the door, and his sister shaking as she held the yellow telegram in her hands. He ran to Dorothy and looked over her shoulder as she read and reread the telegram. A tortured cry was uttered by Dorothy as she tried to comprehend what she was reading.

My dear Mrs. Clark,

Words can be of little consolation at this time of sadness, but I want you to know that you have my heartfelt sympathy in the loss of your husband.

Hiram Clark has made the great contribution to the American way of living. He died while serving as an American soldier and his sacrifice will not be forgotten by those who are determined to bring this terrible struggle to a victorious conclusion.

Again, my deepest sympathy.

Faithfully yours,

J.C. Marshall

Chief of Staff

Dorothy fell to the floor, screaming and sobbing. Her mother simply walked over to her daughter, took the telegram from her hands, and went to her room and closed the door, leaving sixteen year old Dorothy and fourteen year old Joseph alone in their grief. Joe, looking after his mother, then looking at his sister crumpled on the floor, put his hands to his mouth to hold back his own screams, and ran out the back door. Anna remained isolated from her two younger children, ignoring the fact that her two children were left without the comfort they needed in their grief upon hearing the news.

The next week was one that passed in a blur. Anna contacted Hiram's sisters. She made funeral arrangements at the Johnson funeral parlor on Broadway Avenue in Bedford. She accepted food donations from well-meaning neighbors. Anna barely functioned, but she went through all the motions of a woman who was expected to bury her husband and carry on in the name of duty.

The funeral was the largest that the Bedford community had ever seen. Agnes and her husband, the Clark and Hahner relations, postal workers, friends, neighbors, and of course soldiers came to pay tribute to Captain Clark. Hiram was up for promotion to Major in only two weeks, and this added to the sadness that his brothers and sisters felt in his loss. Hank was unable to return home for the funeral as he was serving in Europe. Anna stood in line next to her sisters-in-law, (Rose, Helen, Sophia, and Gertrude) as well as her brothers-in-law, (John and William) and greeted those who came to pay their respects. Dorothy and Joe were left to fend for themselves.

Joe could not bear to look at his father in the coffin and he escaped outdoors, smoking away his grief. Dorothy; however, never left the side of the coffin. Her body was stiff and aching. She had slept a lot since news of her father's passing had come. It was no doubt an effort to escape this reality, but she still felt exhausted. She merely nodded as people talked to her and limply shook hands or endured hugs that were given, but she was paralyzed in her grief. The wake lasted two days and on the third day there was a service at the funeral parlor. The family was the last to view the body, and Dorothy screamed and cried holding fast to the side of the coffin. She was forcibly taken away by one of her uncles and guided into the waiting car. The church service at St. Mary's in Bedford was a blur of tributes and religious sentiment, then a graveside service was held at Calvary Cemetery in Cleveland. Dorothy heard none of it. The coffin was left behind as the family and mourners moved to their cars. Dorothy was turned in the car, staring at the coffin sitting alone in the Calvary Cemetery in Cleveland. There was a reception with food, but Dorothy did not care to eat. Throughout this, Anna still did not reach out to her children.

Upon returning home, her father's sisters came to the house and asked to take all the memorabilia of their father that had been given to Hiram including the family Bible, the war medals, and family photos. Anna didn't argue. She just handed everything over, not thinking that Hank might want to keep these family mementos. Dorothy felt her mother was getting rid of every memory of her father and the things that he held in esteem. She looked at her mother with hatred and disgust, but Anna did not look at Dorothy, or even care about Dorothy's grief. After everyone left, Anna went to her room and closed the door. Dorothy sat on the davenport too tired to cry, too emotionally drained to even think.

Chapter 2: 1943-1944

In her dream Dorothy was lying in the hot sun. Her skin was burning. Dorothy saw herself thrashing about screaming as her skin suddenly burst into flames.

The sudden motion of her body jerking about in her sleep, pulled Dorothy to consciousness. Her body indeed felt as if it were on fire. She pulled off the sheet and looked at her arms and saw bright red welts as if someone had scratched her. Then she looked at her legs and they too were covered with the swollen streaks. She pulled up her nightgown and saw that her torso was covered with the long hateful welts which rose above her otherwise pale skin. She screamed and called out to her mother. Anna did not respond at first, but when she heard Dorothy's continued screaming, she quickly ran to the bedroom. Anna was horrified to see her daughter covered in hideous patches of angry red skin all across her body.

As if coming out of a fog, Anna quickly jumped into action. She was reminded of the fear she had felt when first Emma, then William had died. Anna went to the kitchen and ran a basin of cold water and brought towels to apply them to Dorothy's skin. Anna carefully put the cool compresses on Dorothy's torso, but Dorothy cried in pain as even the carefully placed compresses were heavy on her tortured skin. Anna realized she had to get Dorothy medical care.

There was no telephone in the Clark house, so Anna ran to the neighbor. They called a local doctor who promised to come to the Clark house as soon as he was able. By the time he arrived, Dorothy was complaining of itching and burning in her ears, scalp, and eyelids as well. The doctor examined the welts and determined that Dorothy needed to be transported to the hospital. Anna did not have a car, so again she ran to a neighbor for help.

At the hospital Dorothy was examined, poked, and prodded. All the well meaning investigations of her skin left Dorothy even more stressed than when she arrived. The doctors tried to make Dorothy comfortable and sent for a skin specialist. Her body was wrapped in medicated bandages to ease the swelling and welting. Anna demanded to know what caused this welting. No one seemed to have answers. They first considered poison ivy, poison oak, allergies to soaps, or perhaps allergies to food. Nothing seemed to sit right with her condition.

Finally after the second day, the skin specialist declared Dorothy had erythrodermic psoriasis, which was a very rare skin disorder. The doctor told Anna that the stress and depression could cause this severe of an outbreak. He explained that typically the initial outbreak was the worst, although the diagnosis was that Dorothy would be forever plagued with this disease. Certainly the death of her father was the cause for this initial outbreak. Dorothy remained hospitalized for several weeks. Orders were given to keep her from stressful and emotional situations as future outbreaks would happen specifically when Dorothy was exposed to undue stress. This news was devastating to both Anna and Dorothy. Anna looked at her once beautiful daughter realizing that she would forever be scarred with this disease.

It did not take Dorothy long to learn that her skin was revolting to many people. She overheard several nurse's aides talking about the sores and guessing how she got them. "It's probably because she doesn't clean herself," said one. Another said, "These farm girls run wild and it's probably syphilis. I heard that when you get it your whole body becomes one big oozing scab." One nurse didn't want to treat the lesions and the doctor had to tell her they were not contagious. She heard a patient who had walked into her room by mistake tell someone that she had gone into the "scab girl's room." None of these comments escaped Dorothy's hearing. She cried and felt unclean and unworthy of love. The coal tar treatments and various emollients gave her little relief. One doctor recommended she spend as much time as she could under the sun; however, Dorothy was very susceptible to sunburn, so this advice did not sound promising. Finally the doctor recommended she sit outside from 7-10 AM every day to get as much sunlight as she could without threat of serious sunburn. Ohio's weather was not always cooperative with the provision of sunlight year round, so this treatment would be very limited. Moving to a warmer climate was out of the question as Anna's financial resources were limited.

In the fall of 1943, Dorothy refused to return to school until she felt "normal" again. Her skin was still red. She couldn't face seeing her school friends in her condition, and Anna decided to not press her as this would cause additional stress. Dorothy spent her days reading, doing crossword puzzles, and crocheting lace handkerchiefs. Anna became concerned that Dorothy was not socializing much, so she would give Dorothy money to go to the movies with some of her girlfriends. One positive thing came from this latest disaster: Anna had come out of her moroseness, and became determined she was not going to lose another child.

At the same time, Joe quit school, and Anna surrendered her attempt to force him to go. She had met with the principal who tried to coerce Joe to get his education, but neither he, nor Anna could reason with him. Joe preferred to go to the local race track to work, or even place a small bet, although he was under-aged and had to rely on someone else to place the bet for him. The principal warned both Anna and Joseph that going to the horse track would prove to be a bad decision. Too many young men found their way to unlawful behaviors at the racetrack. Joseph was destined to join their ranks. When Anna tried to persuade Joe that his father would be horrified to know his son was throwing away his education, Joe shot back an angry retort that his father had not cared about him when he was alive and always looked for opportunities to put his job or the Army ahead of the family. Anna's eyes filled with tears knowing that she could never persuade Joe to think otherwise. She admitted defeat and Joe left school.

When it was time for Dorothy to return to school after her skin treatments, she hid from her mother that she was not leaving the house each day for school, but instead was going to work. She secretly forged her mother's signature on the release document and gladly shed the distress of facing peers who could make her feel ashamed and bitter about her lot in life. Without telling her mother, Dorothy sought a job at a creamery. After only three days she quit the job because she and the other girls were already bickering. Dorothy felt they were making comments about her skin and Dorothy verbally shot back at them. The supervisor let Dorothy go. Dorothy was developing an aggressive personality when it came to dealing with people she did not like. Her temper was quickly shared with peers and adults as well. Her next attempt at a job was a salesgirl. She quit that job because she didn't like the work she was asked to do, and she resented working with girls she felt acted superior to her. Finally she obtained a small job at the Marble Chair Factory in Bedford and she carefully put money away in an effort, she reasoned, to help supplement the small widow's military pension her mother received. Dorothy convinced herself by having this job her mother would be able to quit working and live comfortably with the supplemental income provided by her. Anna had taken on a job as a domestic for another family. The irony was that while Anna was taking care of someone else's home, she easily neglected her own. Dorothy reasoned that with the income she was now providing, her mother could quit her job and take care of their house, and the household duties would not be turned over for Dorothy to manage.

Dorothy kept her secret that she had quit school until her mother confronted her about her grades. Dorothy handed her mother an envelope with money in it and told her mom that she didn't want her to work and that rather than go to school she would work and contribute toward the household finances. Anna protested, but by this time she feared Dorothy would once again have an outbreak on her skin and rather than face that probability, she surrendered to Dorothy's decision. Anna had already reconciled herself with the reality that she had very little influence over Dorothy or Joe. Dorothy's generosity was also short-lived. She quickly rescinded her offer of giving her pay to her mother.

The Clark household was typically only occupied by Anna and Dorothy, and an occasional boarder. Joe was constantly away from home, although he was not yet sixteen. He told his mother he planned to join the Merchant Marine, but his absences were typically when he would go to the horse tracks to work in the barns. Within a year a telegram arrived informing Anna that Joe had been placed in a Pennsylvania Reformatory. For some reason, Anna felt a relief knowing Joe was under a watchful eye and she would not have to worry about his whereabouts.

Anna had been left a widow at age fifty, but she had no desire to remarry. Her only goal was to see Hank return from war so he could take over the household needs. She also wanted to be certain Dorothy remained healthy. It wasn't long before Dorothy realized she needed to only act stressed and her mother would surrender any demands she made of her daughter. Dorothy took advantage of Anna's submissiveness.

Anna sought something meaningful for herself. When not working as a domestic, she volunteered as a member of the Women's Relief Corp, the Auxiliary to the Grand Army of the Republic. Anna was proud to wear her uniform as a member of the group. Her cape was adorned with the Woman's Relief Corps Badge which was a Maltese Cross. In the middle of the cross was an American flag encircled in a wreath of stars. There were five figures on the emblem: the Goddess of Liberty, a soldier, a boy, a woman, and a child. Anna was proud of the symbolism of the emblem, especially the woman as a symbol of motherhood who taught mercy, kindness, and extended charity. Anna now envisioned herself as the model mother who cared for her ill child, yet, ironically, she looked for opportunities to escape her house which had robbed her of two children, lost one to delinquency, and threatened to rob her another child of a normal life because of a skin disease.

Sometimes the women of the Relief Corps would visit schools, present flags to the children, or hold patriotic essay competitions. They would visit the Veteran Hospitals, and Anna enjoyed going to the Crile General Hospital which had opened on Easter Sunday, 1944, on Pleasant Valley Road in Parma. The hospital was built by the U.S. Army and named after George Washington Crile who had died in 1943. Crile was an internationally known surgeon and the founder of the Cleveland Clinic. He had served in the Spanish American War, and the present war, and was best known for his work in military medicine. He had researched treatment for shock, blood transfusions, and storing blood to be used for soldiers in the field needing transfusions. Anna was proud to volunteer her time supporting such a cause. Her work in the Relief Corps justified her time volunteering as a way to support the war effort.

Anna dressed for events in the Women's Relief Corp in her white dress, stockings, shoes, cap, and cape. She felt good about herself as she looked at her reflection in the mirror. Her white hair and white attire glistened in the stream of sunlight that entered her bedroom. She knew she would be on her feet all day, so she enjoyed the long ride to Parma on the bus. Upon arriving she was sent to visit the wounded in the 2,000 bed facility. There were seven miles of corridors in the facility where the staff of nearly a 1,000 moved quickly to treat the soldiers and German POW's. Anna came alive with her work at the hospital; however, on her trips home on the bus, her temperament returned to the sadness she had in dealing with her two fatherless children. Upon entering the house, Anna went straight to her room, changed clothing, and she would walk to the kitchen, hoping that her children were not at home so she would not have to deal with them.

Anna's adolescent years had been very protected, thus she never anticipated that Dorothy would be facing challenges she had never experienced. One of the Clark neighbors called on Anna one afternoon, and began asking questions about

Dorothy and her activities. Anna finally confronted her friend and asked her if there was something she knew that she was withholding. The neighbor revealed that a story was being circulated that a teacher from the high school had been going to the chair factory where Dorothy worked and would offer to drive Dorothy home from work. The teacher had a reputation of preying on young girls, especially those who didn't have fathers at home. Some people had speculated that this man was taking advantage of Dorothy, especially since she was naïve about how men can be manipulative and young women's reputations could be forever damaged. Anna was devastated. She immediately remembered the women at St. Ann's and she did not want her daughter to walk that path. Anna had never been one to physically discipline her children; however, as she waited for Dorothy to return home her face became redder with the agitation of her thoughts.

Anna stood by the door waiting for Dorothy to return from work. She saw a car stop down the street and Dorothy leave the car and walk up the street to the small Bedford house. When she entered the house, Anna slapped her across the face. "What do you think you are doing? Who was that?"

At first Dorothy tried to play innocent, and then she lied and said that it was a school friend. Anna stopped her and said, "I know it wasn't a school friend. It was that teacher. I've heard all about it. What are you trying to do? Do you want to disgrace your family and put us all to shame? How long has this been going on? Do you realize that people are talking? They are calling you filthy names."

Dorothy sputtered an angry reply. "Ma, I haven't done anything wrong. He just picks me up and talks to me about how I am doing since Dad died, and what I do with my time now that I am not going to school. He just wants to help me. He actually cares about me and listens to me!"

Anna was not persuaded to believe her. "I will not have you disgracing this family. What would your father say?"

Dorothy's heart sank. Her father. What would he say? Would he be ashamed of her? What if her mother was right and people were talking about her and calling her names? She didn't ask for this. She just wanted someone to care about her. Dorothy said nothing, but went to her room. The next morning she got up and found a note from her mother.

"I am going to the high school to tell that teacher he is never to contact you again. Do not leave the house."

Dorothy stood still. Her face was burning. Were people really calling her the names her mother suggested they were? Dorothy was overcome with the familiar feeling of her skin burning. She began scratching herself again.

When her mother returned, Dorothy was putting the ointment on her newly welted skin. Obviously her stress level had risen and her skin was already reacting. Anna looked at her daughter, and then walked into the kitchen distressed, but determined not to further upset her daughter who was having a reaction to this latest development in their household. Dorothy eventually walked into the kitchen. She sat at the table, looking down at the floor. Minutes passed before Dorothy spoke.

"I'm sorry, Ma, that I upset you. You've got to know that I didn't do anything wrong."

Anna looked at her daughter. "I went to the school and asked to speak to that teacher. I told him that if he ever contacts you I will contact his wife and let her know what he has been up to. You are never to see him again." Dorothy nodded. She sat at the table, and the two did not speak. Silence was now the new guest in the Clark house.

Chapter 3: 1945-1947

The B.L. Marble Chair Company was a major employer in the small Bedford, Ohio, community. Dorothy enjoyed working there. With so many men off to war, there were jobs available for women. The factory had four acres of floor space on Willis Street. For Dorothy, this opened many opportunities to make new friends at the factory. Dorothy's life was now working, going out with friends to the movies and to the roller skating rink, and not returning home until late in the evening. Anna soon gave up asking where Dorothy was and what she had done all day as she knew she would get no answers.

Once the war came to an end, and many of the local boys returned home, many of the women who worked at the chair factory were let go from their jobs in order to accommodate the returning soldiers. Since Dorothy was paid a minimal amount, she was able to maintain her job. She was glad of it because the income provided her money she could use for her own enjoyment. Also, being at work every day gave her an excuse to be away from the house and away from the drama which was always unfolding there.

Dorothy was excited that her brother, Hank returned home from the war; however, he had taken a war bride and they both moved into the small Archer Road house with Anna and Dorothy. During the war Hank had sent his entire pay home for his mother to bank for him so he could begin his new life once the war was over, but upon returning home he learned she had spent it all. Instead of a happy reunion, there was increased tension at home. To pay back Hank, Anna gave him the deed to the house, so long as she, Dorothy, and Joe, who rarely came home, could continue to live there. The tension was thick in the small Archer Road house. There was often a lack of privacy and quiet. To add to the confusion, Anna had taken in a boarder to help supplement the household income. Dorothy often complained to her friends that her family always felt it necessary to constantly comment about her behavior, cleanliness, activities, and what she should and should not be doing. Thus, Dorothy took the opportunity to stay away from the house as much as she could.

It was during this time that Dorothy began to notice changes in her body. Her once lanky body was filling out, and she took an interest in styling her hair like many of the movie stars she saw on the big screen. Not only did she notice a change, but so did the young men. Dorothy was smitten when a young man would whistle at her or flirt with her. Even the boarder at their house would make flirtatious comments whenever Anna and Dee were not at home. In Dorothy's mind, she was like the movie stars who would have people stop and stare in admiration. She had wanted attention for so long, and clearly she enjoyed the attention she received from the young men she met. Sadly, despite these bodily changes, Anna had never had "the talk" with Dorothy, nor had Agnes or Dee.

Dorothy enjoyed the little freedoms small town Bedford could offer. She enjoyed movies, bowling, skating, and going to Geauga Lake. Geauga Lake was near Bedford, and in 1931 they added a race track, bowling alley, and a dance hall. While Joe loved the race track, Dorothy loved the dance hall. Every chance she got she would go there and enjoy the music, dance, and meet many young men. A young taxi driver had taken a shine to Dorothy and offered her a chance to ride in the taxi throughout his entire route. Dorothy would chatter away with him about everything: movies, the young people they both knew, and her family drama. Now that there were plenty of young men home from war, Dorothy would enjoy whatever attention they gave her. At age nineteen Dorothy felt she was now a woman and she resented anyone trying to curb her freedom. Many of her girlfriends were already getting married right after high school, or when their soldier returned home from the war, so Dorothy felt she, too, deserved to make choices that pleased her, regardless of what others might say. Unfortunately, Dorothy never anticipated that her freedom in doing whatever she wanted with no curfew or accountability would actually take away the very freedom she enjoyed.

It was early in 1947 when twenty-year-old Dorothy knew she had a problem. Her period which had been erratic since her father's death had suddenly stopped. At first Dorothy was not certain what this meant, not thinking that pregnancy could be the problem. It took her a month before the reality of her situation truly sank in. It was then that she was filled with anger that no one had talked to her about the risks of having sex. The nuns at her elementary school preached that girls should remain pure, but they never talked about what happened if you weren't. Even at Bedford High School there had been no discussion about sex. Most of what Dorothy knew was from whispered talks with girlfriends. Because so many of her friends were also raised in strict Catholic families, they sustained the idea that being impure was a mortal sin, and even the thought of having sex before marriage would be reason to go straight to Hell. There had been no discussion about sex, even when her mother believed she had relations with the teacher. Her mother gave her no advice, or even warnings about the consequences in having non-marital sex, let alone unprotected sex. Dorothy knew there were girls who disappeared from school occasionally, and rumors flew that they had quickly married and soon appeared pregnant, but no one really talked about it. Dorothy did have some friends who married when they were of age, but they never talked about their private relationship with their husbands. It just wasn't done. Dorothy thought to herself that it was embarrassing that she didn't know enough about sex to fully understand how girls got pregnant. After all, every time Dorothy was with a man she was told that she would be all right and that he knew how to keep her from getting pregnant. Apparently that was not true.

Dorothy was not very brave about sharing her secret sex activities, as she knew that it would put her in the direct path of gossip. All she wanted was for someone to love her, and if having sex would give her that sense of security, so be it. Dorothy never planned on having relations. No nice girl or boy would admit that they planned it. Spontaneity was natural. Dorothy seriously thought that you only got pregnant if you wanted to have children. She didn't, so she shouldn't have a problem.

As days turned into weeks which turned into months, Dorothy was certain she was now pregnant. In tears, she was left to decide how she would handle this problem. Her expanding waistline was making it difficult to wear the clothing she owned. One thing was for certain. She would not tell her mother. Dorothy was bringing shame and disgrace on the family which everyone could see. The only resolution would be to give up the child in hopes it would have a better life than Dorothy could offer. There was no way that Dorothy would reveal to her mother that she was pregnant. Certainly a solution to this problem would present itself and she would not have to admit to anyone that she was pregnant.

Dorothy decided she would continue to work as long as she could, and hopefully no one would realize her waistline was expanding. There was a part of her that wished that the pregnancy would just go away, or that somehow she was mistaken in the belief that she was pregnant. She prayed that God would take care of this problem. God didn't answer that prayer. As the months went by she began wearing layered clothing, saying that she was cold, despite the summer weather. Fortunately, Hank and Dee had moved into their new house which Hank had built across the street, so Dorothy didn't have to worry about them recognizing her expanding shape. It was soon obvious; however, to Dorothy's boss that Dorothy was pregnant and he told her that she could no longer work, but once the baby was born and she was ready, she could return to work. Dorothy would leave home each day and spend the day in the park, or the movies, or taking a bus to Cleveland to avoid seeing people she knew. She went to no pre-natal doctor, and she ate as little as she could to keep her weight down in hopes of keeping her secret. By September she would walk around with a coat or large sweater to conceal her belly. Whenever anyone came to the house she would lock herself in her room, or say she was bathing in order to avoid being seen.

For whatever reason, Anna did not recognize the changes in Dorothy. Perhaps it was pre-occupation with her latest worries over Joe who had been sent to Pennsylvania for a trade school, but got caught stealing a farmer's clothes off a clothesline, and was sent to a Pennsylvania Reformatory; or perhaps it was because of her volunteer work which kept her away from home and interacting with her daughter; or, perhaps it was just denial. It wasn't until Dorothy began screaming in pain that Anna ran to her room and found her daughter on the bed holding what was unmistakably a pregnant belly which was in full contractions. Anna ran across the street to get Hank to drive them to the hospital. The whole way to the hospital Dorothy screamed, Anna lectured and prayed, and Hank kept asking how no one knew this was happening. The thirty minute car ride seemed an eternity, and upon arrival Dorothy could barely walk to the door of the hospital. Hank and his wife had welcomed their first child into the Clark household in March, and the little boy brought much joy to his parents and Anna. How could such joy in parenthood be followed by such shame?

Dorothy was taken into a room and quickly examined. A nurse came in and administered Demerol. Dorothy immediately felt some relief from the pain, but she found that her head felt heavy and her thoughts were muddled. She felt like she was watching a movie of what was happening to her, unable to control anything or to even cry out. When Dorothy was taken to the operating room she was aware of all the activity but was somehow not a part of it. A nurse shaved her and an enema was administered. There came a point where Dorothy had no control of anything and her brain was too foggy to concentrate on what the doctor was saying to her. The doctor kept telling Dorothy to push, but she couldn't control her body to cooperate. Finally the doctor said he needed forceps and he used them to guide the baby out.

Dorothy could feel a relief of pressure in her body. She heard no cry from the baby. The nurses were immediately working on the baby for what seemed like eternity, but in reality was only about a minute. She heard the baby's cry. It was 4:15 A.M. on October 11th, 1947. In just a little over an hour she had arrived at the hospital and given birth.

While Dorothy was delivering, Anna was completing paperwork. She was mortified that her daughter was an unwed mother. Anna had no idea who the father was, and she could not answer reasonably what the plans Dorothy had for the baby. When it was suggested that perhaps Dorothy would surrender the baby for adoption, Anna's face fell. "No. We haven't had a chance to discuss that." When the woman completing the intake records commented that Dorothy was of age to make the decision on her own without her mother's intervention, Anna was heartbroken. Perhaps Dorothy would keep the child. A baby in the household would be wonderful, she thought, yet she truly did not know what her daughter would decide to do.

When the nurse came into Dorothy's room after the delivery, she shocked Dorothy by stating, "It has come to our attention that this is an illegitimate pregnancy. Do you intend to keep the baby, or surrender it for adoption?"

Without a moment's hesitation Dorothy responded, "I don't want this baby. I want to put it up for adoption." The nurse then asked if Dorothy wanted to see the baby, and Dorothy slowly turned her face away from the nurse, shaking her head. "No, I don't want to see the baby. After the nurse left the room Dorothy cried. She asked herself if the tears were for the pain she was in, or for the baby she was going to surrender, or for the shame she felt in knowing her mother and brother now knew the secret she had held for the entire pregnancy. Dorothy couldn't answer, but one thing was certain. She was not keeping this baby.

Dorothy was taken to a room where she fell asleep, no doubt aided by the Demerol she had received during delivery. She awakened later in the day, feeling her now empty belly and remembering she had given birth. Her head was throbbing. She was able to get out of bed and able to walk shakily down the hall to the nurse's station. "When can I leave?" asked Dorothy.

The nurse on duty was abrupt with her. "You shouldn't be out of bed unsupervised. Return to your room. A social worker will be arriving shortly with the forms you will need to complete. Do you have a name picked out for him?"

Dorothy felt stunned. Him? She had a son. She had not thought of a name since she was giving the child up. Being able to pick out a name was something she didn't know she could do. She didn't know that she wanted to either. "You know I am giving him up for adoption."

The nurse looked at her, then sorted through the files on the desk. She found the one she sought and looked it over. "Oh," she said. "I see. Well, there needs to be a name on the birth certificate. The adoptive parents can change it, but there needs to be a name."

"Can I think about it for a bit?" asked Dorothy.

"Yes, but you need to do it today as the agency will be working on the adoption pretty quickly. Do think about the name you want to give him. Meanwhile, do you want to feed the baby?"

"Absolutely not," said Dorothy.

As the nurse watched Dorothy shuffle off to her room she slowly shook her head. The nurse called out after her, "Since you are giving the baby up we will be binding your breasts so that the milk will subside."

Later that day a Miss Bielfelt of the Alice Hunt Center arrived and led Dorothy into a small conference area. She sorted through her stack of papers. "As you know, we have been informed that the infant will be surrendered for adoption. Your signature on the forms to proceed with this is needed. What we need now is for you to give us the information needed in the forms which give the adoptive parents information they would need to know about the child.

The questionnaire asked many questions about Dorothy including information about her height, weight, hair color, eye color, educational background, religion, and health issues.

Dorothy answered questions about health issues with details about the psoriasis she suffered. The next section of the form asked questions about her family. Where were her parents born? What nationality were they? Where did they work? How many children were in the family? What were the family's health issues? Dorothy answered in as much detail as she could, including her father's death from a heart attack and having had two siblings who died of typhus.

The final section of the survey was painful for Dorothy to complete. The first question was "When was your first sexual experience."

Dorothy said, "I was nineteen years old."

"Who is the father of this child?"

Dorothy stopped. She vowed she would never reveal this information to anyone. "I was seeing several boys about the same time." Miss Beilfelt persisted in wanting an answer, suspecting that Dorothy actually knew who the father was. She emphasized that unless they had a name they would be unable to place the baby for adoption. Dorothy refused to look at her inquisitor. Instead she looked at the questions on the form which were about the father's health and his family's health. Dorothy honestly did not know the answers to most of the questions. When she finished tears began to spill from her eyes. Maybe people were right in calling her the horrible names given to girls who get pregnant without benefit of marriage. If she were married she would certainly know her husband's family and things about his family's health.

Miss Bielfelt looked at Dorothy and silently thought of all the girls in Dorothy's situation who she had worked with over the years. A part of her thought Dorothy's obvious discomfort was good as it would make Dorothy think about her actions and her sin and would lead her to making better choices in the future. The other part of her was more reflective. She thought about her own situation. She had never had carnal relations with a man as she felt the potential consequences were too harsh. Yet these girls did not give any caution. She didn't understand how they could be so careless and foolish.

Dorothy wiped away her tears and tried to control herself. "I don't know who the father is," Dorothy finally revealed.

"Are you certain? The information will be interpreted and put into a form which we share with the adoptive parents. They only need to know certain things. They will never know the names of the parents. In that, we will protect you. The father's name will not be listed on the birth certificate as he did not give his consent to having his name on this form, and you are not married. This copy of the birth certificate will include your name and the child's last name will be Clark. Once he is adopted, a new birth certificate will be created with his new name and the names of his adoptive parents. This copy will remain sealed. Are you certain you do not know who the father of your child is?"

Dorothy shook her head and continued to wipe her face. If she knew, she would not reveal it to the case worker. She distrusted the promise that no one would know. Dorothy would not do eye contact with to social worker and continued to deny knowing the father's identity.

"Did you select a name for the birth certificate?"

"Michael Wayne. I have always liked the name Michael, and John Wayne is my favorite actor, so Wayne would be a good middle name."

Miss Bielfelt wrote the name. "The birth certificate will identify him as Michael Wayne Clark. You know he had a bit of trouble at birth. Hopefully he will recover and will be adoptable. I will be in touch when we are ready for the final surrender papers. Are you certain you want to give your child up for adoption?"

Without a moment's delay Dorothy said a firm, "Yes." She could only hope word would not leak out to the Bedford community as her father had been well known and Dorothy did not want his memory to be besmirched.

Michael Wayne was not progressing satisfactorily. Because Booth Hospital had so many patients, they transferred him to St. Ann's Ward B. His movement was not conveyed to Dorothy even though she had not yet signed the surrender papers. When Dorothy found out, she was angry that she had not been consulted, even though she fully intended for him to be placed for adoption. She thought that this was the reason Mrs. Kerr from Booth Hospital and Miss Bielfelt from the Alice Hunt Center came to see her. Dorothy was ready for an argument, but the two quickly told her the reason for their visit.

"We have a more immediate problem. It seems another girl from Bedford, the same neighborhood as you, delivered a baby early this morning. When your mother came in this morning she saw the family of that girl. We need to move you in order to protect your identity and hers. Our job is to keep your situation as confidential as possible and your mother demanded that we move you. Your mother had made a call to a Sister Theresa at St. Ann's. It seems your mother knows her well and asked that she intervene on your behalf. We are going to move you to St. Ann's for postpartum care. It so happens that Michael has already been moved there as they needed more room here at Booth. St. Ann's can better monitor his health there."

"Why wasn't I informed of his movement there?" demanded Dorothy, feeling she should have had a say in this situation.

"The decision was made based on Michael's need. There are more beds available at St. Ann's. Since you are placing him for adoption and have not even consented to seeing him since he was born, we assumed this was the best situation for him."

"I haven't signed the final surrender papers," sputtered Dorothy.

Mrs. Kerr looked at Dorothy for a long moment. "Oh. Are you reconsidering your decision to place him for adoption?

If so, then we will need to call in the financial department to arrange for payments for your and Michael's hospitalization." Dorothy's anger quickly faded. "Have you changed your mind?" asked Mrs. Kerr.

"No," said Dorothy in a much more subdued tone.

Dorothy was admitted to St. Ann's on October 17th. She was to stay in the hospital wing rather than in the rooms where the unwed mothers who were waiting to deliver. It was best that the mothers who were giving up their children were kept separate from those who had not yet given birth.

A nurse came in to see Dorothy. "Michael is still not progressing as rapidly as we expected. Tomorrow he will be baptized, then he will be transferred as a ward of the state. His adoption will be handled by the Children's Services of Cuyahoga County and he will live in the Baby House until he is either adopted or can be moved to the cottages for toddlers." Dorothy listened, but at this point she only longed to be rid of this hospital and the memory of this entire episode. "If you like, you can attend the baptism." Dorothy let it be known she was not interested.

The next morning, October 18th, Michael was wrapped in a tight receiving blanket, and a christening bonnet was on his head. Michael cried throughout the baptism. Dorothy was not in attendance.

On the day that Dorothy was to return home she packed her suitcase and slipped the Bible from the drawer, her scapular, and her father's picture into her suitcase. It was Sister Theresa, a friend of her mother's, who met with Dorothy to do the exit interview. "One of our staff will drive you back to your home. A social service worker will visit you as a follow up to be certain you have recuperated. Your mother had asked that Catholic Charities handle the adoption, however, you need to know that if his health issues are long-term, he will be handed over as a ward of the state and the adoption process will be picked up by Children's Services. You will be notified when you will be needed to sign off final papers. Meanwhile it is expected that you have learned from this experience and you will put it behind you and move on with your life and sin no more." Dorothy nodded her head in understanding. "Dorothy, I know you have done the right thing. Little Michael will have a good life and you will go on, marry and have more children, and you will forget about this part of your life." Sister Theresa pulled a small gold medal out of the desk drawer. "Here is something for you to help you remember to sin no more." Dorothy took the tiny medal and put it into her pocket.

"Thank you, Sister Theresa, for everything you have done for me." Dorothy tried to sound sincere, but she was torn in trying to ascertain how long it would take for her to get back to her normal life.

A social worker drove Dorothy home and Anna was waiting for her at the door. Dorothy could smell food cooking on the stove, but it only made her stomach turn. "No thanks, Ma. I just want to lay down," Dorothy said as she slipped past her mother, avoiding a hug from her. Dorothy went to her room and stayed there for that day and the next only coming out when she used the bathroom. Her mother put a glass of water next to her bed, and put a bowl of soup there, but it went untouched.

After the two days Dorothy finally emerged from her room. Anna was surprised when Dorothy came into the kitchen and sat by the table. Anna waited for her daughter to say something, but she didn't. Finally Anna asked, "Are you hungry? You need to keep up your strength." Dorothy nodded and Anna was relieved to finally have some kind of communication with her daughter. Anna got up and pulled a pot of stew from the icebox and set it on the stove to heat. She busied herself in buttering some bread and making a cup of tea for Dorothy. It was obvious that Anna had something she wanted to discuss with her daughter. As Dorothy began eating Anna decided to broach the topic she had been considering.

"You know, Dorothy. I went to see Michael at both Booth and at St. Ann's. He looks like you and me. He has the same facial features. He has curly blonde hair, blue eyes, and high cheekbones. He is very long and thin. The birth was not easy and it seems he is having some kind of difficulty."

Dorothy didn't know how to respond. Somehow she just thought life would pick up right where it left off before this whole episode. She was not prepared to talk about this and was not certain how to proceed in the discussion.

"I took a christening cap to St. Ann's for his baptism, and I took a small rattle for him, although they don't like to have toys in the cribs. I've been thinking. I could easily take him in and tell everyone that he was a child of a distant relative who couldn't care for her child. No one would have to know he was yours. He will have a good home, Dorothy."

"Absolutely not!" said Dorothy in a most belligerent tone. "I made the decision to give him up for adoption. I do not want people gossiping. I do not want people speculating as to who the child belongs to. You have no right to go visiting him, or giving him gifts, or offering to take him as your own."

"Really, Dorothy," said Anna in a firm tone. "You keep thinking about yourself and your emotions. This is my grandchild and I don't want strangers raising him."

"You have no say in this, Ma. My mind is made up." Dorothy stormed to her room, too angry to even look at her mother. Dorothy stood in front of her dresser and gazed at herself in the mirror. She saw a haggard version of herself in the reflection. She was only twenty years old. She was not equipped to be a mother. Dorothy thought about Hank and Dee's son and although she enjoyed seeing him, she also recognized the amount of work Dee had to do to take care of him. Dorothy asked herself if it was selfishness that she didn't want to keep her son, or had she made this decision because she knew her mother wanted her to keep the baby? She didn't have an answer. Part of it was rebellion against her mother's interference in her life, but there was also a fear deeply ingrained that should she keep this child, there would be gossip about her and ruin brought to her father's name. She had not even told the man she suspected to be the father of Michael that she was pregnant for fear he would tell other people and word would spread throughout the small Bedford community. No, she had done the right thing. She needed to take care of herself and the circumstances had to be right, just like Dee who was married and had a husband to take care of her. No one had ever proposed marriage to her. She certainly couldn't afford to raise a child on her own. For a moment she considered the struggle her mother had as a war widow and constantly trying to survive on the small pension from her father, and the meager earnings she made as a domestic.

Dorothy took a long look at herself in the mirror, and shook her head. If she were to start over, she needed to start now. She studied her hair and realized it was oily. She was also still wearing the same clothing she had on when she traveled home from the hospital. She gathered fresh undergarments and a robe and went to the kitchen. She pulled out the tub and put water on the stove to boil and put together a hot bath. When she stepped into the tub she sunk as deep into the water as she could and took the washcloth and lathered it up and scrubbed her skin until it was red. She wanted to rub off the memory of the past months. She went to her room and applied some of the lotion given to her to keep her skin protected from potential outbreaks. She then looked through her clothing, looking for something that would fit her now shrinking body. She tore apart her room and pulled all of her clothing out, deciding what she would keep and what she needed to alter or get rid of. She took her coat and emptied the pockets and that's when she found the small gold medal. She collapsed on the bed and looked at it. Tears again welled in her eyes. She then straightened her shoulders and took the medal and put it into the sleeve of the scapular and placed it back into the Bible she carried home. She tucked the Bible back into the back of a drawer, looked in the mirror and vowed that she would, indeed, move on with her life. She had a fresh start. No more mistakes.

Dorothy did not leave the house for several weeks while she was going through her adjustment time. The elephant in the room was obvious to both Dorothy and her mother: Dorothy angered with her mother's interference, and Anna's sadness at losing a grandchild.

Chapter 4: 1948

Life seemed pretty good in America in the late 1940's. Bedford, Ohio, also felt the prosperity that the economic boom brought after the war ended. Young men returning from war had many options open to them, including money for college, home loans, and good wages. Many of the factories which had union protection, offered good salaries and benefits to their workers. To the young men of Bedford, this afforded many of them to either marry immediately upon coming home or enjoy "getting established" with a good job, saving money or going to college, and finding or building a home. Hank was certainly one of those young men and he had done well for himself.

Dorothy had vowed to start anew and she began that effort by going to her doctor for hormone shots and pills so she could lose weight. She had also been contacted by Cleveland Clinic to be part of a study on treatment for psoriasis. Dorothy quickly signed up as her skin condition had caused her much embarrassment. The treatments helped keep the skin lesions to a minimum and Dorothy began to feel "normal" for the first time in years. She certainly planned on making changes for the good. She determined that becoming a nurse would be a good profession and she would make a better wage than what she got from the small part-time jobs she held in the past. She got a job at St. Alexis as a nurse's aide, and had also signed up and paid $176 for the Institute of Practical Nursing. She put the whole business of Michael out of her mind and was ready to rejoin the world. Many of Dorothy's friends were getting married and Dorothy was determined to find someone who would want to marry her. Many boys found Dorothy attractive, and this fed into Dorothy's ego; however, none of them were interested in anything more than having fun.

Dorothy found a number of young men to whom she felt attracted. One young man was Eddie, a college student who was also a football player. He towered over her at six feet tall and Dorothy was very smitten with him; however, he was not interested in commitment. There was also Nick, a young man who lived nearby and enjoyed going to the movies with her or driving through Bedford Reservation. Johnny, another young man, played accordion and loved music. He was a good friend of Dorothy's best friend, Josie, and her family. Dorothy loved Johnny's company and his ready smile which she interpreted as his interest in dating her exclusively. The problem was Dorothy was not exclusive to anyone. She cast her net wide in hopes that she would find someone who would commit to her. Unfortunately her inability to protect herself and her reputation would once again become her downfall.

By New Year's Eve, 1948, just a bit over one year since she gave birth to Michael, Dorothy knew she was again pregnant. She had just missed her third period, and her breasts carried the familiar tenderness she felt when she was pregnant with Michael. But New Year's Eve was all about celebrating. Dorothy was invited to her best friend's home for a New Year's Eve party. Everyone enjoyed food, dancing, and drinking. The young people danced to albums which they played on the new Philco Album Length M-15 record player brought to the party by Johnny. It played 33 1/3 albums. Johnny quickly set up the record player to the 1940 Coronado Counsel radio that had an RCA jack that could hook up to a record player. Each album played 20 minutes per side. Everyone was excited about this new invention and Johnny made certain no one touched the equipment but him. He brought all the latest LP albums including Bing Crosby, the Mills Brothers, Dinah Shore, Doris

Day, Ella Fitzgerald and the Ink Spots, Glen Miller Orchestra, Tommy Dorsey, and Gene Autry. Everyone was singing the songs and dancing and laughter filled the air. Dorothy liked this new young man. She loved his playing the accordion and the excitement and enthusiasm he brought to a room with his music. What she didn't expect was that he was not interested in a commitment and that he had heard about her loose reputation.

Dorothy returned home and crumbled on her bed. She didn't sleep at all that night. The fact that he knew about it meant people had been talking about her. There were rumors about her and now she was "that girl" who everyone whispered about behind her back. She thought about all the names girls like her were called and it further shamed her. And now she was certain she was pregnant again which would only fuel the gossip mill and bring shame to the Clark name. What was her plan? She didn't have one, but she would need to figure out what she was going to do about her pregnancy. Once again, it was Dorothy's intention to not tell her mother about her condition. She would again try to conceal her pregnancy for as long as she could.

Dorothy was contacted repeatedly by Children's Services to come in to discuss issues regarding Michael. Dorothy would purposefully miss each appointment. Finally, a call was made to Anna who was still working as a domestic. Anna agreed to come in with Dorothy to meet with the social worker. At the January 22nd meeting Dorothy kept her body very rigid and stared out the window and Anna answered any question posed by the social worker. It was obvious Dorothy was annoyed that her mother was there and that she was interjecting answers to questions which were directed to Dorothy. Finally the social worker pulled Dorothy into a different room, and Dorothy opened up and said her mother was trying to make her keep Michael, but that was not what Dorothy wanted. The social worker explained that Michael had health issues and Children's Services had asked Children's Welfare to take over the case as Michael may not be adoptable. Dorothy appeared to not focus on the discussion of Michael's transfer, or his medical issues, but rather ranted about her mother's interference with decisions Dorothy made. Finally, Dorothy agreed to come in once papers needed to be signed to transfer Michael to Children's Welfare. The worker updated Dorothy's file; however, Dorothy never let it be known that she was pregnant, again.

In February Michael was moved to a sub home in order to be observed more closely, to determine if he did have developmental delays or other health issues. The nuns at St. Ann's repeatedly stated that what Michael needed was more one-on-one attention in a more normal home setting. Meanwhile, the social worker once again tried contacting Dorothy. When they tried to contact her at St. Alexis they were told that she had left the program. It wasn't until March 10th that Dorothy arrived at the social worker's office, quite obviously pregnant again. The social worker was taken aback and stunned that Dorothy was again unmarried, expecting and needing placement for her confinement. "The problem is, Dorothy, we do not yet have Michael as a ward in the Children's Welfare program. If he were, then we could offer you confinement options. We will have to work on this. When are you expecting?"

"I'm thinking sometime in June."

"Have you had prenatal care?"

Dorothy admitted she had not, nor had she told her mother. The social worker knew that for the safety and health of this baby, action needed to take place quickly. Meanwhile, Dorothy was to tell her mother about her condition.

The next morning Dorothy braced herself to tell her mother that she was already six months into another pregnancy, and Dorothy stood still as her mother berated her for being such a foolish woman. "How could you do this a second time? Didn't you learn from the last time? My, God, Dorothy. Now what are we to do?" Dorothy just stood there, unable to talk. The nightmare from not even two years ago came back and all the emotion of what she would face.

"Do you really think some agency that deals with girls like you is going to open their arms to you a second time? Do you have any answers for me, Dorothy?" Dorothy told her that she had gone in to see the social worker and a plan was being put together. Anna went to her room and Dorothy could hear her crying. Dorothy did not know how to comfort her. Dorothy had never grasped how any of this affected her mother. This was her problem and the focus should be on her, yet her mother was clearly upset for many reasons. Dorothy picked up the dishes in the kitchen, washed them and put them away, and then tidied the house. It wasn't much, but she thought her mother might appreciate the small effort she made. Dorothy went to the ice-box and looked at what she could make for dinner.

Monday morning Dorothy found her mother putting on her coat and moving toward the front door. "Where are you going, Ma?"

"I am going to see Sister Theresa. I don't know how I am going to ask for her help again, but I am praying she will help us."

What if Sister Theresa wouldn't take her? What if the social worker could not find placement for her? Dorothy thought of Agnes, but Agnes was getting married after having gone through a bad divorce from her first husband. Agnes was struggling financially to live independently before her second marriage, and once they got married they planned to start their own business. She could not be asked to take care of her sister and an illegitimate baby.

Dorothy tried to think of any relatives who might be willing to help. She considered every aunt and uncle, and even older cousins, but she came up with nothing. Besides, her mother would be furious to know she had taken this dirty secret to their doorsteps. Dorothy had no friends who were in a position to help her. Plus, she now thought that once her new secret was out, it would give even more ammunition to this small community to gossip about her. Her paranoia was increasing each day. Dorothy left the house wearing a large coat to camouflage her expanding body. She walked hoping the brisk air would help her find an answer to her problem.

When she returned home and opened the door her mother was sitting at the kitchen table, waiting for her.

"I went to see Sister Theresa. She was very disappointed that you have made a second mistake, but she felt that she could arrange for you to use their services a second time. Mind you, this is the last time! We will need to get a referral from the Alice Hunt Center and they will take care of the referral to St. Ann's. Do you understand how lucky you are to have Sister Theresa looking out for you?" Anna looked at her daughter and Dorothy merely stood there, defeated. "Do you?" asked Anna, again.

Dorothy slowly nodded her head. She was coming to the full realization that she was solely responsible for the decisions she made and that the consequences of a second mistake would not be as easily forgiven as the first. She was also grateful that her mother was trying to find solutions to her problems. Dorothy knew she would once again be part of the statistics of fallen women.

Chapter 5: 1949

On April 7, 1949, Dorothy was admitted to St. Ann's. Dorothy had the feeling of déjà vu upon returning to St. Ann's. This time it was not Sister Theresa who met with Dorothy in the office. There was a much sterner nun, and she let it be known that Catholic Charities expected the women in this program to actively change their behavior upon leaving and it was obvious that Dorothy had ignored that mandate. If Dorothy was not downtrodden when she came into the office, she certainly was when she left.

Anna looked at her daughter and could see her distress. She quietly asked the nun if Sister Theresa was available as she was a close friend of hers. The nun begrudgingly stood, stared at Dorothy, and then left the room. Twenty minutes later Sister Theresa entered the office. It was explained to Dorothy that a case worker from Children's Services who handled the adoption process would be coming in later to do the initial interviews about this pregnancy.

Sister Theresa tried to make conversation with Anna and Dorothy and explained that the hospital was considered a state of the art medical facility. They had provided care for many women over the years since its opening. On Dorothy's first trip here she was put directly into the hospital wing as she had already delivered her baby. This time she would be housed here until she delivered.

Dorothy obediently signed each document presented her which was not explained in great detail except that she would work at the facility, take classes which could allow her to complete her high school diploma, and that she would release the baby for adoption immediately after the birth. It was also explained that should she change her mind and keep the child, all expenses would need to be repaid. When it was time for Anna to leave, Dorothy asked when she would see her mother next. Sister Theresa said, "We typically do not allow visitors; however, if your mother wants to see you she can make an appointment. It is best that you not be exposed to outside influences and emotions. Your mother will return when you have delivered your baby." Dorothy looked at her mother, imploring her without words to offer compassion and love, but Anna's face was devoid of emotion. This business had certainly taken its toll on Anna. Dorothy reached out and clung to her mother, but Anna merely patted her on the back, then withdrew from the embrace and turned to leave the room. Dorothy was left looking at her mother's back as the door closed behind her.

After Anna's departure, Dorothy moved in a state of depression. How could this happen to her a second time? The words Sister Theresa said were not even heard by Dorothy. She merely nodded her head to whatever was being said, and tears slowly slid down her cheeks. She lowered her head and kept her gaze at the floor. Gone was the happy young woman who enjoyed movies and her friends' company, and even the memory of her interactions with the young men she dated.

Eventually Sister Theresa pulled Dorothy out of her stupor and implored her to follow her. Dorothy dutifully picked up her suitcase and followed after the tall and stately nun, only glimpsing up to take in where she was going. The halls of St. Ann's were clean and bright, unlike the darkness that Dorothy felt within her soul. When Dorothy entered the hallway she saw rooms with four beds in each room. Sister Theresa stopped at a room where Dorothy saw two neatly made beds. Beside each of the four beds was a small dresser, and at the base of the bed was a chest. Two of the beds had mattresses which were rolled up, awaiting the next client. "This floor is where our girls and women sleep. You will store your belongings in your dresser. The chest can be used for your coat, shoes or other outdoor wear. You will be given a package with your hygiene needs. As you need more supplies you will let Sister Mary know and she will secure what you need." Sister Theresa walked to a tall shelf at the end of the hallway and pulled off a set of sheets. She returned to Dorothy. "Go ahead and make up your bed and put your things away. The girls will be returning to the rooms in about forty minutes. We will then show you the rest of the facility and give you a chance to get acclimated. Tomorrow we will meet and create a schedule for you to follow." Dorothy merely nodded, keeping her head lowered.

"Dorothy, we want the girls to use a different name while here at St. Ann's. It is to protect your identity. Do you have a name you would prefer?" Dorothy thought for a moment, and she picked the name Barbara as that was her Confirmation name. "Fine. We will refer to you as Barbara while you are here. Do not share your real first or last name with the other girls." Dorothy nodded. "Also, do not divulge where you live or any other personal information which would jeopardize your family's privacy." My family's privacy, thought Dorothy. She was aware that much of the decision making being done was to protect the family from the shame she had brought them.

When Sister Theresa left the room, Dorothy looked around. The room was very Spartan with little personality. The girls were not allowed to bring personal items to St. Ann's, so it made sense that there were no displays of photographs, makeup, or other items on the dressers. Dorothy looked at the two made up beds and saw one that had carefully arranged the pillow under the blanket. There was an empty bed next to it, and based solely on the hope that the pillow-plumper was someone who liked nice things, Dorothy determined she would set up her belongings in the next bed. Dorothy opened the dresser and found a small Bible in the top drawer. She pulled it out and looked at it, wondering if another "fallen" girl had used it. As she opened the Bible she realized the binding was stiff, and the pages were unbent. She guessed it was a new Bible donated to a girl who had lost her way. She slipped the Bible back into the drawer and unpacked her small suitcase. She reached into the side pocket of the suitcase and pulled out a small photo of her father. She looked at it for a moment and said a small prayer asking her father to forgive her for the mistake she had made. She then slipped the picture inside the Bible in the dresser. She folded her coat and placed it in the chest, and pushed her empty suitcase under the bed. She made up the bed with the sheets that Sister Theresa had given her, and tried to mimic the plumped pillow of the bed beside hers, then sat and waited for the other girls to return.

Not long after she had completed her tasks, Dorothy could hear the girls moving in the hallway. There was the sound of feet and muffled voices. There were a few stifled giggles, then a sharp voice that interrupted. "Stop the noise in the hallways! Now!" There was immediate silence and only the sound of feet moving continued until the group of girls entered the dormitory rooms. Once they were in their rooms Dorothy could hear several of the girls burst into laughter.

Dorothy looked at the girls who were moving in the hallway. There was a wide variety of ages. Some of the girls were obviously very young, probably fifteen at most. There were others who were clearly in their 20's. Dorothy was glad that she was not the youngest or the oldest. Dorothy then noticed that each girl showed a different stage of pregnancy. Some were barely showing at all, while others looked huge and their bellies consumed all attention. The girls furthest along in their pregnancies either moved normally, or some held onto their backs as if they were balancing a lead weight on their abdomen and spine. Dorothy had kept her first pregnancy secret, and as such she tried to walk without displaying discomfort in order to not draw attention to herself. She was already in her last trimester, and she had continued to hold herself erect and didn't allow herself to draw attention to her swollen belly. It was also a way that she could trick herself into not thinking about her condition when she chanced upon a reflection of herself.

Dorothy looked to see if she could pick out the girl with the plumped pillow. Two girls entered her room and both looked back at the doorway to see if the owner of the reprimanding voice would follow them into the room. That's when she spotted Linda. Linda moved quickly and efficiently to the bed next to Dorothy, plopped herself down, rubbed her belly which looked to be full term, and then looked at Dorothy.

"Hey. Hi. I'm Linda," she said with a smile.

"Barbara," said Dorothy, testing out the sound of her new identity. "Hope you don't mind my taking the bed next to yours."

"Not at all," said Linda. "When is your baby due?"

"Not until June."

"Oh. You've got a long wait. This baby is supposed to come sometime at the end of April. I haven't gained a lot of weight, so I think my baby is going to be small. Are you keeping the baby or giving it up?" asked Linda.

"I am giving it up," replied Dorothy, uncertain how that information would be received by Linda, or any of the girls in this group.

"That will be hard. I want to keep mine. I will have some-one to love me all the time. I am pretty excited."

"How is your family going to explain this?" asked Dorothy.

"I've got it all figured out. After I deliver and go home I am going to tell everyone that I had gotten married some time ago. My husband went out to work at a job and I stayed behind with my sister. I no sooner found out I was in a family way, when my husband died in a car accident. Everyone will think that I am so brave to bear such a burden all alone and without my husband." Linda giggled at the thought of how gullible people would be. Dorothy was struck with how detailed Linda's lie was and how easily she felt others would believe her.

Linda quickly changed the subject. "Who did your intake papers?"

"Sister Theresa. She is actually a friend of my mother's."

"Oh, Sister Theresa is very kind. She is always willing to help any of us girls. Now, let me warn you about some of the others. They are not as kind. It is hard to believe they are nuns. I thought nuns were supposed to be all loving and forgiving of everyone. Let me tell you, some of them are darn right mean." Dorothy thought about this and figured the voice she heard in the hallway was probably one of the nuns who was not enchanted with women who had made the wrong decisions in life.

"Most of the nuns are very pleasant and kind, but there were several who did not even attempt to hide their distaste for having to care for someone in our condition," said Linda.

Dorothy considered what Linda had said about keeping her baby. It was nice that Linda's parents were supportive of Linda. It was not fair that any of these girls had to deal with nuns who treated them less than respectfully. Of course, as she pondered that thought, Dorothy realized she was absolutely wrong. If she kept this baby she would have to face every set of eyes looking at her with the same disdain she would see in some of the nuns' eyes. She knew she was making the right choice in giving this baby up for adoption, even if her mother wanted her to keep it and promised to help raise it. Thinking about what the next few months would hold for her drained her of any energy. She knew she needed to refocus.

"What is the schedule for today? I meet with Sister Theresa tomorrow to make up a schedule, but I am just supposed to follow the girls for the rest of the day," said Dorothy, trying to bypass the negative thoughts about how people would treat her.

"Well, this morning most of the girls did school. All the young ones are finishing up their high school diplomas. You can take classes if you want. Did you graduate from high school?"

"No, actually I didn't. I had a medical problem and I quit school at the end of tenth grade. I was taking courses to earn my high school diploma, but I haven't finished."

"Medical condition? Did you have a baby back then?"

"No," said Dorothy, although she thought about the trouble she had gotten in with the teacher and her mother's immediate intervention to make that situation stop. "I had a skin problem that came about after I learned that my father died during the war."

"Oh, that's too bad. Are you ok now?" asked Linda, looking at Dorothy's exposed skin. Her eyes became fixed on Dorothy's elbows and her knees which had the patchy white tell-tale markings of psoriasis.

"It will never go away, but it isn't as bad as my first outbreak. Stress seems to set it off. I mostly have outbreaks on my elbows, knees and sometimes my scalp."

"Is it contagious?" asked Linda, rubbing her belly as if to protect it from some fearsome disease.

"No. It's just something I have to live with. I try to remain calm so it doesn't go haywire."

"Good. Well, you asked about our schedules. You can take classes, or you can go to the library to read. You can write, but you cannot mail out letters unless they are approved by the nuns. They don't want you identifying where you are or asking for visitors. That's part of the agreement here."

"I gathered that at the intake meeting," said Dorothy.

"We typically work for a couple of hours in the laundry or kitchen, or scrubbing the bathroom and toilets. Everyone chips in to do something. They rotate the schedule every week so no one gets stuck with the same job all the time. If some of the girls are not feeling well because of their condition, they are excused from work. We also take classes in how to be a good parent. We learn about how to handle babies and feed them. Most of the girls who are giving up their babies don't take that class. They don't want to think about it." Dorothy thought to herself that she wouldn't take that class because it would just make it harder to give up the baby. She did not reveal that she had already gone through a pregnancy and birth prior to this one. She didn't want the girls to think less of her.

A bell chimed and all the girls straightened up their blankets on their beds, then moved to the doorway. "Time for lunch," said Linda. "I'll show you the way."

Dorothy and Linda left the dormitory, and Dorothy merely listened to Linda as she shared her story. It seemed that Linda grew up in the suburbs of Cleveland. Her parents were very religious. When Dorothy asked about the father of the baby she was surprised that Linda answered she didn't know who it was.

"You don't know who the father is?"

"Oh, Barbara. When the boys went off to war no one said anything about how many girls they had relations with. Why should girls be any different? What about you?"

Dorothy shrugged. She really didn't want to talk about the father of her baby.

"I get that you don't want to talk about it. Some of the girls here talk about their baby's father all the time. Some are like you and they don't talk about it at all. There was one girl that was here who confessed that her brother was the father of the baby, and another told us her uncle was at fault." Dorothy looked at Linda in alarm. At least Dorothy didn't have that problem.

Linda walked Dorothy to the cafeteria. They picked up their tray of food from the kitchen area and moved to one of the tables. "They use this room for our meals, plus they use it for different meetings we have. Sometimes there are groups from outside that come in to use the facility and they use this room as well. When they do we are not allowed to come down to this floor. Best to keep us hidden from the public eye," said Linda.

Dorothy and Linda were eating their lunch when another girl asked if she could sit with them. Dorothy recognized her as the other roommate, but she had quickly dropped off some books then went to the restroom before she could introduce herself to Dorothy. "Sure," said Linda. "This is Brenda. Do you know she was in college and when they found out she was expecting, they expelled her. Can you believe that?"

Brenda shook her head in disgust. "My boyfriend and I were not allowed to buy any kind of contraceptive at the local store or through the campus infirmary. They said that not selling us contraceptives would prevent us from having sex." Both she and Linda laughed out loud. "I saw a study that said thirty-nine percent of unmarried girls had sex before they were twenty years old. Do they think they can stop people from falling in love and acting on it? So now I am labeled a 'wayward girl,' and my family has forbidden me to come home with this baby. I feel like I am being shunned by my own family. I lost my scholarship for college, my parents look at me in disgust, and I haven't yet figured out what will happen to me after I leave here."

"What about your boyfriend's family?" asked Dorothy.

"Former boyfriend. When his parents found out they demanded Eric break off our relationship or be cut from the family will. I found out which he valued more," said Brenda, not looking at either girl as she turned her attention to her tray of uneaten food.

The three girls sat silently, thinking about their own situation and what the future held for them and for their babies.

Little did the girls know that society was readily defining them. Unfortunately, society was led to believe through "research" that girls and women who had no control over their sex lives were psychologically deficient. They had a neurosis which disallowed them to control their sexual urges. Many felt unmarried white girls who became pregnant would be unable to find normalcy in marriage and home unless they relinquished their bastard children and recognized the shame of their mistakes and guilt in making the mistakes they made. Statistics would show that white unwed mothers who found themselves in maternity homes were considered "breeders" for the white parents who adopted their babies.

Despite being sent away to maternity homes, the mothers received very little information about governmental programs that could help them raise their children, nor were they informed about their right to child support. Most often, the male was not held accountable for his part in the pregnancy. Very few women who found themselves in maternity homes spoke with a lawyer, yet were asked, or forced under duress by their own parents, to sign papers to surrender their child. They were not schooled about informed consent or conflicts of interest in the adoption process.

Most maternity homes discouraged the girls to get married to the fathers of their children. Mail was censored and communications were limited with anyone outside the facility. While Catholic Charities in Cleveland was known to be a good center, many of the issues mentioned here were still present there as well. There were many maternity homes which profited from the adoption process. To obtain the signed surrender paper, many mothers were asked to sign while they were still under medication from delivery. Signatures were often coerced, or done under psychological pressure brought on by identifying them as fallen women and sinners.

One day Linda was called with several other girls to attend a special class. When she returned Dorothy asked her what the class was about. "A doctor and nurse came in and told us about the birth process. Some of the girls in the class had seen babies born with the help of a midwife, but most of us had never seen a baby born. They had charts and diagrams that we looked at, and the nurse explained how the baby would move to position and labor pains would let us know that our time was coming."

"Did they tell you what to do about the pain?" asked Dorothy.

"They assured us that they would give us sedatives if needed to help us through the pain. They said we would get Demerol which would make the pain more manageable. They really didn't get into great detail. Seems like we just show up and they take over."

"Did they talk about what happens after the baby is born?" asked Dorothy.

"Briefly. They said we have a choice. The baby could be taken away immediately with or without our seeing it. The baby will be put into the nursery, but we wouldn't have access to see it. Or, we can hold the baby and feed the baby until either we have recovered from the delivery, or until the adoptive parents come in to pick up the baby. They warned us that doing this would make it harder to separate later."

"What are you going to do, Linda?" asked Dorothy.

"I am keeping the baby, so I want to hold it and feed it and love it."

Dorothy thought about this, knowing there was only one choice she would make when the time came to give birth.

Several days later Dorothy was awakened by Linda's moaning. She looked over at Linda's bed and saw Linda holding tight to her swollen belly and dropping her head forward. "Linda, are you all right?"

"I have been having some light pains on and off all night, but this one was not light. I think it is time for this baby to come."

Dorothy put on a robe and slippers and helped Linda into her robe and slippers. She then walked beside Linda as they went to the infirmary. About half way down the hallway Linda stopped and stared at her feet. "What in the world?" she said as she felt water moving down her legs onto the floor.

"Wait here, Linda. I'll get help." Dorothy moved quickly, but was met in the hall by one of the nuns who had heard voices in the hallway. "Linda has water running down her legs," said Dorothy breathlessly.

"Foolish girl. That is a sign that the baby will be arriving soon. Go to the infirmary and tell them to bring a wheelchair," barked the nun. Dorothy dutifully moved quickly to the infirmary. One of the nurses secured a wheelchair, and another nurse on duty got on the phone to call the doctor. Dorothy returned to Linda. "Go back to the dormitory. You are no longer needed here," said the nun harshly to Dorothy.

Linda did not return to the room for the next week. Dorothy learned that when a girl went into labor she was taken to the infirmary and evaluated, then transported to the hospital. She was allowed no visitors. After a set amount of time the girl would go back to the dormitory and pack her things to leave. Dorothy was thankful she was able to see Linda before she left the facility. Dorothy embraced Linda and the two sat down. "Tell me all about it," said Dorothy.

Linda began quietly crying, which surprised Dorothy as Linda had always said she wanted the baby, yet she was leaving without the baby. "I was told my water broke and that is a sign that the baby is coming. They didn't tell us that in the class we took. When I got to the infirmary they put me in bed and did an examination. I was then driven to the hospital where I was dumped off like I was being taken to a dog pound. No one stayed with me when I was put into a room. My pains were pretty steady, at first every fifteen minutes, then between five and seven minutes. That went on for about seven hours. Someone would occasionally come into the room to check on me. When my pains got to be about four minutes apart things got crazy. They gave me the Demerol and even though I was awake I had no control over my body. It didn't hurt any more, but I couldn't even talk clearly or move myself. I was wheeled into the operating room and things happened very fast. I could feel the movement of the baby leaving my body, and I could hear the baby cry so I knew it was all right. The nurse said it was a girl. She asked if I wanted to see her and at first I didn't know how to respond. I finally nodded and they put this little baby on my chest. She was so tiny. I know I started crying. The nurse then took the baby away when someone in the room asked if I had reconsidered keeping the baby. I said I wanted to keep her and I was told I had to pay for each month for the facility, the delivery, plus all other expenses. They asked how I would pay my debt. I said I couldn't. They said they had asked my parents if they were going to pay, and they had said they could not, and even if they could, they would not. My choice was to pay, or sign off for adoption. My head was still spinning from the Demerol and everything I had just been through. I started crying and said I had no money. I signed the papers to give the child up immediately. I could hear the door close when someone took the baby out of the room." Linda stopped and her head dropped and she cried silently. Dorothy just listened and put her arm around Linda's shoulders.

"I remained in the hospital for a little more than a week while my body healed and I was able to walk and take care of myself. I asked several times if I could see the baby, but they said that since I had signed the papers and it would be too painful to see her and they recommended that I save myself from that pain. I cannot believe how much I cried. Plus, my chest hurt so badly. The nurse said it was because my milk had come in and since I was not nursing the pressure built inside was causing the pain. They bound me up to help stop the milk from producing. My chest kept hurting, but I think it was really my heart hurting because I only got to see my little girl for moments before they took her away." Linda continued to cry quietly. Dorothy searched for something to say to make the situation less stressful. She could think of nothing. Finally she asked, "Did you name her?"

Linda looked up and smiled weakly. "Yes. I named her after my grandmother. She is Elizabeth Marie. That is the only thing I could give to my daughter. A name. A name that will probably be changed by the family who adopts her. But for now, at least, she has the name I have given her."

Linda eventually stood up, and Dorothy helped her pack her suitcase. The two embraced and Dorothy knew they would never see each other again. Several of the girls had talked about girls that left and once they left, they never wanted to remember this part of their lives. Linda walked slowly out of the dormitory and Dorothy lay on her bed, trying to make sense out of her life and the decisions she had made.

Dorothy was called to the office to meet with her social worker. The focus would be having Dorothy reveal the paternity of the child. She was overcome with emotion at having to vocalize a name as the father. Dorothy carefully answered, "I don't know who the father is."

"Fine. Please understand that it is highly likely you will be asked to help pay for the costs of your stay here, the delivery, and all other medical and housekeeping costs. If you reveal the name of the father we will contact him and he will be asked to assist in payments. You can return to your room and when you are ready you can return to your schedule. If you remember who the father was, make an appointment to meet with me so we can work on this."

Dorothy went back to her room and lay on her bed. Tears and sobs overwhelmed her. She truly wasn't certain who the father was, but if she revealed a name she was certain everyone in Bedford would find about her pregnancy and the child she was giving up. They might also figure out about Michael Wayne. She would be ruined. Dorothy did not leave her room at all for the rest of the day. When the girls returned at night, Dorothy pretended to be asleep so she would not need to talk to anyone. In the morning, Dorothy was once again covered in red welts. She was taken to the infirmary and treated and the doctor who visited gave her a sedative to calm her down. Dorothy spent much of her days sleeping until the episode subsided.

Dorothy spent her days doing laundry, working in the kitchen, or doing other household tasks. Every week was different. She spent her education time writing poetry, and taking history classes. She was not interested in spending all day in classes to get her diploma as she felt at age twenty-two she was too old to sit in class with the younger girls. She also chose not to be in the class that taught parenting skills as she thought it was unnecessary as she was giving the baby up for adoption. Instead she filled her hours doing things she felt satisfied in doing. She enjoyed memorizing things and focused her attention on memorizing the names of the states and their capitals. Not only could she do this in alphabetical order, she could do it in reverse order both by state and by capital. This time consuming task allowed her to stop thinking about her situation and wallowing in her circumstances. Dorothy was good at memorizing things, like the lyrics to songs or the words to different poems. Dorothy had packed some plain handkerchiefs and a crochet hook and various colors of crochet thread. She found comfort as she crocheted lace on handkerchiefs and did crossword puzzles. The distractions helped her mind escape the impending events which awaited her.

All of the girls were required to go to the religion class. There were parts of it Dorothy enjoyed, but there were equal parts of it that made her feel unworthy. The nun teaching the class was firm and outspoken about sins of the flesh. To Dorothy it seemed she was speaking directly to her, although that sentiment was probably felt by every girl or woman in the class. It was painful to go each day to class knowing that this particular day could be a lesson of morality. After class all the girls went to chapel for either a full mass, or to a prayer service. Dorothy was given a rosary when she was first admitted into St. Ann's and she found the routine of saying the rosary an easy way to pass the time in prayer service. Dorothy stayed to herself and avoided conversations with the other women. Her state of depression worsened as she internalized every comment made about the shame and guilt she should feel for her condition. When reminders were said that they should never become repeat offenders of their sin, Dorothy withdrew into herself, angered because she felt the comments were directed specifically at her.

Days turned into weeks, and time passed slowly. Dorothy made no comment as the girls left to deliver their babies then quietly disappear from St. Ann's, and new girls came to take their place. There was a small library of donated books at the center. Many books were religious in nature, but there was a mix of other themes. Dorothy filled her time reading detective stories. It seemed safer to her to read a non-emotional book about solving mysteries than solving the problems of real life that she was facing.

Dorothy was unhappy during her stay at St. Ann's. She disliked Children's Services and the case workers who had been assigned to her. It seemed that everyone felt entitled to treat her poorly and tell her what to do. When Dorothy received word that her mother had landed in the hospital, Dorothy decided she needed to go see her. Her case worker was not persuaded, and when Dorothy demanded she be allowed to go the case worker told her that she should not exert herself this late in the pregnancy by going to another hospital. She also reminded Dorothy that when she became stressed her skin condition returned. Besides, the whole point of Dorothy being placed in this home was to help hide her from public view and going to see her mother would certainly put her in full view of family and friends who were with Anna. Dorothy was having no part of listening to her case worker's argumentation. Finally a supervisor was called in to try to reason with Dorothy. When Dorothy continued her demands the supervisor snapped and said, "Right now your mother does not need you running out in public. She has enough worry about her own health and should not have to add more worry because you are jeopardizing everything she worked so hard to do for you."

Dorothy retorted, "So you think my mother would be better off dead than to see me?"

"That is not what I said, Dorothy. I said that she needs to put her own health needs ahead of unnecessary worry about you exposing your condition to relatives or friends who might be at her hospital. She tried to protect you. Please understand this is for your own good, and for your mother's good.

"You can't tell me what to do. I want to know who I need to talk to so I can get out of here."

The supervisor was fast becoming angry with Dorothy. "Look, I am telling you that you will not leave this building.

We will let you know how your mother is progressing. You are not in a position to be demanding anything from anyone. You asked for our assistance to help you when you made poor life choices. You are near your due date and our job is to keep you safe and healthy. We cannot do that if you come and go as you want."

Dorothy began to start a new tirade, and the supervisor looked at her and sternly said, "No! That is the end of this discussion. If you leave this building we will void all support we have agreed upon. You will have to find your own housing, and keep your child and make restitution for our costs, and the costs you will endure from delivery and raising your child. If you are willing to do that, then leave. But know this--there will be no coming back."

Dorothy had spent the last year doing whatever she wanted with no one telling her she couldn't do something. While she wanted to just show this supervisor and case worker that she had a mind of her own, Dorothy realized if she left she would add even more stress to her mother, and she certainly didn't plan on raising this baby.

Chapter 6: June, 1949

There were no visitors, no letters, and no kind words. The nuns and the nurses communicated as they needed to, but no one seemed concerned that Dorothy was in the pits of despair and depression. She tried to block from her memory having lost her father, her unsatisfied relationships with men, first one and now a second pregnancy, and being removed from the nursing program because of this pregnancy. This all weighed heavily on Dorothy's mind.

Every day was a trial for Dorothy. She longed for escape from the thoughts which caused such anxiety. Sleep would let her escape, but sleeping was constantly disturbed when her mind looked back into her desperate situation. It didn't take long for Dorothy' torment to manifest itself into another full blown case of psoriasis. If anything, the hateful pain and itching pulled her mind from her other worries.

When the doctor was called to deal with Dorothy's outbreak it was quickly recognized that she was clinically depressed; however, she would be given no medications as she was so far along in her pregnancy. "The sedatives we give her to calm down her psoriasis should help calm her mind and ease this depression," he said. Dorothy certainly hoped it would be true. "Also, set her up for some counseling," the doctor said.

The idea of counseling was having a social worker come in to talk with, or rather, as Dorothy thought, "at" her. A middle aged woman with ratted up hair and bright red lipstick came in every few days to meet with Dorothy. The messages were all the same. "You should be thankful that this agency is taking care of your problem." "You have put many people at a disadvantage because of your illegal sex." "You cannot provide for the baby, so you should be happy that we will provide a good family who is educated and has the financial resources to care for the baby." "Perhaps it was God's will for you to be able to provide this baby for a loving, good family to raise." "If you keep this baby, how will this baby feel when he or she is old enough and knows he or she was born an illegitimate child? You know people will talk." This "counseling" filled Dorothy with more guilt than anything else. No one asked what she wanted. She didn't matter. She was a sinner. She had caused all this unrest for everyone else.

The last month of Dorothy's pregnancy was quiet. Dorothy tried to align her feelings into believing she was doing the right thing. She messed up a second time, but she had learned from this lesson. She could put this behind her, meet a nice man, marry, and have children she could keep. That was the plan.

The weather was unusually hot and the girls felt miserable as many carried the additional weight of full-term pregnancy. It was a relief when Dorothy began her labor pains in mid-June. Unlike most of the other girls who knew nothing about what to expect in childbirth, Dorothy had the advantage of knowing what awaited her. Her pains started and she was quickly transferred to the hospital. In a matter of a few hours, at 2:03 AM, she delivered a healthy boy. This time she had a name picked out. "Lawrence Gene," she said. Again, she liked the name Lawrence because of Lawrence Welk whose orchestra she enjoyed hearing on the radio, and she loved Gene Autry, a movie star and singer. The baby's paperwork was completed. Lawrence Gene Clark. Born June 14, 1949. Mother, Dorothy Clark of Bedford, Ohio. No father's name appeared on the birth certificate.

When asked if she wanted to see the baby, Dorothy hesitated for a moment, but after thinking about all the stress and emotion she had felt over the past few months she decided to not let separation make things worse. She said no. And within a moment, Lawrence was gone.

It was only a short time later that Dorothy was to be sent home. Sister Theresa met with her. "Well, Dorothy. I am hoping that you have had time to think about this experience. I have been praying for you and I hope that you will truly find your happiness. I am hoping that you will put this business behind you and move on with your life. Have you given any thought as to how you will keep this from happening again in the future?"

Dorothy paused, then said. "I said a prayer to God and promised I would not let this happen again. I never break a promise that I make."

Sr. Theresa reached into the desk and pulled out yet another gold medal, exactly like the first. She put it into Dorothy's hand and said, "Go now, and sin no more." Dorothy nodded, stood up and left the office. She vowed she would never make another mistake like this. It was too difficult.

She returned home. She slipped the gold medal into the sleeve of the scapular with the one from Michael. "Sister Theresa is right. Sin no more."

But she did.

Chapter 7: 1949-1950

After Dorothy returned to the Archer Road home, she entered a silent house. Anna had little to say to her. Hank's wife, Dee, had found out about Dorothy and was less than happy that Dorothy had brought shame to the family name. Dorothy avoided seeing her as she did not want any kind of confrontation or lectures on morality. Dorothy was now convinced that everyone knew about her sins. Plural. She had not made one mistake, but now a second. She chose not to expose herself to additional gossip and shame.

Once Dorothy was on her feet again she became a domestic for a Jewish family in Cleveland Heights. There were two children Dorothy was to care for: a six-year-old girl and a little boy. It did not take long for Dorothy to quit that job.

Being around young children every day only reminded her that she had relinquished her two sons. She was confused as to whether she was happy she did not have the responsibility of raising her sons on her own, or if the reality of having relinquishing them made her a bad person. Rather than dwell on it, she tried to put these memories out of her mind.

It was at this time that Dorothy was called into the Children's Welfare office to discuss the two children who had not yet been adopted. The case worker told Dorothy she needed to update the records and asked Dorothy many questions. Dorothy indicated that she was hoping to land a job in the maternity ward of a new hospital which was to open in Garfield Heights. She had been quite certain she would get in as they had originally acted very interested. When asked who her references were Dorothy replied, "The priest at our parish and a family doctor who knew about one of my pregnancies."

At her next visit the case worker asked Dorothy about the hospital job. Dorothy revealed that when she called back there was a change in attitude about the likelihood that she would be hired. The case worker stated that it was highly likely that when they learned she had given birth to two illegitimate children that could have tempered their decision. Dorothy immediately shut down any further discussion of the potential job.

The case worker then tried to get Dorothy to talk about the fathers of her two sons, but Dorothy became annoyed and changed the subject to how bad her experience was with

Children's Services. Her strategy was to divert the attention off of the subject she did not want to discuss and get the focus on the mistreatment she had experienced from Children's Services. The case worker had seen such manipulation in the past and knew it would get her nowhere to pursue this line of questioning at the time.

When questioned about her next plans Dorothy indicated she had picked up pamphlets from the Recruiting Office and was thinking she'd be interested in the Army and working in the Medical Corps. The social worker wondered how Dorothy would fare in a setting like that and whether she would be back to her old behaviors. As Dorothy left the meeting, the social worker looked at her notes and shook her head. Dorothy was certainly a puzzle. She wasn't convinced that Dorothy had learned her lesson yet.

Meanwhile, at home, Anna was busy with Hank's family. Dee had delivered her third son in March and Anna was thrilled that she had three grandsons. Although Dorothy was happy that Hank and Dee had three healthy sons, she felt resentment at her mother's joy. Despite Dorothy's strong objections to keeping her two sons, and resenting her mother for wanting her to keep the boys, Dorothy felt ignored in that she had mothered two boys, yet had no positive recognition for it. This contrary thought process was even a puzzle to Dorothy, yet her emotions were always in direct conflict with whatever her mother was doing: doting on Hank's three sons, admonishing Dorothy for her poor behavior and choices she made, or not giving Dorothy the kind of attention she wanted. To appease her daughter, Anna avoided ever making any mention of her other grandsons. The conflicts between Dorothy and Anna could never be solved without some kind of professional intervention; however, finances and shame in admitting the need for such services would never allow that to happen. It was obvious that Dorothy had a low self-esteem, and perhaps even self-loathing, yet she resented anyone or anything which would force to her face these emotions. It was Dorothy's perception that everyone, family, neighbors and friends, were judging her. If only she could heal these feelings, or come to some resolution for what led to her present state of mind, perhaps then she could truly move on and make a better life for herself. Her only plan was to put the past out of her mind and escape from anything and anyone who would remind her of her misfortunes.

Dorothy's sister, Agnes, came to visit in August, 1950. She was expecting her first child and she was violently ill from morning sickness and constantly feeling exhausted. Anna offered that Dorothy was not working, so perhaps she could move in and help Agnes around the house, and help out at the diner that Agnes and her husband had purchased near a small airport in Northfield. Agnes thought it would be a good idea, and Dorothy, eager to get away from the tension in the Clark household, readily agreed. By the end of August Dorothy had moved in with Agnes. Agnes' home was small and Dorothy had to sleep on the sofa as there was no additional bedroom. She didn't care. This was paradise being away from the prying eyes of neighbors and her mother's disapproval. She would only return home on her days off work.

The diner was located near what had been Sky Haven Airport in Northfield near the intersection of Olde Route 8 and Twinsburg Road. It was listed as a commercial airfield and it had three unpaved, loam, clay, and sod runways. The longest of these runways was 2,500 feet long. There were two wooden hangars on the property. In 1947 the owner, Slim Honroth, lost his lease on this airfield, and then opened another airfield one mile north on Route 8. The original airfield was renamed Welcome Airport. America was entering the Golden Age of Flying, and there were numerous men who had learned to fly during World War II in the CPTP (Civilian Pilot Training Program.) Over 60,000 Americans learned to fly during that training. Many became involved in the Civil Air Patrol which was a civilian group that provided aviation support during the war, along with military aircraft to be freed for the war effort. The Civil Air Patrol flew border patrol, search and rescue, and other non-combat missions across the nation. Their planes were often called tail-draggers, puddle jumpers, and low-and-slow flyers. After the war many former Civil Air Patrol men and aircraft hobbyists in the area owned their own single-engine aircraft or Swifts, and kept their planes at the Welcome Airport. A social group, the Welcomaires, was formed to promote social and flying activities. Between the airport activity and the busy Route 8 traffic, the diner kept a steady array of customers, and often prepared food for the Welcomaires' activities.

Dorothy was put to work immediately in the diner. She cleaned, took orders, and served. Many young men who entered the diner owned planes they kept at the airport. Dorothy was quickly smitten when any of the men coming to the diner flirted with her. None knew her past, and it was like she had a clean slate. Freedom from the prying eyes of her mother and confidence that young men found her attractive allowed Dorothy to once again throw caution to the wind.

A nice looking man visited the diner often. Dorothy thought he was a veteran as he wore a bomber jacket and had a set of pilot wings on his coat. At first Dorothy thought he was a pilot in the Air Force, but she learned he was a Navy veteran, yet he loved flying. The young man was living with a cousin, Shirley, in Bedford, not very far from the Clark household. His full-time job was as a wire cutter at a factory; however, every free moment he would spend at the airport. He would always come to the diner to pick up coffee and pastry before he went to the airport, and he would always eat lunch at the counter of the diner. There was an immediate attraction between Dorothy and this young man. He would tell her to stand outside when he was flying overhead and he would show off doing loop-de-loops in the air. She would stand excitedly watching his antics. He even took her for a couple of flights which thrilled Dorothy as she felt that this man was attractive and a good match. She looked forward to the days he would come to the airfield. Dorothy's brother-in-law didn't take much interest in Dorothy's actions, as long as she kept up on her chores at the diner. Agnes, however, was none too pleased with her sister's behavior. She noticed that too often Dorothy became overly possessive of the young man's time and made him feel uncomfortable. One day Agnes pulled Dorothy aside. "You are out of your class, young lady. He is too good for you."

Dorothy pulled away, angry that her sister was challenging her happiness. "It's none of your business, Agnes. For the first time in years I am happy. He loves me."

"Did he tell you that?" asked Agnes.

"He doesn't have to say it. I know he does," snapped Dorothy. "Just mind your own business."

Agnes measured her words carefully. While she was glad that Dorothy was helping her out at the house and diner, she did not want her sister making yet another mistake. "Dorothy. Take your time with this relationship. If he does love you, make him wait. Don't get yourself in the same situation you've found yourself in before." Dorothy stormed into the bathroom and slammed the door. "That went well," said Agnes to her husband. "That girl doesn't realize that once he finds out her past he will dump her."

What Agnes didn't know was that Dorothy began to feel that this man was not giving her enough attention. He had stopped taking her out on dates mid-October, and began avoiding eating in the diner. He would sometimes drop in to pick up coffee and some food, but he would leave to eat it at the airport in an effort to avoid Dorothy's questions about when they were going out again. Dorothy was angry and she began seeking other friendships with other men who came to the diner, or those who went to a local bar where a band played every weekend, or with delivery drivers who stopped at the diner. The cool fall weather was beginning to change when Dorothy received a message that her pilot wanted to see her. Dorothy was breathless because she, too, wanted to talk to him.

Dorothy carefully dressed and applied her makeup and combed her hair. She looked at herself in the mirror, noting that her waist was still trim and tight. When she heard the knock on the door, Dorothy quickly grabbed her coat and said her goodbyes, but when she stepped outside, instead of an excited meeting, this man put his hand up to keep her from embracing him. "Wait," he said. Dorothy looked at the car and recognized the fact that her evening was not going to have the excited outcome she expected.

After several minutes Agnes told her husband that she could hear the car still running. She went to the window and looked out, but she saw the two still standing on the step outside the door. She looked at the car and there was a woman seated inside the car. Agnes turned to her husband. "This is not good. I think we will be in for a long night."

Minutes later Dorothy came back into the house and went into the bathroom. There was no place else for her to go for privacy. It was not long before Agnes heard her sister sobbing. She waited a bit, then knocked gently on the door. "Dorothy? Are you all right?"

"Go away," Dorothy replied between fits of crying. Agnes and her husband sat down and turned on the radio to drown out the sorrowful noises coming from the bathroom. Eventually Agnes and her husband went to bed leaving Dorothy in an obvious emotional breakdown.

"I told her he was out of her class," whispered Agnes.

In the morning Agnes came to the kitchen to find Dorothy sitting at the table. Her eyes were swollen and red. "Morning." Dorothy did not respond. "Want to talk?"

"He dumped me. He had another date with him. He only came over to tell me he wasn't going to see me anymore."

Agnes didn't relish rubbing it Dorothy's face that she was right about Dorothy not being good enough for this man. In all reality, he probably had heard about Dorothy's sordid past. Instead she got a cup of coffee and sat at the table.

After about fifteen minutes, Dorothy looked up. "Agnes. My period is late."

Agnes was speechless. She couldn't even find the words to respond.

"I know. I know. I am hoping it is just late, but what if I am expecting again? I just cannot do this again."

Agnes paused until she could talk with a civil tongue. "Did you tell him?"

"Yes. He said it didn't make any difference. He said if I were expecting he would help me financially, but he cannot afford much. In June he plans to marry the girl he was with last night."

Agnes didn't know what to say. Maybe all of this was for nothing. Maybe Dorothy was just late.

She wasn't late. She was pregnant. Again.

Chapter 8: 1951

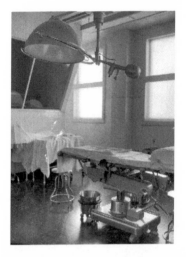

Dorothy begged her sister not to tell their mother about the pregnancy. Agnes haltingly promised, although it became the battering ram she would use whenever she got upset with Dorothy. Meanwhile, Dorothy tried to figure out a plan for having this child and putting it up for adoption.

In January, 1951, Dorothy was to come in to sign the papers to transfer custody of her two sons from Children's Services to the Children's Welfare Board. During the interviews Dorothy felt cornered under the threat that she would have to repay all medical costs of the two sons she surrendered. Dorothy finally named one man as Michael's father stating he was of average height, had straight blonde hair and blue eyes, was of average looks, and she said that even if he hadn't completed high school he could have. She said he was a taxi driver and he would take her for rides around town in the taxi. She confessed that she had never told him about the baby as she didn't want him broadcasting to all the other drivers that she was pregnant. She reasoned that because her father was well known in the community, she didn't want any slander to ruin his memory.

When the worker asked Dorothy about the father of Lawrence. Dorothy responded that he was a football player, six feet tall, and had completed one year of college. She thought he came from a family of eight children. When she spoke of him the social worker felt Dorothy held him in high regard, perhaps because he had attended college and was handsome. She responded that she had not told him about her pregnancy as he had broken off with her and she had no contact with him.

Dorothy then confessed that her mother was still nagging her to keep both boys. She said she had "laid down the law, and said no, and that was that!" Dorothy did not reveal to the social worker that she was already pregnant for a third time.

On February 10th, 1951, Agnes and her husband welcomed a son. Watching the happiness her sister and brother-in-law had for their beautiful child made Dorothy wonder what it would be like to raise her own child. Agnes was not financially well off, but her family was going to make it. Why couldn't she? The reality of her situation hit her hard. Agnes had a husband. They owned a house. They owned a business. The baby was legitimate. Why couldn't her life have turned out like Agnes'?

Dorothy knew she had to go home and face her mother, uncertain as to who would help her this time. She knew she would not be able to conceal her pregnancy from her mother for very long. She tried to come up with a plan. Sister Theresa had said Catholic Charities would not be an option. Two strikes and they were not willing to do a third. She dreaded the dialogue she knew she had to have, but she had no one else who could help her. Just as she expected, Anna was not happy. "What are we to do now? **Where** will you go? How could you do this to us?" Dorothy thought it was strange that her mother thought she had purposely gotten herself pregnant in order to hurt her family. No one ever asked her how she was feeling or what she was thinking.

What she was thinking was that she couldn't do this again. Anna immediately made plans to visit Sister Theresa. Dorothy waited patiently for her mother to return . She thought perhaps her mother and Sister's Theresa's friendship would override the hard line of not providing shelter and assistance a third time. Sister Theresa was true to her word and told Anna that Catholic Charities could not house Dorothy a third time.

"As a repeater, she would make a bad example for the girls. We don't want them to make this mistake again."

Dorothy went to Booth Hospital to see if they would take her for delivery. The Florence Crittenden Home which worked with Booth Hospital was available for unwed mothers and Dorothy was hopeful that they would provide her shelter. She did not expect the answer she received. Dorothy was told that as a repeater she would not be welcomed there. At first Dorothy was belligerent of this response. After all, she had not used the Crittenden Home before, and no one needed to know that she was a repeater. It was explained to her that as a repeater they did not want the first time unwed mothers to think that repeat offenses were acceptable. The Crittenden Home was mostly for first time unwed mothers and Dorothy's third mistake was not acceptable. Financial support from the public was graciously provided for first time unwed mothers, but such donations would not be forthcoming for repeaters.

In early May Dorothy then turned to Children's Welfare, admitting that she knew she was pregnant the last time she met with the worker. When the conversation turned to personal questions, Dorothy quickly changed the subject and she loudly decried the unfair treatment she had received from her former case workers. She did not willingly surrender answers to the questions asked and this time the agency was adamant that she be held accountable. This time the case worker was not distracted by Dorothy's attempt to remove the focus of the conversation to addressing Dorothy's "victimization" at the hands of former case worker. Instead the case worker calmly explained that if Dorothy wanted the help of the agency, she would need to address the costs for the first two pregnancies which had not been met. Dorothy should have to pay toward those expenses. It became clear that if she wanted help from the agency, she would have to make payments toward the boys' expenses. She had no choice. She quickly agreed knowing she had no other alternatives. "Once the boys are adopted then I won't have to pay any more, is that correct?"

The case worker carefully explained that Michael had many health issues and that his costs had surpassed $1300. She also said Lawrence's care cost the agency over $800. For a moment Dorothy sat stunned that there would be any issue with the boys. Dorothy's face turned white. $2,100? Where would she get that kind of money? She couldn't afford that, plus whatever cost this newest child would accrue.

When Dorothy withdrew from the conversation, the case worker tried to pull her back into the business at hand by appealing to Dorothy's sentimentality. "Would you like to see pictures of the boys?" Dorothy half-heartedly nodded. There on the wall were pictures of all the babies and children the agency was trying to place. The case worker pointed out Michael and Lawrence. Dorothy looked, but made no outward sign of interest for fear the discussion would begin anew that she might take the children and raise them as her own.

"I'm surprised neither of them has my dark hair. What are their eye colors? Are they blue like mine?"

"Lawrence's are like yours, and Michael's are lighter." The case worker studied Dorothy's face as she looked at the photographs. The worker felt it was as though Dorothy was looking at pictures of children who had no connection to her. She never asked Dorothy how she felt upon seeing the photos of the boys. Dorothy did not make any comment, keeping her thoughts to herself.

Dorothy changed the subject and said that she was again working at the chair factory. "While you are still working we would expect you to make payments toward the costs accrued for the boys."

Dorothy agreed she could do that and the two sat down to determine a payment schedule. "Once I am unable to continue working I won't have to pay, right?" asked Dorothy.

"Correct, but we would expect you to begin again once you are able to return to work." Dorothy nodded. The two worked out a schedule of payment, and Dorothy remarked that a large portion of her pay would be tied into repaying the agency, leaving very little for her own expenses. It was obvious to the case worker that Dorothy was overwhelmed with the costs and facing additional costs once this child was born. In an effort to give Dorothy an alternative she proposed that since Michael was having a lot of health problems he would be under the care of Children's Welfare, but perhaps Dorothy would consider taking Lawrence and the new baby and living in the projects with help from the Aid to Dependent Children.

Dorothy immediately began weeping. "But I like to work. If I took the children I would not be able to work, and I just got a nickel raise at the chair factory." How sad, thought the case worker, that this woman saw making a minimal wage with a nickel raise far outweighed an opportunity to accept her children and raise them with the assistance of the agency. It was obvious this was an avenue that would not be considered by Dorothy.

Dorothy then ventured a question which was bothering her. "When can I move into the maternity home? If I don't move soon people will start noticing and gossip will start."

The worker looked hard at Dorothy who obviously did not understand the depth of the position she had placed herself in when she made a third mistake. "Dorothy. We can no longer protect you against invasion of your privacy, and hide you from the public eye. In all likelihood, you will not be admitted to the home until shortly before your delivery."

Dorothy pondered this and said, rather hopefully, "I could just tell everybody that my husband had died in an accident. No one would think badly of me then."

The worker just looked at her, speechless, that Dorothy still had not realized she had put herself in this situation with the poor choices she made. The worker went on to tell Dorothy of other obligations she now had to address. "Dorothy, you are going to have to make some more hard choices. Either you go to Juvenile Court with me and file bastardly action against the man who got you pregnant this time, or you will need to contact him and have him come in to arrange payments. "

Dorothy was stunned. "Do I have to?" she asked. "Couldn't you just write him a letter?" The case worker said she would do that; however, if this child were born without a father's name, there would be serious consequences. "Dorothy, you would be leaving the hospital with the baby and be required to make payments for the costs the agency accrues with your shelter, hospital costs, and medical needs for you and the baby. Do you want that?" Dorothy shook her head "no." "Another thing, we will keep the baby for six months then place it for adoption. If it is not adoptable then there will be more decisions to be made." Dorothy did not react to that possibility, but seemed relieved that at least the agency would work on the hospital and take the responsibility of the baby. Finally the worker said, "Remember, you will have to now make payments of $12 a week until you are moved to the hospital, and once you are back at a job, you will continue to pay until either the boys are adopted, or the costs have been paid." Dorothy agreed, saying she would find a way to make payments, but would not cash in the war bonds she had purchased while she was working.

The worker had arranged for her to go to the OB Clinic in Lakeside Hospital starting May 8th. Her appointment was at 8:00, and Dorothy began to complain about the early hour.

When the case worker looked at her with a stern face, Dorothy quickly changed her attitude. Dorothy was asked if she would want to deliver at St. Ann's and Dorothy replied immediately that she would not go there, even if she could. "The nuns there know my mother and they would always be asking me about the boys." Such complications, thought the case worker. She is a three time offender and she doesn't understand that it is through charity that she has gotten help in the past, and yet she expects it now. The case worker kept her thoughts to herself, but marveled at how clueless Dorothy was about her situation.

After Dorothy left the office the case worker began seeking a place for Dorothy to deliver her baby. The MacDonald House of University Hospitals was begun in order to provide obstetric practitioners, both doctors and nurses, a place to learn their trade. Because most poor patients, or unwed mothers, had no money for hospital deliveries, the MacDonald House could serve as a viable option to provide health care for women, while providing medical practice for the interns. Data collected identified high mortality rates among the poor and indigent, so there were more philanthropic and benevolence groups funding these homes to support this population. Originally, the home provided not only physical needs, but also moral rehabilitation. The whole woman was treated: her body, her behavior, and her beliefs. Unfortunately, by the 1940's, the focus of MacDonald House was more in alignment to the teaching of doctors and nurses, and not to the social work of rehabilitating the sinners.

MacDonald House, named after Calvina MacDonald, its head nurse from 1913 to 1933, provided doctors an opportunity to practice on patients gathered in a convenient location. Being next door to the University Hospitals allowed the interns ease for coursework and practice. University Hospitals made it their goal to create a Maternity Home that would furnish "a home for worthy women during confinement and the lying-in period," while at the same time provide valuable experience for their doctors and nurses in obstetrics in the Cleveland Homeopathic Medical College. The medical students were able to witness demonstrations, were taught manipulation of instruments and obstetrical appliances, and conduct at least one case of labor under supervision. It was a teaching college setting. Additionally, there were ten visiting doctors and twenty student nurses providing services along with the students of the college.

Dorothy was almost happy to escape both Agnes' and her mother's homes. Every day was difficult as Dorothy went to work, then came home and helped around the house before she would go to her room to sleep and awaken and begin the process all over again. The weather was getting hotter and she was having a harder time hiding her pregnancy. Her mother's house had constant visits from Hank and Dee and their three boys, and Agnes would bring her son to visit as well. Anna now had four legitimate grandsons, plus two she would never mention aloud. The irony of Anna having all grandsons was not unnoticed. In Anna's rants she often expounded on the idea that daughters could bring shame to the family, discounting the fact that her youngest son had long disappeared from the Clark house and when he came home it was often to loot her handbag for any spare money. Still, in Anna's mind, sons were less stress. Dorothy wondered if this child would be a seventh grandson for Anna.

It was time for Dorothy to report to the MacDonald House for her confinement. Although there were some differences with the intake process at McDonald House, much of the paperwork was the same, with one major difference. Dorothy had identified her pilot ex-boyfriend as the father of the baby. After the agency contacted him, he offered to help pay some of the expenses at the MacDonald House, although he was already engaged to another woman. Dorothy learned from the case worker that some of the paperwork about the father was already filled in. When she questioned the social worker she was told that he had come to the center and had made payment, and agreed to have his name listed on the birth certificate. He also signed off his rights to custody. "He is getting married at the end of June, and he wants this business behind him before he starts his new life," said the social worker. Tears welled in Dorothy's eyes as she thought of this man moving on and starting a new life, but not with her. The social worker waited patiently until Dorothy collected herself, then she ushered her to the dormitory, introducing her by the name she had used in the past, Barbara.

As always, when Dorothy became emotional, her psoriasis reacted. While she was happy that at least this child would have a father's name on the birth certificate, she was also dismayed at the finality of her former boyfriend moving on with his life. Because Dorothy was near University Hospitals she became part of their study on psoriasis and received experimental treatments which helped curb the outbreaks. Meanwhile, her days were spent reading, crocheting handkerchiefs, and waiting. The end of July could not come soon enough.

The baby continued to grow, but by the end of July no baby was arriving. Dorothy was put on daily observations and examinations, all of which were bothersome. "Any day now," the doctor would say. One week passed, and a second week was coming to an end when finally Dorothy went into labor. The doctor was alarmed as the baby appeared to be too large.

Dorothy was wheeled into the delivery room where she was given enough medication to knock out most of the pain. Still, the delivery seemed to take forever. Instead of doing a Cesarean, the doctor insisted that she could deliver vaginally. Unfortunately, the eleven pound, four ounce baby tore Dorothy inside and out.

Instead of immediately closing her up, the lead doctor who was called in far too late asked if Dorothy would mind if they put her in the "arena," an operating room where there was a large glass window allowing doctors in training to watch the procedure. "You've been torn internally and externally, so we will put you out and stitch you. If you agree, this will be excellent training for our doctor practitioners as it is very unusual to have this much damage done to the birth canal. Dorothy was so drugged she didn't care what they did. She was wheeled into the arena, and for a moment she could see the large window. Legs spread for the world to see, Dorothy was filled with shame. Was this her punishment for a third sin? She looked up into the light above her head, and she felt a needle entering her arm, and she was out.

There was daylight streaming into the room when Dorothy struggled to open her eyes. A nurse was checking her blood pressure, and Dorothy could feel a pounding pain within her belly. As she struggled to pull herself awake, the nurse made some comment which Dorothy couldn't seem to understand. Her mind raced. Yes, she had had the baby. She forced herself to speak. "Baby?"

"Yes, you had a girl. The social worker will be coming in to complete some paperwork. I will let her know that you are waking up."

Dorothy closed her eyes again and sleep overtook her. She wasn't certain how much time had passed before she felt a gentle shaking of her arm. She opened her eyes and the social worker's face came into focus.

"Hello, Dorothy. You delivered a rather large baby. She was macrosomia."

"What?"

"That means she was a large baby. Eleven pounds, four ounces. I need to put a name on the forms. Do you have a name?"

"Name?" asked Dorothy.

"Yes. Do you have a name?"

"Barbara," said Dorothy, thinking they were asking the assumed name she had used again during her stay.

"What is the middle name?"

"Louise," mumbled Dorothy before she again slipped into sleep. The social worker looked at the nurse.

"She's under some strong sedatives. She should be more alert later today."

When Dorothy finally did awaken, she was alone in the recovery room. She attempted to stand, but exhaustion and pain kept her from pulling herself upright. A nurse quickly came into the room. "Well, Dorothy. It is nice to see you among the living again. Are you ready to stand up?"

"It hurts," said Dorothy.

"Well, you gave birth to a very large baby. We think you were suffering from some diabetes at the end of your pregnancy which contributed to Barbara's birth weight."

"Barbara? Who is Barbara?" asked Dorothy. She had used that name when she was at St. Ann's during her second pregnancy, and now at MacDonald House, but she had not considered that as the name for this baby if it were a girl. Louise was her own middle name as well as her mother's. "I planned on naming her Doris Gayle. I like Doris Day, and the name Gayle like Dorothy Gale in the *Wizard of Oz*."

"Well, the paperwork has already been done and is already being filed today. If you want it changed you would have to pay for a change to be made."

Payment? She couldn't afford to take care of herself, and she certainly had no money for changing the name of a baby she was surrendering. "Never mind. That's fine."

"Yes. Once we get you settled into your room they will bring the baby for you to see."

"No, I don't want to see her," Dorothy stated as forcefully as she could. She would not subject herself to any more stress. Besides, she was certain her mother would want her to take the baby home, and the case worker had already suggested she take both Lawrence and this baby and live in the projects. There was no way she was going to do that!

Dorothy fought through the pain she was feeling, and was obedient in following the orders she was given. There was no doubt she was in a state of depression, which the doctor said it was not unusual for women after birthing a child. Sedatives were given, and Dorothy welcomed the escape from her mood. Barbara was born on August 13th, and on August 29th, Dorothy signed over custody to the Cuyahoga County Child Welfare

Board. Jean Brown and Sarah Sabor witnessed her signing the document. On the day Barbara was to be removed to be placed in a foster home, Dorothy vowed she would get back to her life as quickly as possible and never put herself into this situation again. She did not want to think about the three babies she surrendered.

Dorothy returned home having no appetite. As a result, she lost a lot of the baby weight she had gained, but she was nowhere near the weight she was before all these babies came along. At home and under the constant scrutiny of Anna who had little patience with her daughter's well deserved discomfort, Dorothy was ready for escape, although she promised herself she would not so easily surrender her body to a man. She would give herself time and allow herself to heal emotionally from the past five years.

In September, only a few weeks after she returned home, Dorothy decided to go to the movies to treat herself out for an evening away from the Clark house. As Dorothy stood in line, a group of young men also joined the ticket line. One of the young men motioned to his friends to look at the girl in line ahead of them. "I'm going to go talk to that girl," said Stanley.

After a short introduction, Stanley ended up sitting with Dorothy at the movies. Stanley G_ was a nice looking young man, and he was very attentive to Dorothy. Dorothy's resolve to stay uncommitted to any man quickly faded.

Chapter 9: October, 1951

During the Russian Revolution of 1905-1907, Kompi, Lithuania, was Russian-ruled. There were nationwide strikes and boycotts against the Russian control. Communism was being pushed, and for the first time, even the poor of Lithuania, became engaged in protests against the Russian led government. Many Lithuanians attempted to escape conscription to the Tsarist army, and to escape the economic and political atmosphere. Most of those who escaped and emigrated to the United States were of peasant origin.

Isadore G_ had emigrated from Kompi, Lithuania (which was later known as Kovno, Poland) in 1910 after the

Russian Army paid a visit to their town, going door-to-door to conscript men for the Russian Army. Isadore and his wife, Helena, had a baby, Joseph, and were able to support their family by working on their own farm and other nearby farms. It did not matter to the Russian officer if the man was married or had children; his job was to take all eligible men, leaving the wives, mothers and children to fend for themselves in an economically challenged town. The mortality rate for soldiers in the Russian army was incredibly high. Knowing that the political atmosphere was hostile, many believed a war, bigger than any they could remember, would soon become a reality.

Once the family heard about the soldiers coming to Kompi, Helen's father called a friend who was an apothecary and asked for something to make his son-in-law ill enough that the officer would be dissuaded to take him immediately, giving him time to make travel arrangements. The medication worked; however, the officer said he would be back soon to collect Isadore. Helena's father made the necessary arrangements to move Isadore and buy him passage to America. The plot worked, and within two years Isadore was set to have his wife and child travel to America. Smallpox had different plans as both Helena and the baby contracted it. The baby did not survive. Once Helena was permitted to travel, she left for America, forever grateful that her father had intervened and saved her husband. Settling in Cleveland, Ohio, they had ten more children, two who did not survive childbirth.

Stanley had grown up in Cleveland and was the youngest of eight surviving children of the Isadore and Helena. The oldest surviving G___ child was a boy, followed by six girls, and finally, Stanley. Isadore and Helena wanted their children to do well in school and become responsible adults. Unlike his siblings, Stanley was always into mischief and found his way into hanging out with other neighborhood boys who were constantly truant from school and getting into trouble. Isadore was called to meet with a judge of juvenile offenders and was told that if Stanley stayed in Cleveland, he would certainly find his way into more serious trouble. The judge recommended moving out of the city. Isadore agreed.

A farmhouse was found on Solon Road in Bedford, and Isadore and Helena moved their family out of Cleveland. Only Stanley and two of his sisters moved to the farm as the older siblings had already married. Eventually, Stanley's brother moved into an upstairs apartment at the farmhouse, and his sister closest in age to him married and moved into another section of the farmhouse. Another sister lived across the street from the farm with her family, and down the street another sister lived with her family. The G___ farm was always active with visits from family. Stanley quickly adapted to the change in scenery and spent much of his time fishing and hunting with his nephew who was only six years younger and living just up the road. Life was pretty great for Stanley. That is, before Stanley faced potential draft into the army.

The Selective Service Act of 1948 made post World War II men, aged 18 to 26, register for the draft. In 1951, the Universal Military Training and Service Act changed the draft. Prior to this, deferments were available to married men, but the law had changed and deferments would only be available to men with children in their home who they supported. Stanley was 18, the perfect age for the draft. Isadore and Helena were overwhelmed when they realized their youngest could be sent off to fight in Korea which reported high casualties. The memory of Isadore's near draft into the Russian Army frightened both Helena and Isadore. Now they were frantic as it was highly likely that Stanley would be drafted for the Korean Conflict.

On one particular night Stanley decided to go to the movies at the Stillwell Theater in Bedford with some friends.

As they stood in line, one of his buddies pointed out a young woman who was standing in line ahead of them. "Hey, that's Dorothy Clark. She was in my brother's class at Bedford. Rumor has it she was a little fast with the local boys. I even heard she was sent away because she got pregnant." Stanley looked at the young woman. She was attractive and she was not trying to draw attention to herself. Stanley excused himself from his friends and went up to speak to the young woman who was startled at his approach.

"Hi. My name is Stanley G_. It looks like you are alone and I thought maybe you wouldn't mind sitting with me to watch the movie." Dorothy looked at the young man. He was obviously younger than her, but he was attractive. She then glanced back at his friends who were all giggling and pushing each other as they watched Stanley talking. She rolled her eyes, and Stanley quickly said, "We won't sit with my friends. They are morons!" Dorothy chuckled, then said that it would be all right if he sat with her. Stanley purchased the tickets and led her to a seat away from his friends.

Stanley and Dorothy sat on one side of the theater, while Stanley's friends kept making immature comments, teasing Stanley. Finally the movie, *Rio Grande*, began, and Stanley's friends settled down to watch the film. Dorothy's attention was both on John Wayne in the movie, and Stanley who eventually reached over and held her hand. She did not pull her hand away but began romanticizing in her mind that Stanley was more than a little interested in her. Reality then surfaced and she feared he sought her out because he knew of her past. After the movie Dorothy wanted to go directly home; however, Stanley convinced her to stop for a soda at the restaurant in downtown Bedford. The two talked a lot about their favorite movies, about their families, and finally, about themselves.

"Were you ever married, Dorothy?" asked Stanley.

Here it comes, thought Dorothy. "No. I was in a couple of relationships that I thought were serious, but they didn't turn out well."

Stanley paused for a moment. Dorothy looked at him and knew he knew. She stood up and gathered her coat and handbag. "I'm sorry, I have to leave."

"No, wait," said Stanley. "I know this is awkward, but I don't care about the rumors I heard. In fact, that would actually be a good thing."

Dorothy looked at him, thinking that he was making a pass at her as he knew she was 'one of *those* girls.' "I will not put myself in a position to make another mistake. I think it is horrible of you to make such a suggestion." It was only a month since she had Barbara and now this boy appeared to be suggesting she make the same mistakes she had made before.

"No, no. I am not suggesting that. I just want to be able to see you again."

Dorothy looked deeply into his eyes, and he appeared to be speaking honestly. "I will let you walk me home. I am not making any promises."

When Stanley returned home he told two of his sisters about meeting Dorothy Clark and was immediately stopped by them. "Seriously, Stanley. Haven't you heard about her? There is rumor that she was sent away to have a baby. She is a ruined woman. You cannot see her again." Stanley was never one to listen to rules, so he, of course, disobeyed and went on to see Dorothy.

Within a week of having met Dorothy, Stanley received his draft notice. Helena cried and Isadore was unable to console her. It was a reminder of what they went through in Lithuania before coming to America, only now Helena was fearful for her son's life. The Korean Conflict was claiming many lives and she feared for Stanley to be drafted and put into such a war.

Stanley immediately went to see Dorothy. What surprised many who didn't know the situation was that on October 6th, Stanley and Dorothy eloped to Richmond, Indiana, only weeks after having just met.

Upon returning home, Anna was waiting for Dorothy, very angry that she had not returned home for two days and Anna was ready to call the police. Dorothy flashed her hand out for her mother to see and a small gold band was on her ring finger. Dorothy informed her mother that she had married Stanley. Although Anna was initially upset that Dorothy had run off without telling her, she was happy as there would now be no more unwed mother business. What she hadn't planned on was Dorothy's next announcement that she and Stanley would be living with her in the Archer Road house.

As to the G_ household, things were a bit different. Stanley's parents were not happy about the match; however, his mother said she would only be satisfied if they at least married in the church. Stanley agreed and a second ceremony was to be held at St. Mary's in Bedford in December. Stanley's siblings were not very happy that Stanley had married a woman six years his senior with a questionable past. This would be the start of a very rocky relationship Dorothy would have with the G_ family.

Chapter 10: 1952-1955

Stanley immediately sought full-time employment, working at the Reid, Clinton Coal Company where his father had worked for many years. He would drive to work, pick up the truck, load it with coal, and deliver it through the coal chutes of the Cleveland homes which still used coal furnaces.

In March, 1952, letter arrived from the draft board stating that while Stanley had married, he was not qualified for deferment. Stanley was scheduled for the physical examination, and he was hopeful that they would say he was flat-footed, or his vision was too poor, which he had heard helped many avoid the draft. His parents were not very optimistic that this would keep him from being drafted. It was at this time that

Dorothy offered the idea of accepting responsibility for one of her children put up for adoption could serve as a reason to be deferred from the draft.

While Stanley worked, Dorothy and Anna traveled to the Alice Hunt Center and St. Ann's to see if either of the boys had been adopted. Stanley indicated he would prefer to have one of the boys as he would enjoy teaching him to fish and hunt. Dorothy and Anna traveled to the various locations in search of information. Dorothy finally learned that custody of the boys had finally been turned over to the county. When the social worker researched further she found that both boys had been adopted by different families in October, 1951, within a week of Stanley and Dorothy having married. That left only the daughter, Barbara.

A trip to see the social worker, Jean Brown, was not very promising. At first there was a question as to Stanley not being the father of the child and whether this speedy relationship was stable enough to support a child in a safe and loving environment. There was also a question as to the stability of the family as they had no place of their own, and Stanley's wages were meager. It was finally revealed that Barbara had not yet been adopted, but was in foster care.

Dorothy confided in Jean that Stanley needed a letter for potential deferment in the draft and with his helping to care for Barbara, it could qualify for a deferment. Jean promised to see what she could do. Typically the process of placing a child up for adoption took six months, but Dorothy was adamant that the wait time be ignored as she was the natural mother and wanted to take custody as soon as possible. It was agreed that Dorothy and Stanley find their own place and that they make the preparations for caring for a child. They were also told that frequent visits would be made to determine if Barbara was well cared for. The two quickly agreed that they would do what was expected. The first requirement was that the couple have a place of their own, which meant moving out of the Archer Road house into their own apartment. Such accommodations were found and the couple moved into a tiny apartment located upstairs from a friend of Stanley's. To access the apartment, steep stairs on the outside of the house had to be maneuvered. The apartment was very meager, having only one small bedroom, a minimal kitchen, and a sitting area. It was best suited for a single person, yet Dorothy, Stanley, and Barbara would now call this their home.

It was arranged for Dorothy and Stanley to take Barbara home for short visits to determine if they could make themselves a family. Although Barbara was tremendously unhappy and often screamed and cried being taken from her foster home, Dorothy would report back that all had gone well, and quickly hand her over to Miss Brown at the end of the visit. It was in May that Children's Welfare determined they would allow Barbara to move in with Dorothy and Stanley. Barbara was nine months old, and separation anxiety was the cause for the crying. For Dorothy, it pushed her away from bonding with this child who appeared to dislike her. Agnes and Dee explained that it was a natural response of all children at this age and that Barbara just did not know her. Both encouraged Dorothy to keep working on the relationship. Home visits from Children's Welfare continued and Dorothy would be certain Barbara was clean and dressed nicely when the visits were made; however, each visit the case worker would find the apartment progressively dirtier. Despite making comments that safety and health issues were to be considered, Dorothy would make empty promises to do better the next time.

Soon after Dorothy and Stanley took Barbara home, Dorothy placed Barbara into a pram and walked to Columbus Road in Bedford where the ex-boyfriend was living with his wife. Dorothy did this against Stanley's wishes, but Dorothy wanted to make certain the father would not cause them problems. She pushed the pram and practiced what she would say to the man she had not seen since he broke up with her. When she arrived she softly knocked on his door, then walked back to the sidewalk to stand beside the pram. A window curtain was pulled aside, and after a few moments, he appeared, looking back into the house as he quietly shut the door. Dorothy told him that she had married and that she and her husband were going to take Barbara out of the adoption process. Would he have any objection? He only looked at her and glanced at Barbara and said he didn't care as he was now married and he and his wife planned on starting their own family. That would be the first and last time he saw Barbara.

Frequent visits were made by Jean, the social worker, to the Egbert Road apartment. Each visit left Jean counseling Dorothy on how to keep house, how to keep Barbara clean, how to learn to cook, and how to build a bond with Barbara. Dorothy would quickly agree to take the advice and act upon it. After Jean would leave, Dorothy would slip back into her same habits.

On May 27, 1952, Jean Brown sent Dorothy a letter.

Dear Dorothy:

I have been thinking about you and thought you might appreciate having the enclosed. The papers are a record of Barbara's early development and increases in weight. I saved her bracelet the day I took Barbara from the hospital and this is something I felt you would particularly like to have for a keepsake.

By now I suppose you have received the draft board report. I am "keeping my fingers crossed" for you, and of course I am hoping the decision will mean you can go ahead with some kind of plan for more adequate housing. It is only fair to yourselves and for Barbara to have a place where you can "spread out" a little more and really keep your house.

My best to you and your family and wishes for continuing happiness.

Sincerely,

Jean Brown, Case Worker

Cuyahoga County Child Welfare Board

P.S. Dorothy, I am sending this on as it was written originally, as I know you will understand.

Dorothy snorted when she read the "advice" Jean had given about her housekeeping and keeping the baby clean, yet another person telling her what she should be doing. She put the letter aside and looked over the accompanying paperwork. The documentation for Barbara's early baby visits showed that she was a happy baby and progressing well. Dr. Randall had kept excellent records of her health, feeding schedules, plan for removal of the mole on her arm, and her vaccinations. Dorothy looked at these and put them into an envelope and placed it into a cedar chest, never to be looked at again unless she accidently came across them when she went into the cedar chest for some reason.

The draft board approved Stanley's deferment in a large

part because of the supportive letter Jean Brown had written on his behalf. The deferment was given despite the fact that Stanley had not adopted Barbara, nor had the couple removed Barbara from being a ward of the state. The rationale for this decision was that should Barbara need any health care, it would be addressed by the state rather than the financial responsibility being placed on Dorothy and Stanley. Dorothy also felt that should something negative happen between her and Stanley, Barbara could easily be put back into the system.

The rent Stanley and Dorothy were paying for the small upstairs apartment on Egbert Road, was an extra expense they could not afford, especially with the cost of a child in the house. Now that the regularly scheduled home visits were over, Dorothy announced to Anna that they would be moving in with her. Anna welcomed the chance to see her new granddaughter.

Anna was an attentive grandmother, much to Dorothy's aggravation. Dorothy did not want her mother doting on Barbara. In Dorothy's mind, Anna never mentioned the two surrendered grandsons, but now she was giving all this attention to this granddaughter. Dorothy didn't appreciate her mother constantly reminding her that Barbara needed fed, changed, or cleaned. She was annoyed when her mother shushed her when Barbara was napping. Dorothy felt her mother had not doted on her, but she certainly went out of her way to worry about Barbara. There arose in Dorothy a sense of jealousy over the relationship building between Barbara and Anna.

For Isadore and Helena, Stanley was saved from going to war. Helena embraced Barbara and was attentive to her when Stanley would visit with her in tow. Helena had never given toys to any of her grandchildren, but she found a discarded doll, cleaned it, and gave it to Barbara. She also lined up Stanley's siblings and warned them that they were to treat Barbara like all the other nieces and nephews, and they were not to mention that she was not of their blood. They complied; however, their dislike of Dorothy was still evident. Dorothy, meanwhile, did not help her situation with her in-laws. She remained aloof and looked for opportunities to stay home when Stanley took Barbara to the farm.

Life went on for Dorothy and Stanley. The couple had been married nearly a year when Dorothy recognized that familiar feeling. She was pregnant. This time it would certainly be different. This time she would be treated with respect as a married woman, and this time she would keep this child and not have it taken from her. Dorothy gave birth to her second daughter, Emily, in May of 1953. She named Stanley's sister and her husband as Godparents, partially out of respect for Stanley, but also to bond with her in-laws. Now Dorothy was a legitimate wife and mother and felt secure enough to finally terminate the consent for surrendering Barbara for adoption on June 26, 1953.

Two years after Emily was born, a third daughter, Susan,

was born. Dorothy and Susan had no sooner come home from the hospital when Emily became violently ill. She had pneumonia and in the middle of the night Stanley and Dorothy had to take her to the hospital. Barbara and Susan were shipped out to other relatives to take care of while Dorothy stayed at the hospital with Emily. The hospitalization and hours sitting beside the struggling toddler gave Dorothy time to think about her life situation.

These past couple of years Dorothy found herself exhausted with the duties of parenting. She had no time to herself. She rarely left the house. There was always someone wanting her attention. The tiny Clark house was indeed overcrowded with playpen, high chair, cribs, toys, bottles, and clothes which were in constant need of laundering. When Stanley came home from work covered in soot from his job at the coal yard, he showered, then added his coal covered clothing to the wash. He would then either sit down to watch the small screened television, or left to go fishing during the few hours of daylight after work. Meanwhile, there were no vacations or escapes for Dorothy. Her only relief was when she would visit with a neighbor, or occasionally enjoy a visit from a relation coming to visit her mother. Since Stanley would often visit his parents, Dorothy would join him, although it was not her preference. When Isadore and Helena were not there, her sisters-in-law often spoke Polish, purposely keeping Dorothy out of the conversation. Dorothy had long before accepted the fact that she could not erase her past and that she deserved the negative treatment she either received, or imagined she received. Her perception was everyone was against her. In her mind, Barbara was a constant reminder of those mistakes.

After Emily's health crisis, a second reality check came to Stanley and Dorothy. Hank had let his mother live in the Archer Road house after he had built his new home; however, he expected Dorothy and Stanley to pay rent. Month after month he went without payment. Finally, he had enough. He needed to sell the house as he was going to start building another house in the Walton Hills area and needed the money from this house as payment for the lot and for building supplies. He was not heartless, but he knew that he could not afford to finance his sister's family. He found them a place on East 44th Street in Cleveland, in a house which was scheduled to be torn down. They could stay there until they found a place of their own.

Dorothy once again was overwhelmed with the stresses of her family, and now moving and finding a new place to live. She looked at her mother and said, "Ma, I cannot support you, too. Stanley and I can't get by with our own family. You need to go live with Hank or Agnes."

Anna was stunned. She had become comfortable having her own room in the busy Archer Road home where she had lived nearly her entire adult life. She had raised her family there, and she was close to Hank and saw Dorothy and her family daily. She needed a plan. She was 58 years old, and the Ohio winters were getting harder on her each year. She contacted Agnes who had moved to Florida with her family, and was told she could live with them half a year, and then return to Ohio for half a year. Dorothy felt relieved. If Hank would take her for three months, and Agnes six months, she would only need to deal with her mother for three months out of the year. Little did she consider just how much Anna had helped her with the children. She also did not consider that her family would now be her full time responsibility.

Chapter 11: A Family of Seven

Living on East 44th Street was interesting. The house sat on the other side of a fence which separated the dead end street from Cyrus Eaton's Republic Steel Mill. Across the street were row houses which were originally built to house the workers for the steel mills. There were more children on this dead end street so Barbara and Emily had available playmates, and the yard was protected by a hedgerow which added boundaries and perceived safety for the children. The house had an upstairs which the family was not allowed to use because of roof leakage. The family, therefore, lived on the first floor.

Despite the house having structural problems, there was much about the house that Barbara liked. The front room had a pretty staircase. Since house on Archer was a one story, Barbara was fascinated with the stairs, and on a couple of occasions sneaked upstairs to look around. There was much fallen plaster from the ceilings, but there were three bedrooms and a bathroom. It would have been wonderful to be able to use those rooms. Instead, the formal dining room on the first floor became Dorothy and Stanley's bedroom, with a crib for the new baby expected that October. The back room, which must have been a main bedroom, became a bedroom for Emily, Susan, and Barbara. It was also a storage room for anything else the family had to store as the basement was also sealed off from use. The kitchen housed a red laminated table with chrome legs and matching kitchen chairs. There was a back door off the kitchen, which had to be kept locked as Emily would sleepwalk and wander off during the night. The front room was large enough for a davenport and chairs, a black and white television, and some small tables which served as end tables. The first floor bathroom had a bathtub, which the Archer Road house did not have. It seemed so much more spacious that their previous home.

The yard was huge and a swing set was left behind by a previous owner. Barbara loved to sit on the swing and enjoyed the yard which was surrounded by a tall hedgerow. One day Barbara was out playing in the yard when two children arrived. Barbara scurried into the house to announce that there were two "chocolate children" on the swings. Dorothy shushed her as she was talking to the "chocolate mother" at the kitchen table. That family only lived in the house across the street for a short time, but the girls were eager to serve as helpers in teaching Barbara how to navigate the first few months of getting to kindergarten.

It was when Barbara was old enough to start school that the discussion came up that Barbara's last name was still "Clark." Now that she was starting school, people might ask why her name was different than her dad's. Stanley filed for adoption on June 2, 1956, and Barbara's birth certificate was changed from Barbara Clark to Barbara G_.

The G_ family was poor, there was no doubt about that. Stanley's minimal weekly pay was barely enough for rent, food, and necessities. Money was spread thin as Stanley supported his young family of three children. Dorothy gave birth to another daughter, Dorothy Ann, on October 11, 1956, the same day only nine years after she gave birth to Michael. The new baby was a "caulbearer," which meant she was born with a membrane that looked like a sheer veil over her face. There was lots of family talk about how unique this was, as it was a rarity. Caulbearers were often credited with being able to predict weather, see ghosts, and foretell the future, as well as being very lucky people. Additionally it was believed that the purpose of caulbearers was to serve mankind. Dorothy Ann was to be like other great caulbearers: Alexander the Great, Napoleon, and Albert Einstein. It was even said that Jesus Christ was a caulbearer. In reality, a child born with a caul merely meant that the amniotic sac was still intact at birth. Such a birth was easier on the mother, causing less bruising and ease in delivery. For Dorothy, she was just relived that the birth was peaceful and less painful than the others.

The G_ family remained in the East 44th Street house for two years. Barbara walked to school each day, maneuvering the complicated maze of streets from East 44th to Mound School, which stood on the corner of Mound Avenue and East 55th street in Cleveland. It was when Barbara was to start second grade, and Emily was to start kindergarten, that the family moved to the house where Stanley had grown up. In fact, Stanley had been born in this house on East 59th.

The house had originally been owned by the parents of Leon Czolgosz, who assassinated President William McKinley in 1901. Although Leon had never lived in the East 59th Street house, his father, Paul Czolgosz, suffered many harassments from citizens because of his son's actions. In a September 6th, 1912 article it stated that, "Paul Czolgosz of Cleveland, Ohio, father of the misguided young man who took the life of President McKinley, has since suffered without complaint from the fame and ignominy brought upon his family, but a few days ago he was taunted too much for his son's 'rash act' by five unfeeling men, and in anger struck one of his tormentors. He was arrested on charge of assault and battery, but was acquitted when the circumstances of the case were made known. Judge Levin, who presided, rightly observed that the father was not responsible for the sins of his son." It was not long afterward that Paul Czolgosz chose to put his home up for sale on East 59ᵗʰ Street.

At first there were no takers. Luckily, Stanley's father had previously purchased the tiny house next door, and when the opportunity arose, he bought the large home vacated by the Czolgosz family. He divided the house into three areas so that his older children could live in the upstairs or back area until they could afford to buy their own homes. Several of Stanley's siblings married and started off life at the E. 59ᵗʰ Street home. Once Stanley's parents moved to the Solon Road farm in Bedford, the E. 59th Street house was put up for rent; however, renters do not always take care of a house. By the time Stanley and Dorothy moved their family to the house it was already in bad repair. Stanley was not much of a handyman, so it continued to fall into further disrepair. He had great intentions of remodeling and making repairs in the house, Projects were typically left unfinished. He also preferred to fish and hunt instead of spending time repairing his home, so projects were started, but not completed, or done "on the cheap" leaving the house with mounting issues. This became the backdrop for the G_ children growing up.

Meanwhile, a fifth child and final child, Gladys, was added to the family in September of 1958.

Whether Dorothy thought about her two sons, she never shared. She never discarded the gold medals given to her when she left St. Ann's after giving up both boys. But the secrets she had remained hers to keep, and no one was to ever mention anything about them. Dorothy's personality became twofold: The outgoing and fun Dorothy who enjoyed parties, movies, dancing, and escaping the trappings of her family; and the secretive and depressed Dorothy, who held tight to her secrets and resented her non-glamorous life.

Part Two:
Barbara's Story

Chapter 12: The Early Years

I believe most of my cousins and family would agree that I was pretty quiet as a child, but eager to please others. I quickly became aware of my role in my family. Much like my Mom's oldest sister, I lost a lot of my childhood because I was the oldest. It did not take long for me to realize that I had to be a people pleaser in order to survive. While I was not successful with my own mother, I found that others did like me because they viewed me as a well-mannered, polite, and helpful child. I always looked for ways to help others. I did this willingly in order to secure some positive reinforcement. What I could not get from my mother, I treasured getting from others. There was also a possibility that if others liked me, perhaps my mother would see what they saw and she would like me as well. Try as I would, my mother, Dorothy, was never able to bond with me.

As a child, your sense of normalcy is what you live every day. I thought every family was like mine where the mother withheld her love and expected her child to earn it. It was the only normal I knew. Yet, as I began to spend more time at the homes of my friends, I saw other mothers doting on their children, or heard them brag about their children. This never happened in our house. I always thought that if I tried hard enough, eventually I would find the magic recipe for gaining my mother's esteem.

Memories of my youth are recalled with extreme clarity. Many of these memories were the ones that helped shape my personality, and even my relationship with others. The good memories have become the basis of the traditions I have built upon for my own family. These memories are still very clear and perhaps were the earliest means of shaping who I was to become. The bad memories have also shaped me. For some people, the bad memories will forever torment them and build an internal anger that can never be extinguished. For others, like me, the bad memories built a sense of resiliency. I had to rise above those experiences and vow to never repeat them with my own family.

My earliest memory is the steep stairway leading to the Egbert Road apartment in Bedford where I first lived with my parents, Dorothy and Stanley. My mother and father repeated the story to me of my constant screaming and crying when I was a small child. Interestingly, as I began writing this book, I realized that many of the tears I cried in those early days could have stemmed from the fear felt in my being carried up this frightening stairway, by people I did not know, into a tiny, cluttered, and dirty homestead where my life was different from the safety I felt in my foster care home where I had lived for nearly nine months. I learned some time later that my foster mother was a Ms. Ingersoll, and I am forever grateful that she must have given me a good foundation which helped establish my personality and resiliency.

Most of my early memories are from our Archer Road home in Bedford. I now know that after my mom and dad passed the "inspections" by the social worker, allowing me to live permanently with them, we quickly moved to Archer Road in the childhood home of my mother. Many people say they cannot remember anything from their childhood, yet I have very strong memories that date back to at least age three.

One memory in particular was of my playing with an old handbag that must have been either my mother's or grandmother's. I had filled it with the Johnson's Baby Powder metal tin cans. I must have dropped it, making a loud enough noise for my mother to come storming into the room, snatching the handbag away from me and giving me a stern slap across the face. I remember sitting on floor crying uncontrollably, either from the loss of the treasured handbag, or the indignity of being slapped so hard. Perhaps both. My crying was bound to awaken my sister who was asleep in her crib. No doubt frustrated with my racket, my mother appeared in the doorway of the kitchen and forcibly threw the handbag at me, which struck me in the head. I fell backward and hit my head on the leg of the davenport. I then had something to cry about as I had a large bump on the back of my head and another on my forehead. There was no cradling me, or kissing me. Instead my mother brought a washcloth with ice in it and held it to my head, and continued scolding me while I continued to cry. I remember being sent to bed inconsolable. I know it is odd, but I clearly remember not being able to fall asleep and thinking it was because of the bump on my head, and I was terrified to fall asleep for fear I would not awaken in the morning. I said prayers each night, as taught by my grandmother, and the words, "If I should die before I wake," terrified me and I was certain the bump on my head would lead me to whatever dying was. My grandmother had told me that to die meant you never woke up again and I fought off sleep for fear that I would not awaken in the morning. My early lesson here was not to do things which would upset my mother. Her temper was not to be taken lightly, and she was not resistant to the idea of harsh punishment, even to one as young as me.

Wasting or spilling food was not acceptable. I remember being held by the arm and being hit on the butt, mostly with a hand, but sometimes with the hairbrush or other kitchen utensil if food was dropped or spilled. I was to know better than to be clumsy and knock over something. Worse, if I refused to eat something I would sit until bedtime at the table, even if my grandmother would try to intervene on my behalf. Part of my mother's harsh treatment was because she disliked my grandmother's interference. To prove to her mother that she would make all child rearing decisions, not only would I sit at the table until bedtime, but then I would receive a spanking before getting into bed. That wooden handled Fuller hairbrush was often the weapon of choice.

I hated that hairbrush! If I didn't sit still as my mother would brush my hair, I would get a quick smack to the head with the back of the hairbrush. The hairbrush was big and clumsy for me to handle, yet I feared my mother brushing my hair as it often resulted in hair pulling and my inevitable vocal outcries which resulted in the knock on the scalp with that brush handle. Little did that door–to–door salesman from Fuller Brush know that the wooden handled and stiff bristled hairbrush, which was more suitable for adults with thick hair, would instead be used on little ones for both for grooming and punishment. We lived with that hard hairbrush for easily ten years or more!

I do not remember my mother ever reading stories to me. Ever. She was a great reader and enjoyed the solitude of her books, but she did not enjoy reading to her children. My grandmother bought a subscription of Highlights Magazine for my cousins who lived across the street. When they would finish the magazine, they would send the magazine to our house. I would look at the pictures and long to know what the words said in the magazine. I would first look at the Goofus and Gallant cartoon and ask someone to read the caption. I quickly learned that Goofus was always doing something wrong, but Gallant always did the right thing. I have to say that Gallant was a good role model for me. He didn't get punished, which was always my goal. I can remember taking the magazine with me whenever we would go somewhere so I could look it over. Perhaps it was with hopes someone would read me some of the stories inside. I also remember sitting with the magazine when my mother would be reading a book. I longed to have a connection with my mother, so I would imitate her sitting and turning the pages of text, even though I was unable to read until I was in elementary school. I realize she had to be aware of my imitation of her action, yet it did not inspire her to help me read my stories. Picture books were my favorite, and although I longed to "read" aloud the story I thought the pictures told, I did not disturb the silence my mother preferred, as to do so would be punishable. My story telling was only done in my head as I learned disturbing the silence, which my mother demanded, was not to be tolerated. Still, having books in my hands became a pathway for me to escape the world and the loneliness of not having a real relationship with my mother.

We had a television, albeit a tiny black and white screen. I remember watching Captain Kangaroo, the Lone Ranger, Lawrence Welk, Mickey Mouse Club, Felix the Cat, and Lassie. My dad loved watching the cowboy westerns, and my mother enjoyed anything with music. Our television time was based on my parents' use of the television. When they didn't have programs to watch would they tune in to a children's show. Of course, television was also used as a treat, and the withholding of it was a punishment. I remember being put on a stool and told to remain there until I learned to tie my shoes, and I was unable to watch television until I successfully completed the task. Once I mastered it at age three, quite a feat as three year olds are not necessary known for their great dexterity, I was then designated to retie my sisters' shoes whenever they came undone! Perhaps this was among my first duties as a caregiver to my younger siblings.

My early childhood wasn't all bad. I certainly had many great memories as well. I remember for Father's Day my mother had bought a bottle of Old Spice After Shave for my dad. She had wrapped it in colorful paper. Presents were a treat, even if they were for someone else. My sister and I had to shake Dad awake so he could open his present. He kept pretending to be so sound asleep that we couldn't awaken him. We then tried to pull him from the bed. This struggle continued for an extended period of time, and once he awoke, we received a huge tickling. Normally this would be a wonderful family moment; however, tender moments often turned to dreaded moments. I hated being tickled; still do. The tickling often continued until I was left screaming for it to stop. I also recall being given a slap for screaming. What started off as fun sometimes turned into a painful experience.

Every holiday my mom would transform our home with crepe paper streamers which she would tack to the corners of the room and twist them as she strung them to the opposite corner of the room. I thought it was so very special. Red and green for Christmas, pink and red for Valentine's Day, and pink and light blue for Easter. I thought these decorations were the most beautiful addition to our very sparse home. She also recycled each year the tissue folded honeycombed red bells, pink hearts, or blue eggs which she hung from the doorway between the kitchen and living room. I looked forward to seeing the transformation to colorful decorations to our otherwise dark and drab home. Our Christmas tree, albeit very small, was always shrouded in tinsel which I found to be fascinating. I loved the glittery look it had and enjoyed seeing it sparkle in the sunlight which streamed through our dirty windows. Our presents were typically items of clothing, or small toys that could be purchased at the local five and dime store. It didn't matter. They were presents and something to open and they brought me great joy.

My mother's time indoors was mostly cooking and house-work and cleaning babies, although, truth be told, she really was not a very good cook, nor was our house or clothing ever in good condition, nor were we bathed in a consistent time frame. Laundry was done in a tub with a washboard and either Fels Naptha Soap or Rinso detergent was used, then laundry hung to dry on an indoor drying rack, or in the backyard on the clothesline, weather permitting.

It did not take me long to realize my mother enjoyed escape from the day to day demands of her life. I remember her complaining out loud to my grandmother, or just to an invisible person in the house. Thinking back on it I realize she just needed to verbalize her frustration with her lot in life. It certainly wasn't very glamorous or exciting. We never took vacations. We never went for walks in the park, or to playgrounds, or even to the public library. As I look back I now realize we were surrounded by available outings which could have been free to use, but perhaps the thought of packing up her brood of children to walk some place was too overwhelming, and such journeys would take her away from the many tasks of housekeeping. It is most unfortunate that she did not have a mentor to help her steer through the role of motherhood.

I believe the biggest hardship of our lives was our poverty. I believe my mother looked for opportunities for relief from the mundane life she lived. It never occurred to my mother that her focus should have been her children, and perhaps by interacting with them she could have actually enjoyed the excitement of her children learning and discovering life.

Instead, her focus was on herself. Her own misery outweighed any consideration of her children's needs. As an adult I realize she practiced what she knew of motherhood. Since my grandmother was not a good housekeeper, cook, or strong in parenting skills, my mother had no role model to follow. My grandmother was a loving grandmother, however her relationship with her daughter was not ideal.

Fortunately children can often entertain themselves. Give them some pots and pans and some wooden spoons and they can begin their own band. Give them paper and crayons and they can become artists and create masterpieces. In our home noise was not allowed. There was always a sleeping child. Crayons could become destructive, so rather than provide them for creative play, they were avoided as to eliminate the need for cleanup. The list goes on. My mother enjoyed our television and often forfeit interaction with her children in favor of watching television while my dad was at work. When the television tubes burned out, we lost use of it until new tubes could be purchased, and such purchases were not high on the list of necessities. My mother's escape was then through technology by playing her 78 rpm record albums on the tabletop record player. The radio was also often turned on and my mother enjoyed the music of her generation. She would also look for any opportunity to go visit the neighbors. It, too, was an escape from the household duties and care of her children. Since her visits were typically as we napped, I would panic when I would awaken to find her not in the house or our yard. Typically she was next door talking to a neighbor or having a cup of coffee with them in their kitchen. Once I figured out her routines I would venture to the neighbor's yard to retrieve my mother when my younger sisters awoke and screamed for release from their cribs.

Dad was often not home as he enjoyed fishing or hunting every chance he got. He would visit his parents at the farm, or his brother and sisters who also lived on Solon Road which was a short distance from our house. Mom didn't always enjoy going, but she always asked if he would take one or more of the children with him so she could get things done in the house. I don't know that she accomplished much, but the alone time was always a welcome reprieve for her.

When the weather was good our yard became my happiness, and I believe it was my mother's as well. Our yard had two outdoor furnishing I loved. One was a little wading pool made of a canvas material. The water was cold when it was fresh, but as the day progressed the water warmed from the sun. The other outdoor furniture piece was a wooden double bench glider with a canopy. I loved sitting in that swing. My mom would sit on the swing as well, often holding one of my sisters, or reading a book. My favorite memory of this swing was when my dad had gone to Wisconsin to fish with my uncle. I was sitting on the swing waiting for him to return. I was only three years old at the time, but I can still remember my excitement of his returning home after having been away for what seemed like such a long time, which was probably just a week. For my mother, it had to have felt even longer as she was left with all the household tasks by herself, along with the care of three children. My grandmother was often busy with visiting her friends, or doing her volunteer work as she also liked to escape the house.

When I first began penning my story I wondered why it was that these are the memories I held tight from my childhood. I think it was because my mother had to be outside with me at these times. Even though she would be reading her books, or doing crossword puzzles, or crocheting lace handkerchiefs, she was still in close proximity. When I think of it now, it fills me with sadness that what was normal for other families was a treat for me in having my mother nearby, albeit not mentally, physically or emotionally interacting with us.

We moved out of the Archer Road house when I was four years old. We then moved to the East 44th Street house, which was to be temporary. The house was condemned because there were roof issues. We were to live on the first floor. The dining room became a bedroom for my parents, and the first floor bedroom became the bedroom for the three girls. We had a set of bunk beds and a small bed in our room, and a huge box for toys, which were typically hand-me-downs, but still treasured. I had the top bunk which allowed me to see out the high set window in that room. I could watch the bridge at the

Republic Steel Mill which was located in a huge depression in the landscape, which everyone called the "Flats." Our street overlooked the mill, and at night from my bunk top I could see the orange glow from the furnaces of the mills, and the constant movement of what looked like a train engine going back and forth across the black bridge that hung above the mill, and the heaving smokestacks that puffed out sooty air and smoke. Two of my uncles worked at the mill, as did many of the men from Cleveland. Instead of night time lullabies or bedtime stories, my comfort was watching the moving train and the soft orange glow of the furnaces. I don't recall bedtime kisses or hugs. In fact, it was not until I was an adult that I began giving my mother kisses on the cheek and hugging her in greeting. It was foreign to me as a child as it was never done to me.

There was some excitement during this time as I was turning five and getting ready to start kindergarten. Although I don't remember all the details, I do remember my mother and father dressing up and my being cleaned up and I believe I even had a new dress and shoes. We went to a large building and there were a number of adults who talked about things I didn't understand. My father held me tightly in his arms and I remember kisses on my cheek. My dad was never outwardly affectionate to any of us, which is why this memory clearly stands out. When I got home I was told that my name was now the same as my dad's. I couldn't quite wrap my brain around how this was any different than before. As an adult I now recognize the importance of this occasion. I would be starting school and it would be important for me to have the same name as my Dad rather than still carrying my mother's maiden name. All this time I had never been formally adopted by my Dad.

Chapter 13: Maid Service

In 1956 my mother's days were filled with three children, laundry which was a constant battle, and keeping house. A new baby was due so my mother was uncomfortable, unhappy, and uneasy. She never enjoyed cooking, nor was she a very accomplished cook. Breakfasts for the children were either oatmeal or Cheerios with evaporated milk with water and a spoonful of sugar. Lunch was Campbell's tomato soup, mushroom soup, and occasionally vegetable soup, or Kraft Macaroni and Cheese. Dinners were usually something cooked in the grease from meats or bacon she collected in the grease jars on the stove. She would use this to "flavor" other foods. Feeding a large family with a small food budget meant looking at meatless dishes. My dad loved to fish, so fried fish was often on the weekly menu, especially in the summer and on Fridays. I can't remember a time when we did not have the very large freezer in our home which was used to store the white butcher paper wrapped packages of frozen filleted fish. Rarely were fresh vegetables served, and meats that were served were filled with fat. I don't remember my mother smiling or laughing very much while we lived in the house on E. 44th Street. She was once again pregnant and the birth was to be in October, so the bulk of her pregnancy was during the heat of summer. What she needed was a helper, and the best she could have was her oldest daughter.

It was at this time that I was given household tasks to do. While I understand it is healthy to have children do chores, I don't believe my mother was trying to teach me a sense of responsibility or organization. I would think young children help carry dishes to the sink, straighten up their beds, and pick up their toys. It seemed that from a young age my mother viewed me as a maid service which would allow her to avoid the typical household jobs she disliked doing. My chores included dusting furniture, and emptying the Curity flat cloth diapers of their waste into the toilet then putting the diapers into the diaper pail to soak before they were washed. Holding the baby bottle so the little ones could eat was also done. I showed early signs of being very organized which could have come from being in charge of putting all toys the away and picking up discarded clothing and putting it in the laundry hamper. I also would wet and rinse out a towel and wipe down the bathroom floor every week. These chores were the beginning of the expectations for me to help with the younger children and maintain the house. I was not yet five years old. As I grew older, so did the list of chores I was to do also grew.

Maternal Failure

September was exciting. I was going to school. Two black girls who lived across the street from us (who I had at first called "chocolate children") walked me to and from school. They only lived there for a couple months. After that I was left to walk to school on my own. I had just turned five mid-August, one of the youngest of my class, and this was quite the feat for one so young. From East 44th I would walk to Sykora, take a left on Chard to a footbridge which spanned the expressway below. The footbridge only had a railing protecting the walker from the expressway below, and I was warned to not mess around, and avoid any of the horseplay which could potentially knock someone over the railing into the fast moving lanes of traffic on the expressway. Winter winds or storms were particularly frightening as I was always fearful I would get blown over the guardrail. After crossing the footbridge I made a right on East 50th, a left on Kirkham, a left on East 42nd, and a right on Mound. Although the walk may have been a little over a mile, it was still a lot of twists and turns for a five year old. In the beginning, walking to school I had the comfort of walking with the two girls who helped me navigate. Walking home after a half day of kindergarten was done alone. I was terrified I would get lost. This necessitated me in gaining some friends so I had someone to walk with along the route. My mother was unable, or unwilling to walk with me as she had little ones at home, and we only had one car, which my father needed for work. There was little other choice but for me to walk alone.

Some might think navigating myself to and from school would be enough responsibility for a child. By first grade my mother added a "shopping list" for me to do on the way home. There was a small store on Kirkham which was along my route and I would take the little list which was typically a loaf of bread, and perhaps a can or two of soups or evaporated milk. The list was inside an envelope which was put into my lunchbox. I was to stop on the way home and pick up the items and carry them home. I don't remember the items being heavy, but it certainly was a responsibility for someone as young as me, and may have caused some clumsiness in trying to manage the paper sack and my lunchbox, as well as anything I was carrying to and from school. It also caused me to lose my fellow walkers as they continued on their route home while I did the shopping, thus forcing me to walk alone for the bulk of my trip home.

I loved school. I loved everything about it. There were many children, and my teachers were truly kind women. My teachers liked me and I loved them. My obsession with organization was often transferred to the classroom. In kindergarten I would take it upon myself to straighten out the full storage wall of blocks by color and size, put all the furniture into the appropriate room in the giant doll house, and straighten out the art supplies and other classroom materials for the teacher. I would be so happy when my teachers would praise me for helping. I understood that my teachers liked my help, but I also understood that my help at home was just an expectation. At home I would often get criticized if I didn't do something right, and receive no praise for anything I did to help. For me, school was my escape! Often it provided me the praise I so longed to have at home

In 1958 we were given notice we were to move again. This time we rented the house my Dad's parents owned on East 59th. Once their children had moved out of the house, my grandparents began renting it to other families. My Dad's sister, Pauline, lived with her husband and two daughter in the back end of the house, and there was a renter in the upstairs apartment when we moved in. We were to live in the front of the house and basement which housed a kitchen, storage rooms, and a bathroom. The house always scared me. There were huge water bugs which climbed out of the water drains in the basement. Every time I would see them I would squeal and run. I would often get hit for this because I was teaching my younger sisters to react badly. I was to set a good example. Bugs were bugs and I wanted no part of them. The house itself was not as pretty as the house on East 44th. Everything looked old. The fixtures were converted gas lights, which today would be treasured, but at the time seemed like old-fashioned eyesores. When the house had been converted to electric, the walls were plaster, so instead of recessing the wiring in the walls, they were run through metal conduit which was then tacked to the plaster walls. The coal furnace left soot on the walls of the rooms, and no one had taken the time to refresh and paint the walls, or wash the windows which were sooty and dull. Sadly, my father also saw no need to do this, so the dingy walls remained in our tenure as tenants, and eventual homeowners when my dad bought the house after his parents died.

In this home my chores expanded. I was only seven and in the second grade when we moved there, but my mother felt I was old enough to help on a bigger scale. We had purchased a washing machine, but no dryer. It became my job at age seven to hang the laundry when I was not at school. In the summer I would stand on a chair outside and pin the clothes to the line which drooped down close to the ground. I would then put the forked pole under the line to lift it up so the clothes would not hit the ground. At first it was the Curity diapers and children's clothes I was tasked to hang. As I got older other clothing was added in. Eventually I was also hanging my father's work clothes, towels, and heavier clothing. In the winter I would follow the same procedure, only climb up and down a chair to pin the wet clothes to the wire clothes lines which stretched across the basement rafters.

I can't remember what age I was when I first learned to sweep the floor and gather the dirt into a dustpan. I am certain I was seven when I took on this task, although it was never done perfectly at that age. I learned to get better at it since I would be made to redo a task that was not done correctly. I also mastered washing floors, sometimes with a mop, but most often on my hands and knees. It was the same with dishes. With a large family, and babies with baby bottles, there were always dishes to wash. I stood on a chair and used the bristle bottle brush to wash the bottles and nipples, and a washcloth to wash dishes. I dipped them into the rinse water, then put them in the rack to air dry. I was too short when I started the task to be able to put the dishes away in the cupboards, but once tall enough, I did that, too.

By eight, my job expanded to feeding the laundry through the wringer of the washer, ever careful to keep my fingers from its hungry grip. One trip through the wringer from the washer into the rinse water, then I poked the laundry around with the large wooden paddle, then another trip through the wringer, and place the clothes ready for being hung in a laundry basket. Sometimes I would accidentally put too thick a layer of clothing into the wringer and the upper portion of the machine would pop up. I would then have to tell my mother what I did. While I am certain she did this from time to time, I was led to believe that I was the dumbest girl on earth and I would either get a vocal lashing, or I'd get hit for not paying attention to what I was doing.

We had a coal furnace for many years. My father would typically handle the job of feeding coal into the hungry mouth of the furnace, but in his absence I was told to go downstairs and add a shovelful to keep the embers burning. I was terrified of getting burned. The handle to the door was often hot, so I would take a washcloth to cushion my hand against the heat. I would then take the shovel, which was nearly as tall as me, and put a small layer of coal on it from the coal room and carry it across the room to the furnace. I would push the shovel into the furnace and twist the handle to dump the coal. I would have to do this several times because I couldn't carry enough coal on the shovel. My five trips was probably equal to one trip by my father. Sometimes I dropped the coal off the shovel, and I would hurry to clean it so I wouldn't upset my mother.

I was also, by age nine, sent to pay bills. I would take the envelope with the money inside and walk to Sears and Roebuck, Western Auto, or to the bank and wait patiently as a receipt was written up. I was always terrified that I would get robbed, or that the envelope would fall out of my pocket. One time I took the envelope from my mother and it didn't feel right. Perhaps there was only a single bill inside, I thought. I went up to the store to make the payment, and when the man opened the flap of the envelope he found nothing inside. I was humiliated when he accused me of stealing the money. When I insisted I had not opened the envelope, he then said I had to have lost it. It was then that my suspicions of my mother giving me an empty envelope intentionally to make the cashier think I had lost the money was correct. This ploy would then buy my mother time to gather the money to pay the bill. Sadly, I would like to say this was an isolated incident, but my mother always struggled with the bills. We just did not make enough money, or money was not allocated correctly. I also knew there was a lack of priorities. If my mother or father wanted something, it came before they budgeted for it. It was not unusual for my mother to give me an envelope with a note inside, and I was to give it to various people identified by my mother. It did not take long for me to realize I was sent as the courier to borrow money from people, and all too often, the loan was not repaid. It was when my mother started having me take these notes to my friends' houses, I finally realized what she was doing. I eventually stopped delivering the notes and returned home to tell my mother the person said "no." Once we had a phone installed in our house, (I believe I was already twelve years old) it began a constant stream of bill collectors calling the house.

We only had one car which my dad drove to work, and typically my mom and dad would do the family shopping on a Friday night. There were often needs for items during the week, and it was too difficult to drag all the children off to the grocery store, so I was assigned the task of shopping. Once we moved to East 59th, my shopping errands were increased. I would take the chrome shopping cart to the local A&P store on Broadway, or the Pick-n-Pay, and pick up groceries, mostly canned foods of evaporated milk, soups, some vegetables, laundry detergent, and occasionally a package of ground meat. I typically would have to take one of my sisters with me so my mom would have a break from watching all the girls, thus making my job both babysitting and shopping. During the summer months it was not so much a problem in dragging the heavy cart home, but it did become a problem in the winter months when I had to drag the cart through the snow.

The shopping cart was also used when I was sent to the Laundromat when our washer or dryer stopped working. In the summer the Laundromat was horribly hot and I dreaded going. There were also an assortment of strange people there which also scared me, especially when I was by myself. As scared as I was, I could never tell my mother about my fears as she had no patience for my worries.

My dad always had a boat since I was little. Most were small two person fishing boats, but over the years he got larger boats which could house four to six people. The boats were pricey and often needed costly repairs. I never had a problem with my dad fishing with my uncles or cousins, but there was always a long line of men who befriended my dad and went fishing with him. They fished, they used the boat, but never once did any of them ever come by to clean the boat after an outing. My dad was very particular about cleaning the boat, and he would always tell my mom that the boat needed cleaning. It struck me as strange that he was so particular about the boat, but ignore the condition of our home. Dad would leave the house and my mother would designate the boat cleaning job to me. I would scour out the floor and seats of the boat with cleanser and hose it out, then repack all the life preservers and equipment. There was never a choice for me to say no to this task. My mom made certain I had done it so that when my dad returned from work it was clean and ready for the next outing. I'm not certain that my dad even knew I was the one who did this. It was yet another chore added to the long line of expectations made upon me. There was never any negotiating to get out of cleaning the boat. I knew better than to argue with my mother.

I probably would have enjoyed learning how to cook as a child. It was, however, not to be. Not only was my mother not a good cook, but we never had the typical staples in the house to make recipes. Our cupboard was home to limited food, and any child "helping themselves" to food that was available was accused of "stealing" food. We would have to ask if we wanted something, and typically the answer was no. Poverty certainly had something to do with this, however I also noticed that my mother would purchase foods she liked and they were only for her consumption. My culinary experiences were mostly canned or boxed foods, fried meat, and breads. Perhaps that is why I love bread so much! I would make bread and butter sandwiches, or bread and butter and mustard sandwiches. Sneaking (or stealing) these items typically went unnoticed. We rarely had leftovers as such a large family would certainly have family members hungry for whatever was left. My mother did get creative with pastas. While she hated spaghetti which she said she thought was white worms when she was a child, she would be creative with ground beef, with sautéed onions and green peppers and tomato sauce, added to some pasta noodles or elbow macaroni. Her younger children nicknamed these dishes "slop," or "garbage" as she threw the ingredients together. She also learned to bake a turkey for Thanksgiving, and a reasonable stuffing. She would add to this mashed potatoes and her interpretation of gravy, and canned vegetables. It was a feast! Easter would be a canned ham which was deli sliced for us, and she would make potato salad, and canned vegetables. She never invited any of us to work with her in the kitchen. Even though she was not a strong cook, I think working beside her would have been a bonding experience, and perhaps, after I had taken cooking classes in junior high, I could have helped her with some homemade dishes.

I cannot remember exactly when I began babysitting my sisters. It seems as though I always had. We were left in the car while my parents shopped and I was to keep an eye on them. My parents would enjoy walking up and down the aisles of the stores, even if they were not buying anything. It was an escape for both of them, yet my sisters and me were left to entertain ourselves in the car alone without adult supervision or protection. Leaving the car was a punishable event, so filled bladders were pushed to the limit, and when nature could not be held off, two would sneak into the store to use the restroom and get back into the car before they were caught. It wasn't just shopping stores where my parents did this. It was also any time they stopped to visit with friends. We were to stay in the car and entertain ourselves. I would sing songs, do memorization games or read stories to my sisters to pass the time. It didn't matter if it was summer heat, or freezing cold, we sat in the car. Every so often my parents would go to an Amish auction out in Burton. They would go into the building, just to see if there were any great buys put on the auction block. It was free entertainment for them. My sisters and I would stay in the car. I hated when we would be taken there in the winter. We would be shivering in the car, the only warmth was our coats and a blanket we would bring along. When bathroom breaks were needed the girls would sneak in to get warm before coming back out to the car. I remember several times going into the auction house and seeing my mom and dad eating sandwiches, yet there was nothing sent out to the girls in the car. If too many trips were made into the building, I would be punished for not keeping the girls in the car.

I was not always the best babysitter. One time I was charged with taking three of my sisters up to the Olympia Theatre for the annual Children's Christmas "party." We watched movies and afterward we each received a bag of Christmas candy. When I turned around, one of my sisters was missing. I freaked out. I asked a neighbor friend to walk my two youngest sisters home, and I searched everywhere for the missing sibling. Finally I went to a policeman, sobbing, and told him I had lost my sister. He put me in the back of the police car and drove me home slowly so I could scan the streets to see if I could spot her. When I got home all of my sisters had already arrived. I got paddled by my mom for losing track of one of them! There was no recognition for my having watched three of them all afternoon, and then problem solving in getting the other girls home safely, or seeking assistance from a policeman. I began to feel like it was "every man for himself" in this household, and survival was the key.

I believe that when I look back on my childhood, my happiness diminished with each move. I was happiest in Bedford, then on East 44th, but by the time we moved to East 59th, I changed. I became quiet and reserved at home, and only when I was outside the house or at school did I truly enjoy life. Perhaps it was because I was becoming more aware of our lack of normalcy, or perhaps that I began to realize that I was never able to have the kind of relationship with my mother that I longed to have. Perhaps it was because my duties at home were becoming overwhelming. I probably would never have given any of this a second thought if only my mother would occasionally give me a hug or kiss or compliment for having helped. That never happened. The cycle of my trying to get my mother to love me was ingrained in my role as maid of the house. My work was under appreciated, and often yet another reason to criticize if I didn't do it right. I strove for perfection, and even in that I could not break through her barrier.

As a child you do not understand why your parents act the way they do. At the time, I certainly did not know my mother had her own demons which constantly plagued her and her self-confidence. I did not fully understand the overwhelming duty she had in keeping house for this large family without any help. I did not recognize the many tasks that she was expected to do as a mother of a large family, living in poverty. It was not until I was much older that I realized my mother did not have a strong role model from her own mother in being a good housekeeper and caregiver.

My mother had faced abandonment when her father died, and was overwhelmed with a skin disease which caused her constant embarrassment. What she needed was happiness and love. Thus she made choices which had huge consequences for the rest of her life. While she had tried to avoid these consequences by giving three children up for adoption, the reality became front and center when she made the choice of taking me back from the adoption services. Perhaps in her mind I owed her something for her having rescued me from my "abandonment." She had provided a home for me with a father. Yet, the reality was that she was in a marriage that did not provide enough financial support to take care of the bare necessities of raising a large family. She did not have a strong support system from family, in-laws, or true friends. Perhaps because her early experience with motherhood was one of separating herself from the reality of motherhood she missed the opportunity to learn how to bond with her children. She did not allow herself to feel the pangs of separation from the two sons she had surrendered, thus she never learned to truly bond with the children she had now. She needed to escape the mundane duties and expectations which her married life had handed her, not realizing that many women in Cleveland had the same financial situations, yet they did not abandon their role as a mothers and caregivers. Choosing to self-gratify whenever she could helped my mother escape the hardships of poverty and motherhood. Her wants often took precedence over the needs of her children. My willingness to serve her provided her a way to escape much of her misery. The more she pulled away, the harder I worked at trying to gain her love. It was a vicious cycle and one which I was too young to understand that I could never win.

Chapter 14: Seeing Another Side of Life

I was often allowed to stay overnight or for a few days with various relatives. For me, I thought these visits were vacations where I was able to go on various adventures. Many of my favorite memories were those "vacations" which became times of freedom from home responsibilities, and often times of attention from other people. They also gave me a glimpse of what life was like in other families.

Several summers I visited Edward and Esther's farm in Canton. Edward was a cousin of my mom's. They had a large family of seven children. I stayed there for a week in the summers, learned to pick beans from the huge garden, and then pinch off the ends and snap them in sections, and then throw them in a bucket to be washed. Esther would then boil and can them. While there I enjoyed Esther's baking and cooking. Her food, although just wholesome recipes, was delicious! Being out on the farm allowed me to enjoy long walks with my second cousins down to my mom's Uncle Rene and Cousin Henry's farm. What stays in my mind is that everyone was kind to one another. Even though Esther had a large family, and plenty of work to do in the house and on the farm, she made time for her children.

My dad's sister, Ann, was a favorite of mine. She always treated me so very well and showed an interest in what I was doing in school. A favorite memory was staying at her house and going on an Easter egg hunt with my cousins. I had no idea what you were supposed to do, but my older cousins quickly shared with me the idea of running and discovering the colored eggs hidden in the field. I am quite certain they sacrificed some of their own goodies so that my basket would have plenty of treats. My cousins were all kind to me and Aunt Annie also maintained a home where respect and support for the children's aspirations came first. Aunt Annie and Uncle Joe always bragged about their children's accomplishments and took pride in their home and their extended families.

Another of my dad's sisters, Loretta, let me stay with them several times. Each time was an adventure. My Uncle Ray was a ham radio operator, and I enjoyed going with the family to the ham radio rallies. There were lots of activities for the children while the adults displayed transmitters and receivers and various transmitting tubes, or bought equipment, and traded cards with their call letters to other operators. In another adventure we all piled into the car and took off. Aunt Loretta packed the makings for sandwiches, and our destination was wherever the one-tank trip would take us. One time it was to Erie, Pennsylvania, where we stopped at a park to enjoy exploring a gigantic ship's anchor which was on display. There was always something fun at Aunt Loretta's house. The family would play board games, do crafts, and host the annual Christmas Eve party where the adults would play penny poker and the children would play games in the basement and hit a piñata filled with candy at Christmas when "Santa" would visit. Also, the latest in technology was always discovered at their house. I saw my first television broadcast at their house, and had an egg omelet made in the first microwave oven I had ever seen. Also, Aunt Loretta made many family wedding cakes with beautiful flowers and designs. Their home was always filled with activities and discovery. My aunt and uncle always considered activities for their children, and the children of their extended families. Both Aunt Loretta and Uncle Ray always displayed great interest in my school progress and activities and they would listen attentively when I told them about school.

Another significant summer placement was to my mom's aunt, Annie, who lived out at Punderson Lake in a home that at one time was a summer cottage for vacationers, but they had made it their year-round home. Aunt Annie was the wife of my mother's Uncle Gus, who died shortly after the war. Annie was stricken with Multiple Sclerosis, and was confined most of her days to a type of wheelchair. I would clean her house and help with whatever she needed. She was very kind to me. When she would ask me about my home life, I would cover and say that everything was wonderful. I was fearful that my mother would be punished by her aunt for any misdeeds against her children, and it was my job to protect my mother. The irony of this was lost on me until I became an adult. Aunt Annie was a great listener and would make me feel so appreciated when I would help out at the house.

Most often I spent time with mom's brother's family. I enjoyed my three older male cousins who always had outdoor games to play, like German spotlight tag, or collecting fireflies. I always enjoyed my Aunt Dee's English tea with milk and homemade cookies. My Uncle Hank was especially kind to me and very protective. In fact, when I was a teenager he offered that I leave my home and move in with his family. Although I knew my life was tough, I was totally dedicated to my family and could never think of leaving them. It is a strange phenomenon of children having misplaced loyalty to parents who are hurtful to their children. In fact, I was confident that if I tried harder I could make my mother love me and treat not only me, but also my sisters, better. I had internalized the belief that somehow my behavior was the cause for my mother's unhappiness and distancing herself from me. I would never betray her by admitting, even to my uncle, that my childhood was difficult, although I came to know, as an adult, that he was fully aware of what was happening in our home.

Such outings were relished and enjoyed by me. These "vacations" usually happened because the other people asked for me to be allowed to join them. I knew to not return home with great enthusiasm as that would be the end of my excursions. I could never make my mom happy, nor could I figure out what I had done that had caused her to distance herself from me. No doubt, others picked up on that as well. What I most appreciated from these outings was learning that there was something more to family life than what I had experienced in my own home. As I got older and began to spend more time at my girlfriends' homes, I learned that most families, even those who were also poor, did not have the emotional dysfunction I felt in my home. I particularly remember my girlfriend, Pattie. Her mother would sit up and wait for us to return from outings with friends, or dates. She would have coffee or tea and cookies waiting for us. She wanted to hear all the details and was enthusiastic about listening to our stories. During the holidays Christmas music was always playing and the house had many decorative touches tucked away throughout the house. Her love of her family had such a positive impact on me and I often think of her when I celebrate the holidays, or when I sit and really listen to my sons when they share the stories of their lives. The positive thing is that I took so many of the examples I saw in other homes and made them my own when I would have my own family, always careful to not repeat the negative practices my mother used on me.

Chapter 15: Emotional and Physical Abuse

Loud and angry arguments would erupt between my parents. I always listened in fear that there would be blame pointed toward my sisters or me. It was not unusual for us to be punished for various infractions of the expectations of my parents, or things where the blame was pointed at us, despite our having no control over it. The greatest injustice was that if one of the girls broke the rules, it didn't matter who the offender was, we all got punished. My mother had collected bottle caps, first as a "school supply" which we used as manipulatives in math class when adding and subtracting. At home, however, the bottle caps became a weapon for punishment. We were made to kneel on them, rough side up, when punishment was issued. Sometimes the caps would draw blood, despite my care in trying to balance my weight so they would not pierce my skin. I believe someone must have said something to my parents when it was learned they were punishing us this way because suddenly the box of collected bottle caps disappeared and that punishment was replaced with something else. Weapons of choice were the hairbrush; but more often than not, a wooden paddle which had long since lost the tethered ball that came with it; or a "Board of Education" paddle my mother found at novelty shop, which was meant to be humorous, but in actuality, it was used to paddle us; my father's belt; or worse of all, the "peeda."

The peeda was a thick razor strap which was originally used to sharpen barbershop razors. I am not certain how my father procured these, but all five girls dreaded being hit with them. Some of the peedas were split at the end into long strips which, when used, would spread out for repeated insult to the skin of the recipient. When I heard that ancient societies used a "cat-of-nine-tails," I knew intimately to what they referred. I remember going to school with angry red welts which eventually turned purple and blue. I always felt that if I hurt so much from being hit with the peeda, then I could not imagine how painful it was for my younger sisters. We would try hiding the dreaded weapon in an effort to avoid the painful beatings. I remember tucking it into the couch cushions in an effort to keep it out of my Dad's hands. I would never totally discard it, for fear that a failed search for it would be reason for serious retribution which all of us would feel. Sadly, my mother would rarely intervene when my Dad was punishing us. My worst memory was when I looked to my mother for mercy, she stood smiling when he went after me. Perhaps it was because my dad had grown up with a strict father who freely used corporal punishment when my dad was disobedient. Dad had a quick temper, and often forgot that his daughters were just little girls. The heartbreaking thing was we rarely found mercy from either parent when one would become angered. I do not recall my mother ever intervening on my behalf when I was the object of punishment, and often stood by encouraging it.

There were times that my mother's behavior toward me was outright sinister. Typically a mother would want to protect her child from situations which would cause them embarrassment or alter their looks. There was no such mercy from my mother. At age eight my permanent front and lower teeth had come in. One of my sisters was jumping on a bed upstairs. Mom told me to go upstairs to make her stop. When I walked through the door a pop bottle sailed through the air, aimed at a chair outside the bedroom. Instead it made direct impact with my mouth. The central incisors on the top and bottom of my mouth were suddenly sheared off. I screamed as each heartbeat caused the exposed live nerve to send horrific shooting pain. My mother grabbed me and walked me to a dentist office, the whole time listening to my cries through the towel I held firmly to my mouth to keep air from hitting the throbbing nerves, and to muffle my cries. The dentist stopped what he was doing and immediately ushered me into a chair. A rubber mask was applied to my face and within moments I was unconscious. The gas stopped the pain, but when I pulled myself to consciousness my head was spinning around and my stomach was throbbing. My tongue explored the spot where my top tooth had been and I found an empty spot. The dentist explained to my mom that because it was a permanent tooth, I would need a replacement tooth in order to keep my teeth in alignment and for aesthetic reasons, as well as my dental health. She said no. The dentist explained there were programs that could help, or even completely pay the cost, but my mom refused. Upon returning home my grandmother, who was at the time staying with our family, said she would pay the cost. My mother again refused. So, I went with no front tooth, and a broken off bottom incisor from third grade through high school. I spent the rest of my school years talking with my hand in front of my mouth to hide my embarrassment. This also began my mom calling me "ugly" when she would get angry with me. A child believes what she is told by her mother. It has an impact on your self-perception. Even today when I look back at photographs of my school-age self I do not see an attractive girl. Never did I consider myself attractive, even when I was a young woman with repaired teeth, and was asked to model clothing and bridal gowns. Even then, I remained self-conscious about my looks.

I was eight years old when my mother pulled me into the basement bathroom and told me to remove my underwear. She had the red colored hot water bottle rigged up to the open rafter in the basement bathroom. There was a long tube with a kind of clip between the bottle and the nozzle. When I questioned what she was going to do, she indicated she needed to learn how to give an enema. The bladder had been filled with hot sudsy, soapy water. When I said no, she pulled me over her lap and my protests were met with a firm slapping. All I can remember was the burning sensation of the soapy water as it entered my body and once the torture was over, I sat on the toilet as my body protested the invasion it had suffered. I sobbed uncontrollably, and I was thoroughly embarrassed. I remember that I stayed out of my mother sight, hiding in the back basement steps with my collection of library books. I never knew whether that intended client was to be her, or one of my sisters, but I had no intention on being an experimental victim again.

As I think about physical abuse, I have to include the lack of food in our home. We were never allowed to take food freely from the refrigerator. If we did we were told we were "stealing" food. I can remember sneaking down the stairs when I was young to open the refrigerator to take a spoonful of something to eat to stop the rumbling in my stomach. No doubt my parents were on a strict budget and tried to provide as much food as they could; however, they always made certain they had the foods they liked and we were not included in eating those items. My mother always packed our lunches and we had a sandwich with either peanut butter and jelly, or mayo and cheese, or ketchup and bologna; a piece of fruit, and a nickel for the purchase of milk at school. I never once in my entire school career bought a school lunch, as they were too expensive, despite being government subsidized and made "affordable" for children. I rationalized that it really didn't bother me that I carried my own lunch as I disliked standing in line and preferred to have more lunch table time with my girlfriends. Once I started babysitting, I would treat myself occasionally to an ice cream sandwich. The supplemental nickel for milk ended by the time I was in junior high school. Despite being poor, we never applied for food stamps. At some point we did qualify to pick up a block of government distributed cheese and powdered milk. I hated the milk, but the cheese was a nice sandwich addition. It is interesting to note that my mother did not like the powdered milk either, so she still purchased regular milk for herself but the girls were to drink the powdered milk or go without.

I am quite certain that poverty and lack of proper role models made Mom and Dad poor parents. What childhood they had was destroyed for both of them: for Mom, the baggage of her three mistakes which could be blamed on her feeling of abandonment when her father died and lack of attention from her mother throughout her childhood. For Dad, he married far too young and his strict father who disciplined too harshly was his only role model. Add to this the responsibility of raising five children on a limited budget, and you easily find two people looking for every opportunity to do things for themselves. Mom's escape was going to the movies, doing crossword puzzles, fishing with Dad, or visiting her friends.

Dad's escape was fishing, hunting and visiting with family and friends. Too often, they put their needs before their children's needs. The tragedy is that they did not see a need to provide their children with educational opportunities, consistent and supportive family interactions, healthy meals and medical interventions. Neither did they protect their young daughters from possible danger.

Although sexual abuse never happened in our house, we were exposed to it. A "friend of the family" lived behind LaDue Reservoir. My parents had befriended the couple, and we were told to call them Aunt Kay and Uncle John. Aunt Kay was a kindly woman who cooked, baked, and always had a tray of candies available when we visited. She had to have been blind to her husband's ways. Uncle John did not know how to keep his hands to himself. I had overheard my parents talking about how he had groped one of his nieces and the parents cut off their relationship with him. Despite this, my parents still befriended them, simply because they could go fishing behind his house. My parents would drop us off to "watch TV" or play outside at Aunt Kay's, but warned to "not sit on Uncle John's lap." It did not take me long to figure out this man was a pedophile, although at the time I didn't know the correct word for it. I would gather my sisters and have them go outside to read, play, or pet the horse at the farm next door. When it would get dark and my parents weren't back, we would retreat to the basement of the house to watch TV in order to escape the biting insects outside, only to have Uncle John at the ready to pull one of the girls to his lap. I was incredibly uncomfortable about this man and when I mentioned to my mother that I was uncomfortable around him she said, "Just stay away from him." That was it? Really? You have five young daughters and you know this man has done things he shouldn't and you think it is ok to leave your young daughters defenseless against this monster? It was no surprise that when he visited our house while my parents were visiting Aunt Kay at her sister's home across the street from us, Uncle John molested one of my sisters. Who got blamed? My younger sister. I was of an age that I did not go on the family outings to their home any longer, and I was stunned that my family continued going there after he had molested my sister. On my wedding day I nearly fell over when I saw my parents had invited Aunt Kay and Uncle John to my wedding. What parents do this? I knew then that fishing and self-fulfillment would always outweigh any protection of the children.

When I was twelve, my mom's sister, Agnes, and her family came for a visit. I was not allowed to sit at the table with the family. I couldn't figure out what I could have possibly done to ban me from the table. I sat at the top of the stairway, straining to hear the conversation everyone enjoyed at the table. After dinner was over, my aunt told my mother that she would never again visit our home because of the way she treated me. Little did I know at the time that the reason for my banishment was because my mom didn't want her sister or brother-in-law to mention that my appearance must favor my biological father. At the time, I was unaware that I had been adopted by my dad. Years later Aunt Ag revealed this story to me, which cleared up the ambiguity of why I had been banished from view and from the table. True to her word, my aunt never again visited our home.

Both parents used emotional abuse on the girls. For me, I was expected to set a good example. I was rather timid out of fear of being hit or paddled, so I typically behaved and failed to "talk back" for fear of being punished. Although my mother had a wide variety of hurtful nicknames for me, her favorite nickname for me was "Queenie," followed by mocking comments that I thought I was better than everyone else. I would protest that I did not feel that way, which only encouraged her to continue to use the name, knowing I hated being called that.

In reality, I only wanted my mother to love me. It seemed nothing I could do would please her. Childhood just led to puberty and the adolescent and teen years which were turbulent at best. I quickly learned that standing up to my mother was not to be tolerated. One time after a fairly long line of belittling and hitting and reducing me to tears, I called her a "horror." That was not what she heard. I thought the hot handprint on my face would remain there when I went to school. It wasn't until I was older that I realized why she had reacted so violently. She thought I had said, "whore," a word I didn't even know or know its meaning. Again, I blamed myself as was it was my fault as I had not enunciated clearly enough and I had deserved to be slapped.

As I said before, school was my refuge. I took great comfort in being complimented by my teachers for my hard work and dedication. In eighth grade, I enjoyed going to school early so I could help the music teacher put the score charts on the board. I enjoyed singing in the choir, and being on student council, and I was allowed to put together the first school newspaper at Myron T. Herrick. I couldn't wait to get to school every day. I also worked in the main office. One day I was called out of class to the principal's office. I had never had a call slip, so I was puzzled as to why the principal had called me. Mr. Jenks looked very uncomfortable when I entered his office. He motioned for me to sit down, and as I looked around the room, I saw my mother sitting there. She smiled at me with a look that I can only describe as sinister. Mr. Jenks began the conversation. "Barbara, you mother came here today because she is concerned that you come to school early. She fears that you are smoking, and that you are hanging out with boys and will get yourself in trouble." My face reddened and a lump formed both in my throat and in my chest.

"Mr. Jenks. I come early so I can help in the music room. Miss Jones lets me wash the boards and put the musical scores on the board for the day. I have never touched cigarettes, and I don't hang around with boys."

Mr. Jenks looked at me sympathetically. "I think it best that you no longer help Miss Jones. I will let her know that you will no longer come to school early." Silent tears rolled down my reddened face. "Did you have any other concerns?" he asked my mother.

My mother stood up. "No, that takes care of what I needed to do." My mom shook hands with the principal, and I stood, head down out of sheer embarrassment, and followed her out the door. When we reached the hall my mother turned and said, "I told you I would come up here and find out what you were doing and put a stop to it."

"I wasn't doing anything wrong, Mom. Why did you do this to me?"

My mom said, "You are just a little guttersnipe." She just smiled, turned and walked out of the building, leaving me standing in the hall crying. When I had time I looked up the word "guttersnipe." I was baffled as to why my mother thought I was a bad behaving child who lived on the streets. I had never given my mother cause to believe I was interested in smoking. In fact, I would wave away the smoke my dad blew in my face when he was trying to be funny. And, as for boys, I had no self-confidence in my appearance at all and was quite certain there were no boys interested in me either, especially at this awkward age. At no time did my mother ever apologize for embarrassing me in this way. I suppose I should not have been surprised. It wasn't the first time she tried to embarrass me in front of my teachers. I dreaded Open House nights as she would always make a negative comment about me when teachers complimented me on my studies or my work ethic. "Really? That's surprising. She doesn't do anything constructive at home." I was almost relieved when she stopped attending Open Houses as it meant I would not have to deal with the embarrassing and untrue comments she would make about me.

By age fifteen I was tall, lanky, and my Toni perm tortures had ended. My hair was straight and long. I wore glasses that I paid for out of my babysitting money, replacing the ugly, pale pink school-issued glasses I had worn since fourth grade. I also bought myself inexpensive outfits with my babysitting money as well as the small paycheck I received from working in the ticket booth at the Olympia Theatre. Our family went on a big camping trip to the Thousand Islands area, camping for a week at Wellesley Island. I quickly met a group of young people close to my age. Among them was a young man from Wooster, Ohio. His name was Donn and the two of us hit it off, laughing and sharing stories about school. His younger sister was under his charge so everywhere we went, she went. One day, he asked if I wanted to go fishing. While I don't enjoy fishing, I quickly accepted an opportunity to sit and talk with him and his sister. We held hands as we walked to the fishing spot. That was the first time any boy had ever paid attention to me, let alone held my hand! We exchanged addresses and promised to write each other when we got home. I walked back to the campsite in plenty of time for dinner, and all hell had broken loose. My grandmother told me that my mother was convinced I had run off with a carload of boys and they were taking me across the border into Canada. Where this story could have come from I have no idea. My dad and mom were out searching everywhere for me. I knew I would be in trouble when they returned even though I had done nothing wrong. When the station wagon pulled up my mother jumped out and began screaming at me, calling me names that I had never heard before. My father followed, dragging me into the tent and paddling me. Other campers nearby stood watching this spectacle, and my sisters cowered out of fear that they would somehow be pulled into this drama. I was told to stay in the tent and my mother wouldn't listen to anything I tried to tell her. First thing in the morning we cut our trip short and packed up and left, two days prior to when we were supposed to leave. I sat by the window staring out the entire way home, wishing I could just die. Upon returning home my mother pulled me by the hair, again calling me all kinds of names, and asked when I had a period. I was told that I was to produce my soiled sanitary napkin when my period started. No amount of protesting and explaining that all I did was hold hands with this boy would appease my mother. The following year was the last time I went on a family vacation. I decided that working and earning money to pay for my high school expenses far outweighed any drama and unwarranted accusations that my mother could possibly produce for me.

At age sixteen I was earning my own money and paying all my expenses including hygiene products and clothing. Still, my mother's hand was often held out asking for money. This went on throughout my high school years. I even opened a savings account in an attempt to hide some of my money to pay for the upcoming expenses I knew I would have for my senior year. My mother said I needed to put her name on my bank account in case there were ever an emergency. I never questioned this as to question it meant my mother would pout and make me feel that I had slighted her. Twice my savings were emptied from the account, until finally she closed the account as she had withdrawn the last of my money. She had never asked for the money, or apologized for taking it. What was mine was hers.

It is probably a good time for me to reveal how the stresses of my childhood affected me as a young person. I am sad to say there were times I wished I could just die. The intensity of the emotional and physical abuse often overwhelmed me. I felt I had no vision of being saved from the emotional turmoil I felt. I clearly remember many times when I just prayed that I would die and it would end the turmoil that was my life. I was too cowardly to ever do anything about it, but I do remember the thought of suicide had crossed my mind numerous times. There were several life-lines I had which truly made a difference for me. One was my faith. Being brought up Catholic, I had plenty of "Catholic guilt," making me believe that my punishments were somehow deserved, yet knowing that I was truly a good person and should not be having such hardships placed upon me. I prayed for intervention. I prayed a lot. I am thankful that I never lost my faith that God would step in and intervene. I knew if I followed the straight path, God would eventually reward me.

The second life-line was filled with people who gave me hope. I was fortunate there were always people put into my path who had the kind words I needed in order to see my way through whatever hardship I was facing. I credit my teachers for somehow knowing when I was in the pits of despair that I needed a kind word. Miss Alinski, my 4th and 6th grade teacher, was one such woman. She spotted the welts on my legs one day and called me to her desk to inquire about them. I was completely protective of my parents and I lied and said that I had fallen. There is no doubt in my mind that she knew it was a lie, but her kind words to me made me feel that, "this too shall pass," and I could and would survive. I believe that is why I became a good teacher as Miss Alinski and other teachers provided for me the lesson that a kind word and action can have a huge impact on a student in distress. There were other teachers who, probably unknowingly, gave me the hope I needed to move forward. They helped me build my resiliency, making me a stronger person capable of moving past the hardships and looking for the silver linings which would certainly present themselves.

Another life-line was actually my mother's cousin's wife, Eleanore. During my high school years I would often call her and cry out my heart and soul about the injustices committed by my parents. She would always listen, never passing judgment, but always giving me the emotional support I needed in order to move forward. She encouraged me to follow my dream and go to college. Eleanore was not the only one. My Aunt Loretta and Uncle Ray were encouraging about my pursuing a college education, as were others in my life. Although I knew I needed to take the challenge to put myself and my future in the forefront, there was a strong need in me not to abandon my parents. I had been a dutiful daughter for years, despite their not being dutiful parents, but the act of leaving Cleveland and moving on in my life was, at least in my mind, a betrayal to my parents and my sisters. The negativity put in my mind by my mother about my thinking I was better than the rest of the family, and other negative comments she would make outweighed my ability to take the bold move to do what I needed to do in order to take care of me.

I was also blessed with friends and acquaintances who encouraged me to move on in my life. The mental and emotional support I received from them gave me the courage I needed to make sound decisions which would forever shape the course of my future. Sometimes it only takes a kind word from someone at a time when you truly need it to make a life changing revelation for someone who is struggling.

I was an overachiever in school. I was rewarded for my hard work and often received awards, and even induction into the National Honor Society. On Senior Recognition Day, my mother never saw me earn a wide range of awards. Although I would give my mother the invitations to the awards ceremonies, she never attended despite all my sisters already being in school and my mom only working in the evenings or weekends. She had taken on a job when I was in junior high. She worked at Jennings Nursing Home. She later left this job and when I was in high school she began working as a waitress at the Brown Derby Restaurant on Route 21. As I think about my mom working I never questioned why her schedule was only for evenings and weekends when her children were at home and she could have spent time nurturing them. Of course, this is probably the very reason why she took these shifts. Just like school was my refuge, work was hers as it took her away from the mundane duties of motherhood.

Despite being a good student in school, I was never counseled about applying for financial aid and going to college. I just assumed I was not smart enough to go to college. Instead, I began working full time after high school and I took classes at night at Cuyahoga Community College. It was natural for me to move into working full time as I had worked throughout high school to pay for my own clothing and personal hygiene products and even food. I knew I had to be able to support myself. Although it would have been nice to have received guidance at school about applying for college, I did the best I could to move forward in my life. As I look back, I wish I had gone to college immediately after high school, but my two years of part time college and working full time made me appreciate my college education when I did decide to make the move. Throughout these two years my mother never let go of making comments about my trying to act better than the rest of the family. My pattern was to always apologize for the choices I was making, yet I was beginning to see that if I ever wanted to really do better for myself, I needed to become self-centered and take care of me. In this way I was like my mother.

My first job was a full-time job at Union Commerce Bank, which stood on the corner of East Ninth and Euclid in downtown Cleveland. I worked in the Trust Department, and my job was to post the interest on bonds, and post the credits or losses from stock or bond sales on the client's accounting sheets. I had to balance to the penny at the end of the day. Although I was very good and efficient at my job, I did not like accounting. In a short span of time, one of my bosses was leaving the bank and working at an office furniture store. She asked if I would go with her, and for an increase in pay, I accepted. Sadly, she had not told me that the company would be going out of business and most of my job would be calling clients for their delinquent payments. I really did not like this work. When the closing of the store was coming close, I took a job working for the Teamsters Local #507 and Baker's Local #19 in downtown Cleveland.

My working for the Teamsters made my dad happy. He was a union man and thought my working for the union was the best thing I could ever do. He was so proud that I worked in their offices. My bosses were Al Friedman and Jackie Presser. I made fantastic money there for a girl with only a high school diploma, but the working conditions were entirely too strange. Every phone call was monitored and was to be logged. Any time one of us would go to the files, one of the union bosses would watch over us. No girl could identify her last name. In fact, I wasn't called Barb, but "Babs." It took me forever to recognize my name when it was announced that Babs had client calling. We each had a tiered scheduled start, lunch, and end time in an effort that none of us would be able to have conversational time coming in or out of the office. I found out years later the reason for all the secrecy at the Teamsters 507 and Bakers Local 19 office, as Jackie Presser ended up being an FBI informant for the illegal activities done by the union, and Allen Friedman ended up in prison as well. My father was furious when I left there to go to college full time. When the stories were released about Presser and Friedman my father was certain it was a conspiracy against them!

Throughout the two years I worked after high school, I

saved every penny I could after paying for my night classes. My first expenditure was to have my teeth repaired. I had spent my entire youth covering my mouth when I talked, embarrassed at my missing tooth, which caused my teeth to shift together, leaving a gap in the front of my mouth. I was humiliated when I saw my high school yearbook display a photo of me with the gap in my teeth. It was not my senior picture and I have no idea to this day who replaced my senior picture with that one. I remember when the dental work was done I was overwhelmed with joy that my smile was no longer an embarrassment and I no longer had to smile with my lips tightly closed. I expected my mother to make some kind of positive statement about my decision and the result of the dental work. My mother never made a positive comment about the change in my appearance.

After paying off my dental bills, I continued saving, and was excited to surprise my parents with a special purchase. I went to Kronheim's in Cleveland and picked out a new living room ensemble for my parents. I bought a sofa, chairs, coffee table, two end tables, lamps, curtains, and throw rugs. Everything matched. I was so excited to do something wonderful and unexpected for them and for the family. Sadly, it didn't take long to realize they didn't appreciate it as they let the hunting dogs sleep on the sofa and chairs, and even rip apart the throw pillows from the sofa. The new end tables just allowed more surface area to leave dirty dishes and assorted garbage. I had started dating and I knew I would never be able to invite a young man to come into my home. I cleaned, and I cleaned, and I cleaned, but it always went back to disrepair and filth.

My parents' inability to keep house was a huge embarrassment to me. They did not set a good example for my younger sisters. As I look back on this time of my life, I felt guilty that I began thinking only of my own survival. I had younger siblings and they had it just as bad as I did, if not worse. My only escape would be leaving the house. At first I considered moving into the upstairs apartment in my parents' home. I painted the cabinets and started taking stock in what I would need to do to make it a home. I bought dishes, china, silverware, and pots and pans. My dream was to make an apartment even my parents would admire. Despite my careful financial planning, making that apartment suitable to live in was beyond my scope of ability. The negativity I constantly received was overwhelming. I knew that to make a difference in my life I needed to leave.

College would be my only ticket out of the lifestyle I had growing up in Cleveland in the 1950's and '60's. Although I had spent two years taking night classes, the location of the college was in a risky neighborhood. When I got chased twice to my car, which was parked away from the campus as I could not afford the parking fees, I decided that it was time for yet another change. A young man I was dating took me to Kent State to show me the campus. Kent State was well known for their teaching program, and it was my desire to become a high school English teacher. Kent was a great match. My friend then made an appointment for me to meet with the Financial Aid Office. No one had ever explained to me that I would be eligible for financial aid. Not only did Kent State provide me financial aid, they offered me a job in the Financial Aid office. My experience in the bank provided the kind of accounting experience they needed in logging work study hours and income for students on financial aid. My friend also set me up to room with one his friend's girlfriend. Everything fell into place and I was ready to make the move.

My father did not speak to me for the three months between my acceptance and starting date at Kent State. He felt there was no reason for me to go away to college. My mother continued calling me Queenie and constantly made negative comments about my trying to be better than them. I believe it was their hope that if they wore down my resolve I would surrender and not go. That did not work.

It was my father who drove me to my room off campus, not talking to me the entire trip to Kent. I stared out the window as the air was thick with a mix of emotion. For me, there was excitement about my new adventure, yet fear that I could potentially fail. For my father, I now realize, his emotions ranged from anger to sadness and fear for my safety. When we arrived at my building I set to unpacking the car by myself, my father visibly acting as if he were dropping off an unwanted piece of baggage, not wanting to soil his hands in the task of ridding himself of it. Finally when I finished unpacking the car by myself, I looked in the car window to say goodbye. "Well, I guess that's it. Goodbye, Dad." He gave no response. As I turned to walk into the building he called out after me.

"Are you hungry?" my dad said. I hopped back in the car and we went to a fast food place to get a burger. I am certain he knew this was going to be my break away from the family and he was uncertain what would become of me. This was only a year after the Kent State shootings, and I am certain he was convinced I would either become a hippy, or I would be killed, or I would be another statistic of drug use. Of course this made me aware that even though he didn't know how to vocalize his concerns, he did love me. His stubbornness, and often times violent outbursts had always worked as a means of controlling my behavior, even though I never practiced irresponsible behavior, but for the first time, I withstood his authority.

Once I moved to Kent, I only came home twice, once at Thanksgiving and once at Christmas. When I did the house was a disaster, my younger sisters were mostly left on their own to fend for themselves, and there was little food in the refrigerator. Any sense of normalcy was gone as my sisters, ranging in age from 7th grade through 11th, were raising themselves. I knew I needed to distance myself from this. I was in survival mode. Many times as an adult I looked back at my behavior and felt I had abandoned my younger sisters. I have felt extreme guilt over this, but I also knew that I had to take care of myself before I could take care of anyone else. Time and distance became a stumbling block, and once I completed college, I married and started my own life leaving my sisters to figure out how to survive on their own.

Leaving home made no major change in my parents still coming to me to borrow money. In fact, my college money was borrowed twice when I was at Kent, leaving me to take out additional loans. As it stood, I had financial aid only because I had to beg my mom and dad to fill out the FAFSA forms for me. When they would be close to the deadline and still not have the forms submitted, I would contact my mom's cousin, Eleanore, to help them complete the forms on my behalf. Eleanore did their taxes every year, so she was familiar with their paperwork. My financial aid package was enough to pay my tuition, but room and board were left to me. I worked two or three jobs each semester, and one of them was working as the doorkeeper for the location where I lived. I would clean the common kitchen, and I would have to be on duty to lock the main doors at 10 P.M., and be alert to open the doors in case any girls forgot their keys after lockdown. My savings from my jobs would help pay for my books, school supplies, food, utilities, clothing, and household expenses. To have my money borrowed would put a serious cramp in my ability to buy food. My typical purchases were for cereal and milk, some canned soup, a loaf of bread, and small supplies of luncheon meat. Since we used a common kitchen it was not unusual for food to disappear, so I tried not to have too much in the refrigerator, which wasn't a problem since my budget did not extend very far. My parents never gave me any monetary support for college, which was not even expected by me because they still had four children at home and their income was based on unskilled labor hourly rates. Only once did my mom bring down a small bag of canned fruit. It was diet fruit and she didn't like the taste. I certainly didn't need diet food at that time, but the fruit was a nice addition to my meager food supply.

As I began my own family and remembered the negative lessons of my youth I fought hard to build a family of love and support for my children. I always found myself saying to my husband and to my sisters, "I love Mom and Dad, but I don't like them." I put a stop to their borrowing money from me because I made my mom ask my husband to borrow money. For some reason, she was intimidated by this, so her borrowing stopped. In fact, when we bought our first home, my parents used their tax refund check to help pay for a new refrigerator for our home. I was overwhelmed at their generosity and truly touched. I had never asked them for anything, so this event stands clearly as a break from the selfishness I had experienced over the years. In fact, it puzzled me as this went against every remembrance I had of our relationship.

I would like to say this was a turning point, but it was short lived. In fact, when my oldest son was born I had a horrible delivery. My back had been injured during the birth process and I was unable to stand up and walk unassisted. My son, who was a month premature, had a bad case of jaundice. Both of us remained in the hospital for ten days. I was placed in intensive therapy for my back. My parents never visited until the last day we were hospitalized. When they came into the room, Mom asked if our friend was going to do the taxidermy work on the deer my dad had shot that season. When I told her no, that he couldn't because he was too busy, both Mom and Dad pouted. At no time did they ask how the baby was doing, or how I was doing. My husband asked if they would like to walk to the nursery to see our son. "Later," my mom said. My husband and I struggled to create small talk, mostly about them, how my Dad stalked the deer, and the bingo games my mother had won. Finally they walked down to the nursery. I was still unable to walk very well, so I waited for their return. I was stunned that the talk went back to hunting and bingo and there was no comment about the baby. My husband was always respectful of my parents, and never said negative things about them to me. I knew he could get angry at their treatment of me, but he kept his comments to himself. After they left the hospital that night, my husband gave me a look I would never forget. I could tell he was hurt, and he was hurt for me. I think at that moment he fully realized what my childhood was like.

I rarely spoke much to my friends about my childhood.

Very few knew I grew up poor and the strange relationship
I had with my mother. It was my baggage I carried around.
To all outward appearances, I was a college-educated woman
who had a great work ethic, and had set high goals and met
them. These are all traits of someone who was raised with
these ethics and support. Dr. Ruby Payne, an expert and
author of *A Framework to Understanding Poverty*, best
described the lie I carried within me. Families in poverty
often felt threatened by a member of the family "raising up"
above the poverty level, and the child who made the bold
move is left feeling she betrayed her family and felt shameful
of her past. It took me a very long time to unveil my mask of
normalcy and let very few into the reality of my childhood.
Only a few of my friends ever knew the "real story," and even
then, I veiled most of the details. Nancy, a teaching colleague,
was one of my friends who knew my story. While teaching, I
put together a Faculty Follies in an effort to raise money for
scholarships for our students. I wrote the majority of the skits
and acted in many of them. It involved nearly all of the faculty
and administration in some part of the show. I bought tickets
for my mom and sister to attend the evening performance.
At the end of the two hour production the faculty presented
me with a huge bouquet of roses and credited me for putting
everything together. I had not wanted any attention brought
on me as it was a faculty effort. My "acceptance" speech was,
"Thank you, everyone, for supporting this worthy cause by our

faculty, which will provide scholarships to our senior class." Immediately afterward I went to the lobby to seek out my Mom. I was still hoping to get some kind of recognition from her about my work. Instead, she took the roses from my arms and said, "I never get roses." Nancy was standing nearby and witnessed this transaction. Then my sister pulled the roses from Mom and said, "These belong to Barb." My mom's face turned to a pout. After greeting other folks who stopped by to compliment the show I asked Mom how she liked the show. "Good, I guess. But I was surprised that you didn't announce that your mother was in the audience." Again, Nancy witnessed this. I was stunned and speechless. Nancy later shared with me she was saddened by what she witnessed, but she better understood how I became the person I am. As I reflected on this afterward, it occurred to me that in my mother's mind my accomplishments were her accomplishments. I believe she felt she had produced a child who had done well, and she was to be congratulated for her good work. For many years I was resentful that she couldn't recognize how hard I had worked, but as I began to better understand why she became the woman she was, it made it easier to make excuses for her behavior.

I do want the reader to know that my life was not one of total despair. As a teacher I had many students over the years who suffered dysfunction in their families and hardships I could not even imagine. My life was a "day in the park" by comparison to some of their experiences. My poverty was not as horrible as some of their poverty as a good number of my former students were homeless or lived with sexual and horrifying physical abuse, or alcohol and drug abuse. Some had parents who were imprisoned. Many also grew up with illnesses which eventually took the lives of their loved ones, and some suffered illnesses which ended their lives far too soon. I count myself lucky that I did not experience any of these things. Perhaps my experiences helped me become a better teacher as I was far more understanding and compassionate to the circumstances many of my students faced. I was blessed to have the love and attention of extended family, friends, and teachers. Because I became a resilient personality, I was able to look at the "silver linings" in my life and not wallow in the negative memories of my past. Just as my mother's childhood and upbringing made her into the person she became, my childhood made me who I became, and I celebrate that I was able to use those experiences to shape the kind of adult I wanted to be. My resilient personality helped me overcome the negativism that was my relationship with my mother.

Chapter 16: Revelation

On May 10, 1965 there was a death. My mother knew about it, and fearful that someone else would tell me, she decided to tell me herself. I had spent the night at my Uncle Adam and Aunt Eleanore's house, and upon returning home my mother asked if they had said anything to me, and I had no clue what she was talking about. She then stunned me with a revelation which I was not prepared to hear. "Your father is not your natural father. Dad adopted you. Your birth father just died." My mind was spinning. I was adopted? My dad wasn't my real dad? My natural father had died. She said that he no longer lived around us, but she wanted to tell me. She said Dad had adopted me and given me his last name. I was allowed a few moments to let this information sink in, although at age thirteen, I didn't have much of a reference as to what all of this meant. When I asked how this man died, she brushed me off and said, "I think he was electrocuted on the job." She had no details, and if she did, she was not sharing them. I was then sent on my way. I took one of my many borrowed library books and sat to read; however, my mind was overwhelmed with what I was to do with this newfound information. When my dad returned from work I was summoned and my mom announced that she had told me about my natural father. "What have you got to say to your dad?" asked my mother. I had no idea how I was to respond. I finally hugged my dad and said, "Thank you for adopting me." I was then dismissed so my parents could talk.

I was soon to realize that any attempt to talk to my mother about anything related to my natural father was off limits. If I asked, she would either get angry, or she would shut down and totally disengage. There finally came a time where I stopped trying to gather information. At no time did I ever say a word to my sisters that their father was not my natural father. I only knew them as my full sisters and my dad as my dad. I wasn't certain if that would make my sisters look at me differently. I had enough to worry about with my mother's inability to love me. I didn't want my sisters to not love me.

The next time I brought up the topic was right after I got married in 1974. My mom was looking at some photos from the wedding, and I said, "I have to admit, I looked around the church and expected to see someone I didn't recognize sitting there."

She pondered this statement and then said, "I did too." My radar went up as I thought this was different than the information she had told me when she first revealed I had been adopted by my dad, and that my bio-father had died in an electrical accident.

I was then emboldened to ask her some questions. "What was my natural father's name, again?" I asked.

She paused for too long a length of time. She then said, "Ed." When I asked his last name, there was again a long pause. "Faith. Just remember to 'Have faith.'"

When I pushed for additional information, she once again retreated back into her silence. Was he alive or was he dead? She was not going to open up and share any further information.

It wasn't until nearly ten years later when I had children of my own that I finally approached the topic again with my mother. My youngest son had a tumor. The "c" word kept circling my brain, and I was hopeful my mother would give me some health information as to my natural father, and if he had died, what was the cause. I was fearful that he may have died of cancer.

"Mom, you know Mark is having surgery on his jaw to remove the tumor. I really need to know any information about my natural father. I know his last name was "Faith," but that's all I really know."

"Where did you get that name?"

"Oh, I thought you told me that name."

"I never told you that!" What a realization that my mother outright lied to me about something I felt was so important to me. It was at this time that she told me my father's name, Edwin M_, and she shared a few details about him. She met him at the Welcome Airport where she worked at a nearby diner. When she was going to tell him she was pregnant, he already had met another woman and wanted to break up with her so he could marry the other woman. She said he did pay some of the bills for the pregnancy, but that was the extent of his involvement. Other than these few meager details she revealed nothing else. She then closed the subject from any further discussion. The door was closed, and from experience, I knew she would not open it again. I knew that what I needed to do was to find out what I could on my own.

I learned that in Ohio, children who were put up for adoption could open their records if they were born before 1964. After that, records would be forever sealed. Since I was born in 1951, I could apply for my records. I did, and what I received shocked me to the very core. I excitedly opened the records, and I saw my original birth certificate. I carefully absorbed the information. There was Edwin's name, his home city and state, his age, and his occupation. But what threw me was a number located at the bottom right corner of the birth certificate. "Number of prior births—2." All my life I was the oldest child. Now all the sudden I learned I had two siblings born before me! Sadly I knew I couldn't ask my mother about this. Instead I called my mom's sister, Agnes. When I asked her about what I found on the form, she at first hesitated, then she asked if I had asked my mom. "You know she will not talk to me about this," I answered.

After a very long pause she said, "You have two brothers." Once the information sunk in, she continued with some vague information. "The oldest boy was born Michael Wayne Clark. She loved the name Michael, and she loved John Wayne. That's how she picked the name. The second son, well, I don't remember the name. I believe both boys were put up for adoption through Catholic Charities. Because she had already made two mistakes, Catholic Charities would not handle your adoption. I think maybe yours went through the Salvation Army. I don't know." I then asked her if she knew my natural father. "Yes, your mother was dating out of her class. I told her that. He was a nice young man. He had a plane and he flew out of the small airport which was near the diner your uncle and I owned. I remember he wore a bomber jacket, much like the airmen who flew planes during the war, but I don't know if he flew planes in the war. All I know is that he didn't want to marry your mother." My aunt made it very clear that my mother had embarrassed the family with her behavior. She went on to tell me that my mother always used her "charm" to get her way. There was an amount of resentment that went back to their childhood. I didn't question any of this as I understand that in family dynamics there was always an amount of jealousy, resentment, and wrongs that were not righted; especially in childhood, and many of these injustices carried their way into adulthood. Instead, I appreciated what my aunt shared with me because it gave me a bit more of an insight into my mother's personality and behaviors. It was evident that my aunt, and the family, had been humiliated by her actions. I thought about that and felt we are still there as a society. Any young woman who has had three illegitimate children with three different men, without benefit of commitment to marriage, was and still is discredited as a respectable person. Things have not truly changed very much.

I did try calling my mom's best friend, Josie, but she said she would not tell me about anything until my mom passed. Sadly, Josie passed before my mother did, so that line of information was forever closed.

Anything I was going to learn would need to be learned on my own. I realized that my mother's continued emotional manipulation of me would only continue, and I knew I could not disrupt her peace of mind by investigating this information further. I would put future research on hold. That was in 1986.

Chapter 17: Extended Non-Bonding

My mother could not bond with me, nor could she bond with my children. My boys would run to my husband's parents and immediately be peppered with hugs, kisses, and questions about their activities. When my boys would run to my mother and hug her, she would move her head aside and continue with whatever conversation she was in prior to their arrival. My in-laws would call and ask about the boys. Often. My mother never called to ask about the boys. Ever. In fact, when my youngest had the tumor and I phoned my mother and tearfully told her how fearful I was about the surgery on my little two year old. My mom answered me, "Well, you had a tubal done after he was born, and now God is punishing you and going to take him away from you." I stood speechless. I quickly hung up the phone and found a quiet place to cry. How could she say such a thing? I had told her my doctor had recommended a tubal as I had such difficult births, yet she was using this information like a hammer to hurt me. What mother would vocalize such a thing, even if she thought it? It wasn't like my mom was super religious. In fact I have only a few memories of her ever going to church, yet she held on to the old Puritanical belief that we have a punishing God, and I was deserving of the most severe punishment God could issue.

When the boys were little it became clear just how disengaged my mother was with my children. We gathered every year for Christmas, and on one particular holiday, we met at my sister's home. My mother and father had purchased Sesame Street table and chairs for one nephew, and a table and chairs set for my niece, and for my oldest nephew they bought a larger gift. For my two sons they got one Sesame Street chair. No table. Only one chair. There were also other gifts for the other grandchildren, but my youngest only got a teething ring and a rattle, which wasn't horrible as he was not very old. My oldest son only had a couple of small toys, mostly from my sisters, and he had to sit while everyone else was opening many more gifts. I had to keep holding him back from going to the tree to look for presents to open. He only wanted to open things like everyone else. Now, my parents didn't have a lot of money, so it wasn't like the gifts needed to be expensive; however, it was obvious to my husband and me that our oldest was not being treated the same as the other grandchildren. Afterward my mom approached me and said, "Your kids have other grandparents and they will get gifts from them." Her words burned me. While driving home my husband, who truly never said anything against my mother, ever, said, "We will not be doing that again next year." I love family and traditions, and I could not bear to think we would no longer do Christmas together. The following year I began hosting our family party at my house, and I told my mother that I would do all the shopping for the grandchildren. I wanted to make certain that my children were treated equally. This was the beginning of my "loving grandmother mythology." My mom didn't remember my children's birthdays, so I would get a gift and a card and sign it from my mom and dad to present to my children. It wasn't as though my children were bad kids. My mother just could not bond with them. I would always invite her to birthday parties or special events for the children, but rarely would she bring a card or gift. I always had my "stand by" gift and card ready to give.

My dad (Stanley) had died in 1988. Upon his death I learned the frightening reality of just how much debt my parents had. My mother didn't even know what some of the bills were. I sorted through all of the bills, closed out bills that were in my father's name, and worked out a budget to pay off all the other debts. To do this we sold the house, which was nearly given away as the water had not been turned off when my mother was hospitalized and the pipes burst, causing massive damage to the walls and floors throughout the house. We sold the house "as is," and bid it farewell at a ridiculously low price as my sisters and I could not afford to bring it to code. My mother also had the deed to a camper and lot in Pymatuning, Pa. She didn't want to go there without my dad so we sold it and used the funds to pay bills. It took me several years, but all the bills were paid and my mother was living debt free. She was not happy that I was using her money to pay off bills, but I stood my ground and said that the bills had to be paid off if she wanted me to help her. She begrudgingly agreed.

As my mother aged she became more and more disengaged from me, although after my dad died, I was the one who found her an apartment near me, and helped her decorate it. I will never forget taking her to the store and asking what colors she wanted in her bathroom. She couldn't make up her mind. I said, "Pick out a shower curtain you like." After looking through all of them she found a pretty peach one. I began throwing sets of peach towels, hand towels and facecloths into the cart, as well as other peach colored accessories. I turned and she was crying. "Mom, if you don't like peach, we can do a different color."

"It's not that," she said. "I just never had matching towels before." She was right. Most of our towels came from Breeze laundry soap, or a bargain basement bin. They certainly were not the thick quality of the towels I was presently tossing into the shopping cart. The towels from Breeze and facecloths from Rinso were always an assortment of colors and textures, fairly thin, and I remember their having little absorbency. My heart melted for her and I continued shopping with her for a sofa and loveseat, a kitchenette table and chairs, and bookcases. We turned her small efficiency apartment into a very pretty home. In fact, the apartment manager asked if they could show her apartment as a model for other people seeking to rent there. Of course, this ended about two months in when the manager called me to complain that the apartment smelled and was dirty. That began my trips over to clean the apartment. Foolishly I believed that with the nicely decorated apartment my mother would want to keep it looking nice. Our childhood home was always in a state of disrepair and disarray. In fact, it was filthy. Once most of the girls left home, so did the housekeeping, and my mother did nothing to care for the house. Now she had a nice apartment which was close to me and close to shopping areas. The building was filled with ladies and gentlemen of her age group and they had monthly gatherings, parties, activities, and even bus trips. I paid an additional deposit so she could keep her cat, Bootsie, and also had him de-clawed. Everything was done so that she would have a fresh start. Sadly I didn't realize she really didn't care about the fresh start.

I was constantly in a struggle to keep my mother healthy and often had to step in to make decisions to keep her financially sound, medically healthy, and dodge constant threat of eviction because she would not keep her apartment clean. Although my sisters tried to help with my mother, they, too, had little influence on keeping her safe, healthy, and sheltered.

My mother never wanted to be tied down to the apartment and looked for every opportunity to do bus trips with the "button box" bands, or go polka dancing at Karlin Hall in Cleveland which I didn't mind and, in fact, encouraged, but she refused to take care of her apartment. I was becoming a parent to my parent. I would hold her feet to the fire in keeping on budget. She would complain to my sisters that I was mean and kept her money from her, although she never told them that I gave her a healthy and reasonable budget within her income limits, and she had spending money allotted for each week. I was always the "bad guy." I made certain all bills were paid, made certain she had food, medicine, and money for Bingo, bus trips, and shopping for incidentals. Unlike the life she had before when she was always in debt and borrowing money, never to be paid back, she was now living within her means. But to her, I was "mean."

Things became grim for my mother when her grandson, Norvell, died from a freak accident in 1996. She was particularly close with Norvell. I believe the closeness was because he was the oldest grandchild, and he had been born illegitimate to my youngest sister, Gladys. When she was pregnant, my mom called me asking me to talk to my sister into keeping the baby, which she did. I never spent much time thinking about it at the time, but I believe her extra attention on Norvell could have been a way for her to make up for her having given up her own two illegitimate sons. Norvell's death left her devastated.

Then two years later in 1998, her youngest daughter, Gladys, died of a heart attack. It became evident that my mother was falling into a deep depression, and at times I wondered if she had a death wish. She would fight me when I interfered when she did things that I felt would jeopardize her health and safety. It was as though she were a rebellious teenager, and she would go out and do the very things I begged her not to do.

My mothering her was extended even to the point where I had to sternly warn her not to do things that could endanger her life. I warned her not to go to Cleveland on a day where an ice storm was moving in, but she went anyway. In the middle of the night I got a call that she was in the hospital. She had driven to Cleveland in the driving rain and by the time she got to Karlin Hall, everything had turned to ice, just as the weather reports had indicated they would. She tried to get out of her car, slipped, and fell. People were leaving the hall as they were canceling and closing because of the dangerous weather. Two men picked up my mom, got her back into the driver's seat, and she assured them she was fine. She wasn't. She had broken her pelvis. Don't ask me how, but she drove through the elements, and got to her apartment. She quickly realized she couldn't move to get out of her car. She at least had the foresight to drive to a police station where she sat in the car flashing her lights until an officer came over to help. An ambulance took her to the hospital where she remained for over a week. After that there was no more polka dancing, nor was there driving. She could no longer drive as it was too painful to use the gas and brake pedals. Her constant companion would now be a walker which was needed to shuffle along when she walked. She was none too happy with me when I took away the car keys. I learned later that she complained to everyone who would listen that I was mean and I didn't give her money and now I had taken away her freedom. Of course, none of this was true as I remained as obedient and respectful as I had always been in the past, but when it came to driving, I refused to give in. She could very well kill herself, but if she killed others because of her not being able to drive safely, that would be my fault because of my cowardliness in not taking away the keys.

Despite my life already being very full, I took on added duties, taking her out weekly for grocery shopping and out to lunch so she would have a break from her apartment. She could not get into my minivan, so I sold it and got a car which would be easier for her to enter and exit. Occasionally I would take her to get her hair cut and styled. I also arranged for the Passport Program and Meals on Wheels to be certain she had company, a hot meal, and someone checking on her vital statistics as neither my sisters nor I could be at her apartment every day. Things took another turn for the worse in May of 2000. Mom tried to move her Lazy Boy recliner by herself. The bottom kicked out and knocked her to the floor. Because of her damaged pelvis, she could not right herself.

She managed to pull the phone off the shelf and call me. It was back to the hospital, this time with a broken arm. Her right arm. Not good. Mom's bones were fragile as she had a bad case of osteoporosis. Her pelvis had never healed after her fall on the ice, and now her arm was broken in several places. There were more trips to the hospital and to the orthopedic surgeon to set the arm and for checks on the healing process.

At this same time my sister, Dottie, was getting married and the wedding would be in Buffalo, New York, in July. We had to make all the arrangements so someone could handle Mom and make certain she was safely transported everywhere. She was unable to take care of herself as her right arm was useless. Showering, drying her hair, putting on her clothing, brushing her hair, basic hygiene needs...everything was impossible. My mother's need for everyone to take care of her added to her annoyance when someone was not available every moment. My sisters and I were all working, and Dottie and I had our own families. Emotions were also running high as Dottie planned on moving to Florida a few months after the wedding. Now my mother had to face her issues with abandonment, which further pushed her into depression. The wedding was beautiful and we were all so happy for my sister, but my mother remained sad and aloof throughout the night of the rehearsal and the wedding. We had to keep her in a wheelchair most of the time, just to make moving her from place to place easier on all of us. My sister, Susan, fortunately, handled all the transporting of mom to and from the rehearsal dinner and the wedding. Afterward she even included some side trips in an effort to distract Mom from her depression. Thinking back on it, Mom's body was probably in a state of rebellion from her emotional and physical issues, and her lack of handling her medications properly. Among her ailments was diabetes, and when clear-headed she would religiously take her insulin injections. I learned that once her arm was broken she was not taking her insulin as prescribed. She was also on blood thinners because of the by-pass surgery and replaced aorta valve, and she was not following the changed protocols in medications as prescribed by her physician. Her body was a mess, but at the time, I thought her mind was clear. I never thought she was unable to make healthy choices with her medications. Apparently I was wrong.

Once we all returned home from the wedding, I discovered that she could not draw her insulin into the syringe with her left hand. I would go over, draw the medicine, and put the syringes in a cup in the refrigerator. I would return to fill more syringes, only to find that she was not giving herself her insulin shots as prescribed. She was groggy and wanted to sleep all the time, either because of mistakes in her medicine, or as an escape from the new reality that one of her daughters would be moving out-of-state. Eventually, she again fell at her apartment and was transported back to the hospital where it was discovered that she was taking old pain pills as well as the new pain pills she was prescribed for her broken arm. She was taking a wide assortment of old prescriptions instead of discarding them when new ones were prescribed. I do not believe it was intentional. I believe she became confused with the mix up of medications. When I arrived at the hospital she was spitting up blood, no doubt caused by the incorrect self-medicating. Once they controlled the internal stomach bleeding, she was moved to a nursing home for rehab as she had to learn how to take care of herself, stand and balance herself, use her left hand to dress herself and to take her medications, including her insulin shots, and how to do simple hygiene tasks. Her right arm would be useless for at least another month. I noticed immediately that her mind was once again clear and she was able to communicate and was coming out of her depressed state.

I would visit her as often as I could. On one of my last visits we had a serious talk about whether it was time for her to move permanently to assisted-living where they would handle her meds, cleaning, and cooking. Her biggest concern was for the care of her cat, Bootsie. It is sad to say that you can be jealous of a cat, but my mom loved and cared for that cat more than she did for me, or my children.

My last visit to the nursing home was on the Wednesday before she was scheduled to be released to go home. I had the most miraculous visit with her. For the first time ever, she asked about my boys. For the first time ever, she sat and chatted with me about my job, about my activities, about my family. How sad that this was a day that is forever etched in my mind because it was so unusual. This had never happened before. Ever! We talked about things that normal mother-daughter relationships visited. We laughed. We smiled. She told me she loved me. I didn't want to leave.

I went home and told my husband that I thought someone had kidnapped my mother, but I certainly enjoyed my visit with the woman who was in her room! He laughed and I was light hearted all evening and looked forward to her coming home. Something had changed. Perhaps with my sister Dottie moving to Florida my mom realized that she not only needed me, as I was a caregiver for her, but she might actually find that she had a loving daughter in me. Perhaps it finally struck her that I had been available to her all my life, just waiting for her to see me as a daughter, not a maid, babysitter, errand runner, bill payer, grocery shopper, or whatever other role I played. I imagined we could finally begin acting like a normal mother and daughter. Needless to say, that dream was quickly crashed. She was to come home on Friday. I received a call from my sister, Dottie, on Friday morning and she said Mom's coloring was not good, and they said they were going to postpone her coming home until Saturday. Instead she landed back in the hospital.

I arrived at the hospital and she was in the ER. I brought with me a stack of papers to grade as I figured this would be another long day of waiting for tests and then eventually either having her move to a room in the hospital, or she would be released to go back to the nursing home. She couldn't talk as they had a tube down her throat. I told her it was the same thing that happened before so they just had to get her stomach to settle down. I did not realize that this time they could not stop the internal bleeding caused by her long-term mismanagement of her medications. I was taken by surprise when doctors brought a crash cart into the room and began speaking loudly, asking if she wanted to be resuscitated should she stop breathing. Her eyes widened in a panic. I called my two sisters to get to the hospital immediately. Dottie arrived and together we stood bedside until my mother slipped into unconsciousness. By the time Sue arrived they had moved her to a quieter room, changed her gown, and we called our sister, Em, in Iowa so she could speak to Mom on the phone, which we held to her ear knowing she was no longer responding. Mom passed with three of her daughters standing at her side. It was September 10, 2000.

It happened that I was taking a graduate course that fall. It was in adult psychology. My mother died on September 10th, right when I had to decide what I would make my focus for the two required papers for my class. It was not a tough decision. I knew it would be about my mother and my relationship. Perhaps it was God's timing for me to address this topic in order that I might understand why my mother was the way she was. Perhaps it gave me insight as to why she acted the way she did, not only with me, but with my siblings. Perhaps it would answer for me the question of why my mother couldn't love me. The good thing was that my research for these papers helped me heal. My research helped me put things into perspective and move forward with the emotions I was left with upon my mother's death.

My mother could have been the poster child for abandonment theory. She felt abandoned by her mother, by her father, and by the men she had relations with over the years. She sought love, and even though she had children and grandchildren who would have given her all the love she could ever want, she was damaged by her experiences, thus making her unable to relate to us.

When I decided to write this book I knew immediately that my title would be "Why Can't My Mother Love Me?" which was the question I asked throughout my growing up years. As I wrote this book, I finally came to the conclusion that no matter what I did, nothing would change my mother's inability to love me. She couldn't love me because she couldn't love herself. Thus, the title of my book changed to a more declarative statement of, "Why My Mother Couldn't Love Me." It was during the editing of this book that it was suggested I consider "Maternal Failings," a term referring to a woman who had a personality disorder which disallowed normalcy in relations with her children. I settled on Maternal Failure as my title.

When authoring a book it is essential to have a book cover that actually summarizes what the reader will discover within the pages. I knew immediately what my book cover would be: a photograph I had remembered seeing as a child of my mother. It had been torn into four pieces, then taped back together. I believe the photograph was taken prior to my birth. At first I was going to have the picture photo-edited to eliminate the tape marks and better align the picture. Instead I left it as it was. My mother had torn this picture years before I had ever discovered it. Perhaps it is just the English teacher in me, but I always look for the symbolism in things. I thought the photograph was significant that it was torn into four pieces: her childhood and upbringing, her choices during her young adulthood, her challenges in parenting, and her firm grip on the secrets she kept throughout her life. The book cover displays the photograph in an elegant frame. Frames are purchased by the person framing the photo and reflects her feelings about the person in the photo. The elegant frame is because I put great value on having a good relationship with my mother, despite her inability to see value in me.

I am hoping that my words and the stories I shared help my readers to better understand not only my mother, but perhaps other people who were unable to love their children. I had my students over the years reflect and write a creative piece that addressed their philosophy of life. I, too, completed the assignment. I wrote that there are two kinds of people in this world. One gets handed a bouquet of roses and everyone ooohs and ahhhs over the beautiful flowers. Others get handed a roll of toilet paper. Now if you got the toilet paper you have two choices. First, you can sit on the "curb of life" and cry and bemoan the indignity and injustice of getting worthless toilet paper while others rejoiced with beautiful flowers. Or, you take the roll of toilet paper, tear apart the sheets; accordion fold a small stack of the sheets and tie them in the middle with string. Then, separate the sheets and fluff them up. What you get is a paper rose. You can scent them with a spritz of perfume, and even add some color to the tips of the tissue sheets. While those with the real roses are eventually left with dead and forgotten blooms, those who made paper roses have a lasting keepsake of their having taken a bad situation and making something beautiful out of it. I am such a person. I have made many, many paper roses.

It took me a long time to realize my mother couldn't love me because she could not love herself. Counseling and medication could have helped my mother address her issues, but these were either never suggested or offered or afforded. I count myself as blessed that my faith provided strength to carry on, despite the despair I often felt as a child. I was also blessed that there were people put into my life who provided me the positive role models, support, advice, and love that I so desperately wanted. I often credit my upbringing with making me a much stronger person and as a teacher, someone who could provide that missing care that some of my students may have needed. My upbringing also made me a better mother as my children have no doubts in their minds that I love them as I often tell them, and show them by word and deed that they are loved.

Part Three:
Uncovering Dorothy's Secrets

Chapter 18: What is Fiction and What is Truth?

Much of what I write in the portion of the book will be repetitious as I felt it was necessary to outline my thought process when uncovering my mother's secrets. I apologize for the repetition, but I think you will agree it makes my journey in uncovering my mother's secrets make more sense. That being said, my first steps were to determine what did she tell me that was truth, and what was a lie.

It had been my lifelong habit to never do anything that would upset my mother. There are many times I regret this as I think had I been more demanding, I might have had more answers not only for me, but for others as well. Having no backbone can only be credited with my constantly wanting my mother to love me, and to upset her only made her pull her love away even further, constantly out of the grasp of my searching heart. The results of my inability to confront my mother meant that if I wanted to know anything I would research and explore without ever allowing my mother to know I was hoping to uncover the many secrets she held.

It is important to know that my memories are clear and sharp when it came to any tidbits of information my mother did share with me. Perhaps it was because these moments were rare instances of my mother talking to me about me, or things that affected me. It is sad to note that one of my earliest memories was just that. I had to be no older than four years old when my mother stood in the kitchen at the stove and I stood in the doorway. I have no idea why her conversation drifted into the direction it took, but my memory picked up with my mother telling me that my father would fly a plane overhead. In an animated motion her hand circled in the air as she looked up, her eyes seemingly watching this man doing loop-de-loops overhead. Her face was relaxed and she was smiling. I don't know where the conversation flowed afterward, but that very distinctive memory stayed with me. In fact, I can still see it quite vividly in my mind. Imagine my surprise years later when my mom said my dad (Stanley) had never stepped foot in a plane, nor would he. I remember my confused mind trying to sort out how he could have done loop-de-loops if he was never on a plane. I tried to discount my recollection as a dream, but I knew my memory was true. I just filed this away as perhaps my mother was just play-acting a scene she wished happened.

Another memory was when my mother was driving a car, which had to be when I was in junior high. I believe it happened after I was told that I had been adopted by my dad

(Stanley.) My girlfriend, Sandy, and I were in the back seat, probably talking about various boys, many of whom had the same first names and we had to say the last name so we knew which boy we were discussing. My mom interjected into the conversation that she had dated three "Eddie's," all at about the same time. Because my mother rarely shared much information of her youth, that tidbit of information also stuck in my brain.

When I was actually told about the adoption all my mother revealed was that my biological father had died. I questioned her as to the cause, and she said she thought he was accidentally electrocuted. Once this conversation came to an end there was no invitation to ever revisit it. If I tried, she immediately shut down and would pout, her typical means of making me regret having pushed her for more information. She would remain aloof for days afterward as I tried to make amends for broaching on an uncomfortable topic of discussion. I was rarely confrontational with her. I would immediately know "my place" and not question her any further.

When I was in high school there was a rare conversation I had with my dad (Stanley.) It was uncommon for my dad to talk about anything sentimental. It was not in his nature, but I had actually built a little bond with him as I would get up at 4 AM and make his lunch for work, and make certain that he was awake because he often overslept. As a thank you he bought me a new clock radio, which was wonderful because my alarm was just a wind up clock, so now I would be able to play AM music in my room. After he gave me my present, he just wanted to chat. I'm not certain as to how the topic came up but he was talking about how I would scream when they first brought me home. He said people would look at them and think they were beating me. I listened politely, not knowing if I should apologize for such rude behavior, but then he continued. "You know, when we brought you home your mother went against my wishes and wheeled you down in the baby buggy to where your father was living. She told him that we were taking you out of adoption services and wanted to know if he had any objections. He said he didn't, but he didn't even look at you or offer to hold you. He just wanted to be left alone." Again, this information was filed away in my brain as one of those rare instances that I learned something about my own past.

After I got married in 1974, my mother and I had a rare moment. I shared that I expected to see a stranger at the church, she said , "So did I." I immediately remembered that she had told me my biological father had died when I was thirteen. I took my chances and asked her what his name was. "Eddie." I asked for a last name and again waited while she thought. "Always remember to have faith." Again, I held onto this scrap of information recognizing that she may have lied to me at age thirteen saying my father had died, but now I had a name and it appeared she thought he might have shown up for my wedding.

Fast forward ten years. Opportunities never arose again to comfortably bring up the conversation about my biological father until 1986. My youngest son had a tumor and I was terrified. I was terrified the tumor could be cancerous. I cornered my mother when no one was around and told her I needed any medical information she could provide to me about my biological father. "All I know is that his name was Eddie Faith," I said.

She looked at me startled and said, "Where did you get that name?"

I said, "I thought you had told me that awhile back."

She continued, "His name was Edwin M_." My head went into a tailspin as the last name she said was not Faith! I realized her annoyance with me was why she opened up, and I figured I would use this to my advantage and pursue questioning. I plunged in and asked more questions about him realizing she had lied to me ten years ago and she could give me more fictional tales, but I was hopeful that at that moment I could get more of the story out of her. She told me that he was kind and that he had helped pay for many of the doctor expenses involving my birth. I asked if he had ever married, and she said she supposed so. She also revealed that he moved to Sarasota, Florida, and thought he flew cargo planes. She revealed that she met him at the Welcome Airport in Northfield at a diner her sister owned. She said she had worked there while her sister was pregnant with my cousin.

This was far more information than she ever shared before, although I was still suspicious as she had lied to me before. I stored this new information in my head to decide later how I would use it. At least this story went with the loop-de-loop conversation I remembered from my early childhood. I asked if Edwin had other children and she responded that she didn't know, but she figured he did. She also repeated the fact that he had died at age forty, but she didn't know what caused it. This conversation would be the last that I ever had with my mother about Edwin. Whenever I tried to explore the topic again, the veil of secrecy took over and she would shut down.

Now that I had a name and some information, I figured I needed to act on it. Perhaps he was not really dead. When I had said I looked around the church on my wedding day, she said she did too. I would have to take what little information she provided and try to unravel the truth to it. I knew she was annoyed with me when I had broached the topic, but often when she was angered she let her guard down and revealed information not previously shared.

It is important to note here that often people who are adopted have a strong curiosity to learn just who they are. What is my nationality? Who do I look like? Are there family health issues? Are there inherited talents and traits? Some adoptees have no desire to find their birth parents, or possible half siblings. But others, like me, wanted to know as much as possible. I was so different from my mother both in looks and personality, and I didn't really resemble my blue-eyed sisters who either looked like my mom, or they resembled Dad's family. I wanted to know more about my biological father.

My first attempt at finding information about Edwin was to write a short note addressed to the Welcome Airport (which was still open in 1984) asking if anyone had any information about Edwin who stored his plane at that airport, and flew from that airport in the early 1950's. It was not until late November in 1984 that I received a phone call from a woman named Shirley who identified herself as a second cousin to Edwin. She said my note had been posted on a bulletin board at the airport and one day she chanced upon it and decided to contact me. She asked why I was trying to find information about Edwin, and I told her I had been adopted by my dad, but my mother had just recently revealed to me that an Edwin M_ was my actual birth father and he had flown a plane at the Welcome Airport. Shirley was startled, but openly shared what little information she had on her mother's cousin. Her family lived on Union Street in Bedford, and Edwin had lived with them for a period of time which matched the time prior to my birth. I asked her a lot of questions about Edwin, and although she was surprised by my revelation, she gave me answers to my questions. She remembered him as a nice looking man, not real tall, dark hair, brown eyes, and that he was always kind. He had taught her how to fly, and she still went out to the Welcome Airport to practice flying long after Edwin moved from their home when he got married. She revealed that he had married Myrtle, and had a young family when he died. He had flown for a commercial company. She knew he died young, she believed from a heart attack, and that his family still lived in Florida although her family had long since lost contact with them. The information Shirley told me matched much of my mother's information, so I felt like I was on the right track. I wrote a follow up letter to Shirley, who now lived in Rittman, Ohio, thanking her for the information; however, the letter came back unopened and stamped, "Return to Sender." I sadly felt that she may have thought I was trying to disrupt Edwin's family. I never tried to contact her again.

Perhaps because my mother had lied to me in the past, I began to wonder if I was being misled and Edwin was actually alive and Shirley was trying to protect him from an uncomfortable situation. Perhaps my mother and Shirley knew each other, and when Shirley saw my note on the bulletin board she had contacted my mother and the two wanted to throw me off track. How sad that I had now become suspicious of anything involving my mother.

On a whim I called Sarasota, Florida information, and asked for a phone number of Edwin M_. The number was unlisted. I probably wouldn't have done anything with the information, yet I longed to know more information, particularly as I was terrified about my son's heath and desperately wanted to know what my paternal side's health history was.

It was not long after these events that an article appeared in the newspaper about adoption records. I learned that if the adoption occurred prior to 1964 in Ohio the adoptee could open and copy their records. I immediately set to work to do this. I learned that every state has different rules about the sealing of adoption records, but in Ohio an adult, or direct descendant, can file to open and copy the adoption records. It all had to be done through the mail. I wrote to the Office of Vital Statistics in Columbus, Ohio at Ohio Department of Health, Office of Vital Statistics, P.O. Box 15098; Columbus, Ohio 43215. I was given the instructions needed to get copies of my files. I sent in my request. Shortly afterward I received a letter including my state adoption record number and the fact that the record was open for reviewing. At that time you had to travel to Columbus to review the files. I contacted them indicating a trip to Columbus would be difficult to plan as I had numerous obligations during the work day. I was then allowed to send the materials in to receive photocopies of my file. I had to include a notarized Application for Adoption File, two pieces of identification, and a small fee which covered the cost of photocopying and mailing the documents. It would take up to a month to receive the file. (Today the only way you can receive copies is to submit the application via the mail. They no longer offer the in-office review.)

When the package arrived my heart skipped a beat. I would be looking at a page out my mother's history, and my history. I was breathless as I tore open the envelope. What I received was my original birth certificate, a Consent for Permanent Custody and Adoption, a Statement in Regard to Adopted Child, and a Final Decree of Adoption, Dispensing with Probationary Period. My first attention was drawn to the legal documents of adoption. My mother had signed off custody of me on August 29th, 1951, sixteen days after I was born. On June 26th, 1953, when I was nearly two years old, she terminated the agreement, thus I had remained a ward of the state until I was nearly two years old. Even though I had been placed in her home when I was nine months old, my mother never terminated the adoption process, thus allowing the path to be open if things didn't work out and she didn't want to keep me. The enormity of this revelation left me feeling empty and sad as there was no romanticizing the reality that she had kept her options open in case things didn't work out. The paperwork showed me she had a built in escape clause so I could be returned to the system.

The next document was the adoption papers. My dad (Stanley) adopted me on June 2nd, 1956, so up until that time my name had remained Barbara Louise Clark. I had not realized that my mother had not terminated the surrender of me for adoption until I was nearly two. He, too, had an escape clause as I was legally a Clark, and even after he and my mother had two other children, and were expecting a third, it was only then that he moved forward to formally adopting me as his own. The feeling that my parents didn't want me, and kept an escape clause at the ready was truly sobering and painful to me. It further established in my mind my mother's inability and unwillingness to bond with me. If you know that you might "give back" a child to the adoption process it would behoove you to not build a strong bond and attachment as it would then be easier to cut ties. There would be limited emotional residue in separating from the child. I can vaguely remember the day my dad (Stanley) adopted me. There was the sense of excitement, and my dad's rare display of affection, although I was not aware of the significance of what was happening. It makes sense that there was necessity in changing my name to his name as I would be starting school that fall. To not do so would cause many additional questions which my mother would not want posed to me, or to her. It saddened me that the formal adoption took so long. For both of my parents it did not seem to bother them that my last name was Clark, yet my two younger sisters had my dad's surname. Only when it would have been awkward to register a child for school with a name different than the parents during a time era that had few divorces did it seem necessary to finally take an active step in adopting me.

The document which I examined last was the one which stopped me in my tracks. It was my original birth certificate. All the details were in place. There on the line for Father of Child was Edwin M_'s name, along with pertinent information about his age, his occupation, and that he was born in Michigan. But there, at the bottom of the form, was a section titled "Children Previously Born to this Mother." Under it, a number "2" for other children now living. At first I thought that by the time I was adopted two of my sisters had been born. It quickly occurred to me this was my original birth certificate and I was the first child. Or was I?

I wanted to call my mother and question her, and in hindsight I wish I had confronted her. Perhaps I would have far more answers and would not have wasted so many years in my effort to find the truth of her secrets. But, a lifetime of not being confrontational pushed me back into passive-aggressive behavior when dealing with my mother and allowing her to keep her secrets. It would be up to me uncover the truth.

My first call was to my Aunt Ag, my mother's sister. It was quite evident that my aunt had never softened her stand on my mother's actions. When I asked about the "2" listed on the birth certificate she asked if I talked first to my mom. I told her that would get me nowhere, and most likely would even further distance our relationship. My aunt revealed to me that I had two brothers. What she knew was that the oldest was named Michael Wayne Clark. My mother liked the name Michael, and John Wayne was her favorite actor. I remember thinking to myself how hard it had to be on my mother that I married a Michael, and my oldest son was a Michael. Also, my sister, Dottie, married a Mike, and she named her son

Michael. I wondered at how my mother would have reacted and felt when that name kept reappearing in her family, and perhaps she thought we purposefully had done this to further antagonize her.

As to the second boy, my aunt could not remember his name, and perhaps thought my mother had also named him Michael Wayne. She did say that both boys were put up for adoption through Catholic Charities. When she got pregnant with me, Catholic Charities refused to handle the case as she would set a bad example for other girls as a repeat offender. I asked my aunt about my father and told her the name on my birth certificate. She said that Edwin was a nice young man who came to the diner. He had an airplane, and my mother was out of her class dating him. She said she knew he was a veteran, and thought he was in the Air Force because he wore a bomber jacket like the Air Force men who came to the diner to fly their planes after the war had ended. She really didn't have much more information than that. She also shared with me that she and her sister had a chasm between them because of Dorothy's behavior, and because of her treatment of me. She said both she and her brother were outraged at Dorothy's lack of affection and attention toward me. She told me the story of the last time they ever came to our house and my mother refused to let me sit at the table. She revealed that my mom said she didn't want any chance conversation that would come up about my looking like my biological father.

My aunt was furious. True to her word, she never came back to visit my mom.

I thanked my aunt, and now armed with a bit more information, I decided to call on my mother's best friend, Josie. For as long as I could remember, Josie had been a good friend of my mother's. I figured she probably knew my mother's secrets better than anyone else, except my Grandmother, who had long since passed away. After I finally located Josie, I called her and asked about the brothers and about my own father. Josie asked if I had talked to my mother, and I said I couldn't because there was such a wedge between us and that would only further damage our fragile relationship. Josie said that as long as my mother was alive she wouldn't tell me anything. She was true to her word. She guarded my mother's secrets, and sadly, she passed before my mom, so I could never learn what she knew. If I were to learn anything, I would have to depend on my own resources.

Acting upon my Aunt's comment that Edwin was a war veteran, and possibly in the Air Force, I sent an inquiry to the Federal Aviation Administration in Washington DC. I included a copy of my original birth certificate with the inquiry, stating I was seeking information about my biological father. My inquiry was then forwarded to the FAA Aeronautical Center, Airmen Certification Branch, AAC 260 in Oklahoma City, Oklahoma. They sent back a Request for Information Form indicating the only airman which they had by the name of Edwin R. M_ was a man who lived in San Mateo, Florida. They provided the address. My first thought was that the airman listed was my biological father, and my suspicions of a cover up may be true. I carefully crafted a letter to the Edwin identified by the FAA, and included pertinent information, what I was seeking, and my contact phone number. I did not include my last name, nor my address as I wanted to protect myself in case the contact was something I did not want to pursue past a phone call. I sent the letter to the address provided. About a week later I received a phone call from Edwin R. M_. He was intrigued with my story; however, he was only forty-seven years old, which would not match the age of the Edwin I was seeking, and he was not at all related to my biological father. This query now established that my biological father was not at all in the Air Force. Another door closed in my search.

By this time my son's surgery was successfully finished, and there was no sign of cancer. With the immediate danger avoided, I put my inquiries to rest. My life became busier than I could ever imagine. I was a wife. I was a mother of two active boys. I worked full time. I was doing my graduate work. I was also active in my community as well as advisor to many clubs and organizations through my job. We also built our new home. Needless to say, my life was overwhelming, and seeking out any further information about my biological lineage went on a back burner.

Chapter 19: The Search Begins Anew

My story fast forwards to my mother's death in September of 2000. There was now nothing keeping me from returning to my exploration of who my father was and finding information about the two half-brothers my mother had surrendered years ago. I would begin uncovering the secrets my mother held all of her adult life. I had uncovered some of the truths in 1984, but since then I had done nothing to move forward.

After my mom's funeral I contacted Hildegard, a close childhood friend of hers, who had come to the funeral. I asked if she knew anything about my two half-brothers, and if she knew anything about my birth father. Hildegard was shocked. "I knew of only one of your brothers. There was a Bedford High School teacher who was known for going after the girls. He went after your mother. He was eventually found out and kicked out of the school. He and his family moved to California. I had no idea about another boy, and I thought Stanley was your father. I know Stanley and Dorothy had sought out the boy that was given up because they wanted to adopt him. That's all I know." What Hildegard provided me was the name of the teacher, and that he had taught in Bedford. I had nothing else to go on. Perhaps he was the father of the oldest brother, and I estimated that since my mother dropped out of high school in her senior year, which is what she had told me, perhaps the teacher had impregnated her, thus causing her to quit school in her senior year.

I had kept my mother's secret about having given up two sons since 1985. It was time for me to share with my three surviving sisters the fact that we had two half-brothers. They were shocked. I explained that I couldn't bring myself to tell them before Mom had died as my relationship with her was strained. I shared with them the evidence I had and said I would research further in trying to find them. I did not tell my sisters that I would also be researching my biological father's family as well. I didn't want my sisters to feel that I did not solely value my relationship with them.

By the year 2000 the internet was a wonderful thing. You could find so much information, but you just had to figure out where to look. The first thing I did was search for adoption websites where birth mothers, fathers, siblings, or adoptees could list information in hopes of connecting with each other. Both my sister, Susan, and I posted that we were looking for two half-brothers. At the time I thought the oldest boy was born around 1945, as my mom had dropped out of school her senior year and I figured it was because she was pregnant. I also calculated that the second boy was born sometime between

1946 and 1950. I included information that my mother had lived in Bedford, Ohio, and the kind of information I had on my original birth certificate. I put the pertinent information into the website and hoped for the best. Although I had a few hits, none of them panned out with the half-brothers I was seeking.

Since finding my half brothers might prove to be difficult, I decided to move on with my biological father through genealogy software. My first program was Generations. Within the package of materials was a Social Security Death Index. Through this software I looked up my natural father's name, the year I calculated when he was born, and the state listed on my original birth certificate as the state of his birthplace. The software pulled up a file for him giving his birth date and his death date along with his social security number. It was some relief to discover that my mother had not lied about his dying at age 40. I felt a bit guilty that I had doubted my mother when she said he had died at that age.

Meanwhile, I began my search for information on my birth father. I shared with my cousin, Denny, what I had learned from the Death Index and he indicated that with the information I had, I could apply for a copy of Edwin's Social Security application. On that form I could find even more information. I immediately researched how to go about applying for this. I sent in the request for a copy of a Social Security application, attaching my original birth certificate and the required fee. On December 18, 2000, I received a copy of Edwin

Ralph M_'s application for a Social Security Card. There, in his own handwriting, was the information I needed to start my research. Sixteen-year-old, Edwin lived on First Street in Milford, Michigan. His birth date was listed, and the names of his father and mother were also listed. He signed it in 1941. I stared at this for a long time. It was a connection to someone who provided me half of my genes, half of my ancestry, and half of my personality. I couldn't wait to learn more.

I went back to the internet to search for possible phone numbers of his relatives. I looked up the last name and the city where Edwin had lived as a child. I found a number. It was for Edison M_. I put together my "script" as I didn't want to call and fumble around searching for words. I carefully dialed the number. A gentleman answered and I carefully stated my purpose. "I am hoping you can help me. I am searching for information about the family of Edwin R. M_. He would have been born in 1925 and died in 1965." The voice on the other end said he was an uncle to Edwin, but he could get me the phone number of Edwin's brother, Lawrence. I was stunned. My first call and I hit pay dirt. I sat down and composed myself and made a list of the questions I hoped to get answered.

I dialed the number, and Lawrence answered the phone. I carefully introduced myself and Lawrence, who went by his middle name, Don, said, "Could you wait a minute? I have to sit down." Over the next hour and a half this man who was the brother of the man listed on my birth certificate as my father, answered all my questions, and gave me even more information about his brother than I asked. He also gave me an address for the oldest son of Edwin, who was named after his father.

A sibling. A brother. I sat shaking for a few minutes. I told my husband what I just learned. He coached me on some questions I should write down before I wrote my letter to my brother. I carefully crafted my letter to Ed, knowing it would be shocking to hear that his father had another child. I put together a package which included a copy of my birth certificate, pictures of me growing up, and pictures of my family. I was careful to say that although I had long ago found the phone number for Myrtle, his mother, when I had first opened my adoption records, it was never my intention to upset her, so I had never called during the past fifteen years. I mailed it and waited.

Weeks went by with no answer. Every day I checked the mailbox, but there was no reply. There were no missed calls on my answering machine, and no messages. I decided that this was a dead end and that I would never learn more about my natural father. Then, after six weeks, I received a phone call. It seems my package had found its way to the bottom of a larger stack of mail, and Ed had only now uncovered it. Our conversation was wonderful. He shared the few memories he had of his father, and told me that his father was not in the Air Force, but had been in the Navy during the war. He had been at Normandy on the amphibious landing craft that carried the tanks to shore. He also told me how his father had received a minor injury during the war, and how his father had saved lives by intercepting a floating live grenade and tossing it away so that the soldiers would not be injured. It was obvious that Ed admired his father, and he had fond memories, although he was only eleven when his dad died of a brain aneurysm.

Edwin's brother, Don and his wife, Eleanore, sent me a full printout of their family tree, and even some photocopied pictures of Edwin and his family and the obituary. I had always wondered where I got my looks. I felt I could see a resemblance when I looked at Edwin's picture. Ed provided me the addresses of his sister, Linda, and brother, Jeff. I made packages of photos of myself and my sons, then mailed them to my other half-siblings.

In the summer of 2002 my husband, youngest son, and I planned a trip to Florida to visit with my sister, Dottie, who lives in Port Charlotte. Much to her dismay, I had also planned a visit to meet my two brothers and sister from my father's side. She was not happy with me, but it was something I needed to do. I had questions that I wanted to ask and I wanted to see if I would find family resemblances, and I wanted to learn more of Edwin's health history. My sister was upset with me. I understood her dismay, but I was not abandoning the only family I knew. I just wanted to know more about who I was--biologically. Unless you lived your life not knowing who your biological father was, or having an insight to your medical history or familial background, it would be difficult to understand the feelings of uncertainty an adoptee carried throughout his or her life. For me, perhaps, I was too much like my father, and that could be why my mother could not bond with me. It could be her disdain for his abandoning her, and if my traits were like his, it would be easy for her to turn her anger toward him against me. I didn't know, but this was an opportunity for me to learn more.

Our visit with Edwin's children did not go as well as I had hoped. It was awkward. I brought with me photos to share with them. I had asked them to bring pictures of their father and of them growing up. I was hoping I would see family resemblances with my newfound siblings and in the pictures they shared. They came empty handed, and I felt it was obvious they were ill at ease in meeting me. My new sister was fearful that her father had only thought of me when he looked at her. I assured her that this was not true. My dad had told me that when he and my mother took me out of adoption, my mother wheeled me down in a baby buggy to where Edwin was living on Union Road in Bedford, to tell him of their decision. My dad said that Edwin didn't attempt to pick me up or touch me. He had moved on with his life and did not want contact with me. I understood that there was a level of skepticism by Edwin's children, which was to be expected when someone dropped out of the blue and announced, "Hey, I'm your long lost sister." Although I was never that glib, I totally understood their hesitation. Linda ventured that she would feel more at ease if there was scientific proof that I was related.

In an effort to provide that scientific proof, I researched companies which did home DNA tests using a cotton swab. The two brothers took the test and I did as well. The test cost nearly $400. When the test results arrived it showed that the boys were brothers, but was inconclusive as to my being their half-sibling. If I had been a boy it would have been able to show if we were siblings, but the tests were not sophisticated enough in 2001 to provide me positive proof of half-sibling relation. I would not be able to provide the scientific proof I had hoped to get. I had a meeting in Twinsburg the day the DNA results arrived and on the way to my meeting I stopped at the cemetery and stood screaming at my mother's grave. I asked the questions which I should have asked her when she was alive. Why couldn't she love me? Was it because of my biological father? Why didn't she ever tell me more about him? I believe my tirade went on for about ten minutes, but it took all my energy, and my face was covered with tears. Exhausted, I wiped my face and left to go to my meeting.

During the following years my communications with my half-siblings were rare. Meanwhile, I attempted to learn more about Edwin. I wrote to the National Personnel Records Center at 9700 Page Avenue, St. Louis, Missouri, in June of 2003, requesting the military records for Edwin R. M_. When the package arrived I couldn't believe the wealth of information I found within the

Navy's records. I learned that Edwin had worked as a clerk from June of 1939 to July of 1943 at the A. W. Johnson Grocery Company in Milford, Michigan. He enlisted on July 23, 1943 and entered into service a week later on July 30th. He served in the Navy during World War II for two years, seven months, and fourteen days. The information in the records included information about his medals (Victory Medal, American Area Campaign Medal, and European African Middle Eastern Area Campaign Medal). The forms also indicated he entered the Navy as Apprentice Seaman, and moved to S2c, Seaman 2nd class, and then S21, Seaman 1st class, and finally QM3c, Quartermaster 3rd class, during his tenure in the Navy. There was also a summary of his service. From July 31-October 14, 1943 he was at USNTS, Great Lakes, Illinois. From October 15 to February 17 1944, he was at the Armed Guard School in Gulfport, Mississippi. Edwin was trained for amphibious landing craft and landing ships and was authorized to wear the approved amphibious insignia. Edwin moved from New Orleans, Louisiana to the Receiving Station in New York, New York where he boarded the U.S.S. LST #497 on February 29, 1944. On April 10th, Edwin was transferred to the base dispensary on the USN AAB Southampton, Hants, England, for medical treatment. He returned to the US LST #497 on May 5th, 1945. His ship was then at Normandy on D-Day. Edwin remained on the USS LST #497 until December 19, 1945. He was then at a Naval Operations Base in Norfolk, Virginia for much of December of 1945, then finally on the USS Whitley from

January 4, 1946 to February 28, 1946. He was transferred to Brooklyn, New York to separate with an Honorable Discharge from the U.S. Naval Service. I loved that I was getting a glimpse into Edwin's life through these records. This man was my father and I was proud of his military records. I made a copy of them and sent them to Linda.

My communications with my newfound siblings continued to be rare. I would send holiday greetings, and remember them on Facebook for birthdays. What I learned was that adoptees can have many different experiences when reaching out to biological families: some biological families will welcome them with open arms and quickly accept them into their own families; some will either not want contact as they have moved on and want to keep that secret from their present family, or not deal with the memories of that time in their lives; some will keep the adoptee at arm's length, not certain how to interact as the truth of the adoptee's existence disrupts the memories and family normalcy. For me there were occasional phone calls, but there was no real attempt to blend as a family. The most excitement occurred when the wife of one of my half-brothers became angry with her mother-in-law, and sent her the packet I had sent when I first made contact. My half-sister called and said that her mother wanted to talk to me, and she confided that her mother was surprisingly calm about the revelation that her husband had another child. I had two conversations with Myrtle and she was most pleasant to me. She was genuinely interested in my family and me. I had been nervous about talking to her, but she soon made me feel at ease. She even made the comment that she had no grandchildren and my children would be like step-grandchildren to her. I told her that was a kind thought and afterward felt she truly did care about me which was surprising as I thought the announcement of my existence would have sent her into a tailspin of resentment and anger at her husband's deception.

Years later Myrtle died and my half-sister contacted me. In a conversation she had with her oldest brother, she asked if he thought their mother knew about me prior to the packet arriving at her doorstep. He said their mother did know. When he was old enough to start dating, his mother warned him to be careful as his father had an illegitimate child. Myrtle kept that secret from her daughter and held it to her grave. This information had never been shared with my half-sister knowing she remained skeptical about her father having another child. The revelation that Myrtle had known all along that I existed, allowed for a few more communications than in the past. Thirteen years had passed since we first met and we had never visited during those years, and our phone and email communications were limited. We promised we would work at building a stronger relationship. We had an occasion to meet up with my youngest half-brother and spent a lovely evening together talking.

Meanwhile, there were other secrets of my mother's which were unraveling.

Chapter 20: Following the Paper Trail

In September of 2012, I lost a second sister, Emily, to heart disease and other health issues. In one of our last conversations Em had asked me if I had ever learned anything else about our two missing brothers. After Emily's death, I started thinking about how to proceed in my search. I had never received any communications on the adoptee websites where I had posted shortly after my mother's death. Now I needed a new plan.

My first thought was to contact the national office of Catholic Charities. My aunt had told me that they handled the adoptions of both brothers. I figured that they would have put my brothers up for adoption away from the Cleveland area to keep siblings and biological family members apart from the adoptee.

After I had mailed my inquiry I received a message from a woman who was working with the adoption records of Catholic Charities and trying to reunite adopted children and birth families. She gave me the contact information for Cleveland Catholic Charities. I made contact with them in hopes that they might be able to provide information on the births of my two half-brothers. The request was turned over to Sandy F_ . She said she would try to find any information about the brother who I could only guess was born around 1945, and was named Michael Wayne Cark. There was a $50 fee for researched information. I figured searching for Michael would be easiest as I had at least a possible birth name and possible birth year to research. Sandy promised she would keep in touch with me.

On September 30, 2013, a bombshell happened. I was in Florida tending to my sister, Dottie, who had a bad injury from a fall. While there my sister Sue called and said, "Get on Facebook right now. There is as message you need to read. I think our brother has contacted us." I expected it would be from Michael Wayne as I had been working with Sandy F_ to find him. Imagine my surprise when the Facebook message was not from Michael Wayne, but for my second half-brother. He had opened his adoption records and had sought out information through adoptee website postings. He found two listings, one by my sister, Susan, and one by me. My email had changed and I had never in the past thirteen years updated the adoptee website posting with my changed email address. With the encouragement of his daughter, Christy, they then searched Facebook to see if they could make the match. They did. A message was crafted and sent through a Facebook message to both Susan and me. I was stunned as I read the message from Richard who believed he was my brother. At first I thought it was Michael Wayne and that his adoptive parents had changed his name to Richard. Upon closer exploration I learned that this was Brother #2.

I was so very surprised as I had been working to find information about our oldest brother, and I had no name or birth date to work with to find the second half-brother. Now here was Brother #2 who just happened to be searching for us at the same time I was searching for Michael Wayne. I responded to Rick and said I would make contact once I returned home from Florida. The following week I made phone contact, and planned a face-to-face get together on October 14th, 2013. The plan was for Rick and his wife and my husband and myself to meet at a restaurant. Expecting a strained meeting like what I had previously experienced with Edwin's children, I was totally shocked as we had a three hour dinner and talked non-stop.

Rick revealed that he had no interest in pursuing his biological roots while his adoptive parents were still alive. After both had passed, Rick's daughter persuaded him that it would be nice to know their heritage. He applied for his adoption records and learned that at his birth he was named "Lawrence Gene," and was born to a Dorothy Clark of Bedford, Ohio. No father's name was listed. Rick had been adopted and his name was changed to Richard Alan. In his youth he had lived not far from our Cleveland home. I would never have expected him to live so close to his biological family. His family later moved to Maple Heights and the family went to the same church as my aunt's family. We gasped as we realized we could have been in the same places at the same time as I would go to midnight mass at St. Wenceslas, which Rick would also attend. Additionally, Rick shared that his band had played at the Agora in downtown Cleveland, and I revealed that I went there often with my friends when younger. Rick shared that he had gotten married in the church which was across the street from the nursing home my mother had worked in during the years when he married! Wouldn't it have been amazing if she had actually seen the wedding as she entered the building for work? We had an immediate connection. By the end of the evening, Rick and I were finishing each other's sentences. For our second meeting we invited our children to join us. Everyone was animated and enjoyed the meeting. Observers would have thought we had all grown up together as we laughed and even teased with each other!

I stayed in contact with Sandy F_, notifying her that we had made contact with Richard, but we were hopeful that we would be able to find Michael. I also shared with her that Rick had opened his adoption records to learn that his birth name was Lawrence Gene Clark. I asked if she would be able to find any other information about Rick's adoption as it might help in locating Michael's records. It was only about a month later that I received the following email from Deb W_ from Catholic Charities:

> *Barbara – I found some information on your old-est brother, Michael Wayne Clark, this morning.*
>
> *I am trying to enter all the old adoption information into an excel sheet. This morning I*

came across an adoption file for your brother, Michael, which we had no record of as he was not listed in the excel log. Apparently he was adopted by a family through Cuyahoga County. He was born in 1947, and was placed in St. Ann's. He had some health issues, so custody was transferred from Catholic Charities to the County.

At lunch I happened to mention to my supervisor, Sandy F_, how much time I had spent on the first file I opened this morning: there were too many babies/birth moms named Clark. That's when she mentioned that she had heard from you. Nice coincidence.

I think Richard's adoption was also through the county, because I had no idea what his adoptive name was: just his birth name. Michael had not yet been placed for adoption when Richard (Lawrence) was born, and since custody of Michael was being transferred to the county, they may have transferred custody of Lawrence/ Richard at the same time.

There is not enough information to make it worth you sending in $50 and a request for info. If you do have additional questions, please call me at 216-xxx-xxxx. Ohio does have an adoption

sibling registry, so that might also help you find
him. Are you working with Adoption Network
Cleveland?

What welcome news this was. I called Deb and thanked her for her work researching to connect adoptees with birth families. Deb promised she would seek out Michael's contact information. The next time I heard from Deb she had contacted Mike. She told him that she had been in touch with his half-sister and that he has five half-sisters and a newly found half-brother. She told him that his sister and brother were anxious to meet him. Mike wanted to wait until after the holidays were over to make up his mind if he wanted to pursue meeting us. By January that contact was made, and a face-to-face meeting was planned.

Again, it was a wonderful meeting when Rick and his wife, and my husband and I met with Mike and his wife. My husband whispered to me when we were seated at the restaurant that Mike looked like my mother! During our dinner we talked about where Mike had lived as a child and where he now lived. He had moved quite a bit over the years, but has lived in Chesterland, Ohio, which is a little more than an hour away from my home, and closer to Rick's home. Our meeting went so well we planned to meet again very soon. As time passed, frequent visits were planned, and each visit was filled with further discoveries. It did not take long for our siblingship to develop and true interest in each other's lives to be investigated.

Mike had not opened his adoption files like Rick and I had done. Eventually Mike opened his adoption records so he could verify that he was indeed our brother. Neither Rick nor Mike would get to know their two siblings who passed (Glad and Em) but I quickly put together visits with Dottie and Susan, who both lived in Florida. My sisters and I have not only gained two brothers, but also two nieces and a nephew, and a great-niece.

I was so very thankful to Catholic Charities for helping to give both Mike and Rick at least some answers. Not only did Catholic Charities help my mother back in the 1940's when there was little recourse for a woman who needed assistance in providing homes for children she could not raise alone, but the agency today offered assistance in helping solve at least some of the lifelong mysteries of my family. At least they assisted in *some* of the mysteries.

Mike, Barb, Rick

Chapter 21: Needing To Know More

Of course, I was not content with just having met my brothers. Yes, now they knew who their mother was, and they met three of their half-sisters. Sadly, neither Mike nor Rick would know who their fathers were. It was the policy of Catholic Charities that the father's name was not to be added to the birth certificate. It was again a case of Adam versus Eve. Eve was the sinner and she led Adam to sin. The father would be forever protected as his name would not appear on any records. How very unfair that neither of my brothers would know who their fathers were, and if they had additional siblings on their father's side. It wasn't fair. I had always been a champion for the truth. I now had a new mission: Find information on Mike and Rick's fathers.

Many of my friends questioned why I felt the need to pursue finding my brothers, or being bothered in trying to uncover my mother's various secrets. They couldn't understand why I was not at rest and now wanted to pursue finding information on my brother's fathers. "You are who you are. Knowing who their fathers were would not change who they are!" Perhaps not, but it helps to put a heritage behind us in letting us know "the stuff we are made of." Those who are adopted always live with the questions about who they are. For me, my father's name was listed on my birth certificate because he had agreed to have it placed there, and since I had been in contact with his family I had at least learned some information about him and his heritage, and it gave me a heritage (English, Welsh, and Scottish) to embrace.

I kept in contact with Deb at Catholic Charities. Here is the letter I sent her in hopes that she would be able to help further in uncovering the mystery. I was looking for the "intake papers" for my mother's three pregnancies through the various agencies. Intake papers are records of interviews, various paperwork, and anecdotal information by social workers on both the mother and children in the adoption process.

> Hi, Deb,
>
> It has been awhile since I last wrote. It was two years ago that my two older brothers and I connected (with your help in locating brother #1.) Mike, Rick, and I have gotten together often and this past summer I hosted a Clark reunion where my cousins from Florida and southern Ohio came to visit and meet both Mike and Rick. Needless to say, I am very much connected to both of my brothers and we have been making up for our 60+ years of separation.

What has since transpired is I finished writing my second historical novel and my niece, Christy, (Rick's daughter) persuaded me to write my next book about my mother. Since I never talked to my mother about my two older siblings, and since she had the smallest of details to give me about my own birth, I am left to make a "thinly veiled" book about her experience. I have been doing a lot of research but I have some questions I am hoping you can help me answer.

What I am trying to find for both Mike and Rick (born Lawrence Gene Clark) is what information was given and recorded in the intake papers when my mother came to St. Ann's. I have talked to both of my brothers about my researching and writing this book, and they, too, are interested in any information I can discover. I want my book to be accurate and detailed and I have found some great information, but knowing the specifics of Mike and Rick's files would be most beneficial. I am trying to be as true to the story as I can be. I have also been in contact with Ann Fessler, author of THE GIRLS WHO WENT AWAY, and she has been helpful in providing leads on the historical aspects of the 40's and early 50's for girls who got pregnant and surrendered their children for adoption. My research has already had a healing effect on me, and when I shared my discoveries with Rick, he also felt it helped him better understand why he was given up. I think this book will help others who experienced having given up their children, or beneficial for the adopted child in best understanding why these decisions were made.

Is there a way of getting my mother's actual records? I know St. Ann's was run by the Sisters of Charity and their main headquarters is now at St. Augustine in Richfield, Ohio. I have sent a request to them to see if they have archival information. I was hoping with your detective work you may know how to best access any records.

Thank you, Deb, for all of your help. I look forward to hearing from you.

Barb Baltrinic

Deb was fast to act. She searched every file she could, but she told me there was nothing about Mike's or Rick's fathers. My cynical self felt that there were things in the files that would not be shared, regardless of how persuasive I was in my quest to find the information about my brothers' fathers. I learned there was a program called the Cleveland Memory Project at the Michael Schwartz Library at Cleveland State University. I felt certain that the intake files on my mother when she entered the system would have included information about the fathers. Bill Barrow was the contact person of the Cleveland Memory Project. I contacted him and shared my reunion story with my brothers and my quest to uncover information about their fathers. He responded that he, too, had been reunited with a half-brother late in life. He recommended that I check with the Sisters of Charity at St. Augustine who might have the information I was seeking.

Although the Cleveland Memory Project was another dead-end, I was still driven to continue searching. My next route was to contact St. Augustine. Supposedly both Catholic Charities, St. Ann's and DePaul's archives were sent to St. Augustine for storage. I contacted Sr. Mary Denis Maher who was the archivist for the Sisters of Charity which ran the adoption services for Catholic Charities. This was her reply to my initial inquiry:

> *Barb: If you go to our web page www.srsofchar-ity.org, click on Archives, under the history tab, you will find a page saying "frequently asked questions." There you will find a suggestion where you might find adoption records. As you may or may not know, the State of Ohio previously had many records sealed. Those are now*

open. Also the Cleveland Adoption Network might also be useful.

Sr. Mary Denis Maher, CSA, PhD
Certified Archivist
Sisters of Charity of St. Augustine

I responded immediately with the following:

Sr. Maher: What I am hoping to locate are the **intake records** for my mother when she came to Catholic Charities for two different pregnancies. My oldest brother was born Michael Wayne Clark on 10-11-1947; and my second brother was born Lawrence Gene Clark born on 6-14-1949. Both were put up for adoption through St. Francis DePaul in Cleveland. I was reconnected with these two brothers in October 2012 (Lawrence Gene) and January 2013 (Michael Wayne.) Their original birth certificates which were included when they opened their adoption files from Columbus had no father listed. The files had only the limited legal paperwork for the adoption, but nothing about parentage except for my mother's name on the original birth certificates. Both are hoping to locate information about their natural fathers. I said I would seek the intake papers on my mother during the births and adoptions of both Mike and Rick (formerly Lawrence.)

I am truly hoping you can help me with this information. I look forward to hearing from you, and would also enjoy a face-to-face meeting with you to talk about the records from Catholic Charities.

Sister Maher then responded:

Barb: Well, I do not have intake records, and I do not know if any still exist. It is possible that Catholic Charities in Cleveland could be able to help or direct you. In terms of what the young women did while living in confinement through Catholic Charities, much depended on their age. If they had not finished high school, then there were arrangements through the Cleveland Public School system, I believe, to work with them to finish. Certainly there were various child care classes. They did help around DePaul Home as well as caring for their baby, depending on circumstances. Not all gave their baby up for adoption, nor not neces-

sarily right away. If the child did not go home or was given up for adoption, they stayed there for a period of time. There was St. Edward Home in Parma, across from Parmadale, where the toddlers stayed.

There is a book "And Sin No More: Social Policy and unwed mothers in Cleveland, 1855-1990" by Marian Morton, Ohio State University Press, 1993, that you would find helpful. It does have a chapter on DePaul Home and probably can answer most of your questions.

Right now until after Christmas, I don't have any time to meet with you, but after the New Year, I could.

Sr. Mary Denis Maher, CSA, PhD
Certified Archivist
Sisters of Charity of St. Augustine

I was sad that the intake records were nowhere to be found. I was certain the information I wanted was within them. My next thought was to follow the paper trail. If the actual adoptions of both of my brothers were turned over to the County, perhaps the intake forms were also transferred from DePaul and St. Ann's. I had a new avenue to pursue. I learned that many of the records for the Cuyahoga County Children

Services' records were moved to Applewood. I once again turned to Deb at Catholic Charities. Below is her response:

From Debbie

OK. Here we go.

If you can find St. Ann's records anywhere, please let me know. I've been trying to figure out where they went to but with no luck.

Here's what the file says:

"10/15/47 Miss Bielfelt of the Alice Hunt Center called after Mrs. Kerr had called in regard to Dorothy. It seems that this girl, who had been brought into Booth in practically an emergency situation, had found a girl in the home who was right from her own neighborhood. Therefore, both Mrs. Kerr and Miss Bielfelt were asking for post partum care in our Maternity Home.

10/17/47. Dorothy was admitted.

Dorothy's baby was born on 10/11/47 at 4:15 AM at Booth Memorial Hospital. Dorothy's baby was placed temporarily on Ward B at St. Ann's Hospital until it was baptized. That was October 18th. It was named Michael Wayne, and then taken over to the Baby House."

So it sounds like Dorothy went to Booth right

before delivery, but because there was a girl there that she knew, she was transferred after delivery to DePaul. She was dismissed 11/25/47. Michael was not dismissed until 4/7/49 but I can't tell if he went to St. Ann's or DePaul. One note card makes me think it was St. Ann's. County Child Welfare had assumed custody of him on 11/9/48, and upon his discharge was placed in a boarding home. He was hospitalized at Rainbow's Babies and Children in June of 1949, seriously ill (suspected celiac disease, in case Michael wants to request those records from the hospital).

On 4/7/49 Dorothy was again admitted to DePaul. She went by the alias of "Barbara" (thought you'd appreciate that). She had again been referred by the Alice Hunt Center. Lawrence was born on 6/14/49 at 2:03 AM. The file states: "On dismissal from St. Ann's this baby was given an examination." This raises the question for me: am I looking at DePaul Maternity Home records or St. Ann's? I honestly don't know. His baby record clearly states that he was born at St. Ann's Hospital. He was discharged from there to the baby home on 8/7/49. Custody was given to the county, since Michael was still in county custody.

The index card we have states: 8/13/51 Barbara Louise – born at MacDonald House. Expecting another baby in May '53. Going to St. Alexis.

I had always assumed that all the old records/index cards we have were from DePaul. But these records make me question if we have some old records from St. Ann's.

OK – just Googled this out and found this out. In response to the need for a maternity hospital and foundling home, the Sisters of Charity opened St. Ann's Hospital (Saint Ann Foundation) in 1873. A new building for St. Ann's, adjacent to Charity Hospital, opened in 1876. The hospital moved to Woodland Ave., where separate buildings housed a foundling home, hospital, and home for unmarried mothers. By 1947 St. Ann Hospital moved to the Leisy estate on Fairhill Rd., and in 1950 the name of the building on Woodland was changed to DePaul Infant Home and Loretta Hall.

Let me know if you want to talk more about the old records. I'm glad you've read "The Girls Who Went Away." Excellent book. My cell is xxx-xxxx. Let me know if you have additional questions

My research continued and I eventually learned that many of the records from this time era were sent to Applewood Center of Cleveland. They handled Social Services and Foster Care service. I immediately contacted my brothers to determine if they wanted to pursue this lead.

January 8, 2016:

Mike and Rick: I've been doing research and found out that all the Cuyahoga County Children Service records were moved to Applewood. It appears that all three of us (Mike, Rick, and me) were put up for adoption through Children's Welfare.

I looked up the information on Applewood, filled out an information form, and got a call from Lori from Applewood who I talked to at length. She said my records would have been destroyed since I was pulled from adoption. (Hmmmm...My dad (Stanley) adopted me...so I think the records are still there. I will pursue this.)

Meanwhile, she said that both of you can call her and she will email them the application for records.

Records are on microfilm. They will STILL not give the name of parents...only non-identifying

*information. They will give **health history of
parents/child, nationality, education.** (I
had found out from Deb W_ of Catholic Charities
that Mike had been ill at birth, and was hospitalized for serious illness when he was not yet
two years old.) All of this information would be
included in the reports. Cost is $50.*

*Lori's number is xxx-xxxx. Mike and Rick
would have to call and ask for the forms to be
emailed to them. Forms would be completed,
notarized, and then mailed in with the fee.*

Let me know what is decided.

Your sister, Barb.

It turns out all three of us were interested in pursuing this
lead. Applications were completed and I sent in the forms
and fees. I was horrified when I received word that all records
older than twenty years had been destroyed. Destroyed? How
could that be allowed? I was once again left with no leads.

I went back and reread all my communications and notes
I had taken during my research. Where could I look to find
additional information which could potentially shed light on
my brothers' parentage? I figured that perhaps if I could find
my own intake records I might find information mentioned
about my brothers.

In one communication I had contacted Deb to learn if MacDonald House, where I was born, was connected to a maternity home. It was not. I assume my mother had gone without a maternity home and was just working through the county's social service organizations, or perhaps another agency which would handle the adoption. In an effort to see if I could learn the specifics of my birth I contacted MacDonald House to determine if I could get a copy of my mothers' and my hospital files. It seemed these, too, had been destroyed. For me, I had met a dead end with records of my foster care being destroyed at Applewood, and my mother's hospital records at MacDonald House also being destroyed.

In a communication with Deb she learned, *"Regrettably, DePaul recordkeeping was not initiated until 1948 and St. Ann's Foundation, which has information on microfilm only, follows the practice of destroying all recordings after 25 years."* It certainly seemed I had hit every dead end possible in discovering files and paper records of my brothers' intake records which could, perhaps, shed light on who their father or fathers were. My mother's secrets appeared to be quite safe.

I received a note from Deb that she would be laid off from Catholic Charities. I was saddened that I would lose her valuable insights to my research. In one last communication, Deb shared this: *"Sandy and I talked this over some more. I may have sent you on a wild goose chase. Michael's records might be at Cuyahoga County Dept. of Children and*

Family Services. Call Andrea G. Cuyahoga Co DCFS used to be called "County" in the old records. Applewood used to be Children Services/Child Welfare. Applewood should NOT have destroyed old adoption records, but their records are separate from "county" records. I thought Children Services and county were the same, but they were not. Sorry!"

With one more lead to go on, I planned to continue my search through Andrea at the Department of Children and Family Services of Cleveland.

Chapter 22: A Veil of Lies

October, 2016, was filled with drama and stress. I was facing retirement at the end of October as a full time employee after forty-two years of full time work in education. I was in training for consulting work which would be my retirement part-time job. I also broke my foot two weeks before my retirement, thus complicating my life by not being able to drive for two months. Add to this my sister, Sue, suffered a massive heart attack and nearly died. Every day was filled with calls to my sister, Dottie, and to the hospital in Florida to check on Sue's constantly changing progress. She did not get home from the hospital until after Christmas.

Add to this that my brothers and I had all done our DNA tests through Ancestry. I was hopeful with the new technology we would be able to get some "hits" on Mike and Rick's DNA matches which could potentially lead us to their fathers. We had jokingly called my brothers members of the "Who's Your Daddy?" Club. Our goal was to kick them out of that club membership. When Mike and Rick's results came back there were no immediate Ancestry.com DNA Match hits (other than us matching each other as 'close family.') The closest Rick had were relations in Canada who were third cousins. I know my mother never traveled to Canada in the 1940's, so this was not very promising. What I didn't expect, however, was that my DNA pie chart (wheel with percentages of heritage from various locations) indicated I was 52% German. Now this was medically and biologically impossible as Edwin R. M_ was English, Scottish and Welsh, or at least that is what was told to me through the family trees shared. I had a grandmother and a great grandmother who were German, but in no way would this account for 52% German ancestry. I contacted Edwin's daughter, my half-sister, and asked her to do a DNA test. When the test results arrived it indicated, quite clearly, she was not German in any way. The most startling fact revealed was that we were not sisters. I was put into an emotional tailspin. For more than half of my life I had believed Edwin was my father. Now I come to learn that my mother had lied on my original birth certificate. I immediately contacted my half-sister who I just learned was not related at all. I told her my news and apologized for my mother's deceit, as well as my having disrupted their family with my belief that I was related. She was very kind and offered that we remain friends, but my guilt for having pursued my mother's lie was over-whelming. First I disrupt their lives and memories of their father by introducing myself as their half-sister. Add to this that Myrtle M_ also believed I was the child of her husband.

Both Edwin and Myrtle went to their grave believing this lie. I was overwhelmed that I had caused such disruption to the M_ family. I was angry with my mother for her deception, and myself for having acted upon it.

While I had sympathized with my brothers, Mike and Rick, that they would probably never know their bio-fathers, now I, too, was in that same position. To ease the emotion I was feeling my husband joked that now I, too, was placed firmly into the "Who's Your Daddy?" Club.

With the start of 2017 I decided I had to move forward. I had been in a writing and researching slump for this book for several months, plus now that I was retired I wanted to make the best use of my increased free time as I was only working part-time. I went back to my notes and realized I had never contacted Andrea at the Department of Children and Family Services in Cleveland. I made my call, not exactly hopeful that I would find any new or useful information when suddenly the door burst wide open. I had nearly confined myself to the belief that I would never uncover the answers I was seeking. In fact they were darn near impossible! My best hope would be discovering the intake papers completed during each of my mother's interactions when giving her children up for adoption.

I dialed the number I had in my possession for months for the Department of Children and Family Services of Cleveland. After several calls back and forth trying to connect, Andrea and I were finally able to talk. Andrea took the information and within minutes called me back and said the intake records I had been searching for were within her reach! I sat dumbfounded that I had not again fallen into another dead-end. Hallelujah! So many doors had closed in front of me, and now there was a glimmer of hope that some "non-identifying" information might be shared that would help Mike, Rick and me in our search for our natural fathers. I shared everything with Andrea and she, too, felt the excitement of the search and potential outcomes within our reach. Would we learn enough information that we could extend our search and actually come up with at least one of the three fathers my brothers and I sought?

Andrea blocked out the identifying information in each packet she mailed to my brothers and me. Each packet focused on the information of that particular baby although much of the information overlapped. My brothers and I met together and poured over each file and pieced together a timeline and life history of our biological mother. The files were incredibly accurate, providing dates when interviews, court dates, transfers and other adoption topics were documented. We learned a lot about Dorothy. Much of the information which I have included in the first part of the book was obtained through the observations and notes kept in the intake papers. They also revealed a lot of information about each of our births, and how my mother reacted to each. Each record also indicated information about the man identified as the fathers of Mike, Rick and myself.

For me, my information indicated that Edwin, the pilot she was seeing, was the father, although his name was blocked out. Sadly I now knew this information was not true. The records did state that she had dated several men around the same time. The problem is, information about the other men were not included in the records. Since I already knew that Edwin was listed as my father on my original birth certificate, the information which was not blocked out was not totally surprising. It was interesting that Edwin went to the interviews freely, agreed to have his name on my birth certificate, paid his share of delivery costs, and was polite in all aspects of the interviews. The information shared included his going to the Welcome Airport, meeting Dorothy at her sister's diner, and had stopped seeing her romantically in mid-October. He also indicated he didn't think he was the father, but he did not pursue this any further. Math alone should have been a tip that my mother had not given the correct man's name as Edwin indicated he stopped seeing her in mid-October, and I was born mid-August. I would have been a ten-month pregnancy. Sadly, my DNA report did not have any leads that were closer than 4th-6th cousins, which are nearly impossible to trace. I was not hopeful that I would ever discover who my bio-father was.

The intake papers indicated Rick's father was a football player, in college, and coming from a family of eight children.

When I asked Andrea about this man's heritage she indicated he was not of Italian descent. Since Rick is 36% Italian, I am pretty certain my mother's identification of this six foot tall football player is also incorrect as the Clarks and Hahners were mostly English, Scottish, and German. There was no Italian from my mother's side, so Rick's bio-father had to have strong Italian heritage. In the intake papers my mother did indicate that she was dating several men at the same time as the football college student. Again, there was no questioning her about the other potential men who could have fathered Rick. I would have to rely on Ancestry's DNA test to try to determine if I could find any connection to Rick's father. Ancestry gives DNA matches from people who have done their DNA through their services. Rick's matches include names who would be 3rd cousins to him, with family trees loaded with Italian names; however, none of these matches are of people in Ohio, or even the U.S. To search we would have to figure out the family trees of the Canadian matches and cross check to see if any records could be found of anyone coming to America, and eventually to Bedford.

It was a harsh reality to learn that my mother had mis-identified the fathers of both Rick and me. Whether she did it intentionally, or purposefully, we will never know. Perhaps she listed the man she most wished had fathered each child: a college student for Rick, and a pilot for me.

By the end of February, 2017, I had become disheartened and believed that I would never find the fathers of Mike, Rick and myself. Now Mike, my oldest brother, had the same story line in his paperwork. Again, Dorothy indicated she was seeing several young men at the same time. The man she identified drove taxi in the Bedford area and she drove with him back and forth on his runs. Mike's DNA states he is 34% Great Britain, 33% Western European, and 18% Scandinavian, and 7% Irish. In his paperwork it says that Dorothy didn't know much about the taxi driver's background. Dorothy refused to tell him about her pregnancy for fear that he would tell everyone about it and word would spread and ruin her father's good name in the community. He was never contacted by Children's Services and held accountable for the expenses of Mike's care. Through a source I cannot mention, I learned the name of the taxi driver. I did some research on Ancestry and in the census records and tracked down information on this man. I then searched Mike's DNA report and found that there were a large number of distant cousins with the same last name. I held onto the idea that I would at least be able to discover at least one of our fathers!

I had tracked down the man who my mother had identified as Mike's father, a Donald E_. I searched on Facebook members with that family name who lived in or near Bedford, Ohio, and found a young man who lived in Twinsburg, Ohio. I messaged him and he sent me the contact information for his aunt, who coincidentally lives in my own city, not even two miles away! I contacted her and shared my mother's story and her family's connection to the birth of my brother, Mike. I also shared with her what I learned about Donald E_, her uncle. I had researched the entire family tree, looking at census reports and birth, marriage and death records. I learned that Don E_ who was named in my mother's intake papers never had children of his own, and even found where he was buried. A name was not enough proof. I needed to be certain I had the right connection. Every fiber in my being told me I was right. I met with the woman who lived near me, and her brother at a local restaurant. Her brother had agreed to do a DNA test and both were excited at the possibility of a long lost cousin between them and Mike. I mailed in the DNA test and waited for the results. On May 2, to my dismay, I learned the DNA was not a match! Once again my mother had not identified the correct man as the father of one of her children. My emotions once again went into a tailspin as I was so certain that I had uncovered Mike's birth father's name, only to learn that not only had she lied about it, but she was obviously more promiscuous than I had previously believed.

I had come to terms that my mother had children by four different men: Mike's dad, Rick's dad, my dad, and my four sister's dad (Stanley.) I never anticipated that I would uncover that she had been with more than four men. I know that sex was not invented in our time and as a teacher I know that many of my students openly had multiple sexual partners while dating in high school. Sadly, that was not even surprising by the time

I retired from the classroom. But, when thinking of your own mother, no one would want to face the fact that your mother had been as open about sex, especially when she was a young woman in the 1940's and 50's.

In other considerations, it is maddening to know that Ohio has opened adoption records, yet the birth father's name did not appear on the original documents unless the man consented to allow this. Ohio has now opened adoption files; however, in the case of intake papers, they still protect the identity of the father by blacking out any information which could help identify him. It certainly seems unfair, and to me it was unfair when trying to identify paternal lines. Now, I understand in the case of the men named in Mike's, Rick's and my paperwork, my mother gave false information, whether intentional or not, we will never know. This is probably why men are protected because women could name any man as the father. Hospitals would know who the mother was because she gave birth; however, there was no proof back then as to the identity of the father. DNA was not available. My cause-bearing appeal that it was unfair that men's names were hidden and kept secret was quickly shattered upon realizing my mother was part of the reason such rules came into play.

I had jokingly said one time that my mother was my birth control. She had treated me so poorly growing up and I blamed this on her having had me without benefit of marriage. I had resolved to never put myself in that position. The differences between my mother and myself was enormous. We were so very, very different. When I began writing this book I wanted to be compassionate about her circumstances, but through the discovery of the false information given about the parentage of my brothers and myself, I was faced with the fact that my mother's secrets from her past were far more complicated than just having given birth to three illegitimate children. The writing of this book forced me to look at my mother and her many poor choices. I will always love her, but my dislike for her behaviors and her inability to bond with me, and even my sisters, will always be unsettling to me. She was unable to "move on" and make her own "paper roses." She was stuck in her own regrets and let those regrets and secrets temper her personality and relationships with those she should have loved.

There was definite regrouping to be done in my own mind as well after my discovery of my mother's deceit. The reality was that the man I thought was my "birth father" was not my birth father, and that my mother had uprooted his life and his wife's life with her lie. I had further uprooted his family by reaching out to his children and claiming siblingship. I had used this man's health history as my own. When I broke my foot my doctor reviewed my medical records which were red-flagged with health issues I would have inherited from Edwin. After my foot healed I had to go back and change my records and my children's records to erase Edwin's health history, and list "father/grandfather" as unknown. I had lived with misinformation about my father's identify for more than half of my life. I now had no paternal "story," no heritage, no family tree, no health history, no paternal relations.

My mother lied to Edwin, lied on the birth record, lied to me, and most importantly, lied to herself, perhaps in an effort to believe this man would be her best chance at a good marriage. Although I am overwhelmed with sadness for myself, and for my children who were also brought up believing this man was their biological grandfather along with his health history, I am mostly sad, surprisingly, for my mother. How awful that she truly didn't know which man impregnated her. I truly believe she thought he really was my father, or she at the very least hoped he was.

God bless my husband. Michael, in an attempt to appease my shock, said that perhaps my real biological father had perfect health so my constant fear of health issues were unfounded and I had a new "lease on life" as perhaps longevity was indeed in my gene pool after all! The trouble is, I felt I would never know. I had no leads as to who my bio-father could be.

My husband was certain my mother may have left some clues. She didn't save many pictures from her youth, but there were several of her and a married man who was a brother-in-law to the sister of my mother's best friend, Josie. My husband became convinced that this might be a lead. The picture of him and my mother, wrapped arm-in-arm, just months prior to my conception, could be a clue, or it could have just been a coincidence. He was of German descent. My husband remarked that he saw facial resemblances, although I was resistant to see any. Although I wanted to know who my biological father was, I certainly did not want to repeat what happened with Edwin's family. I would not jump to any conclusions. I would pray that Ancestry.com would provide me with a DNA match closer than that 3rd-4th cousin matches which I could not trace.

Chapter 23: The Wonders of DNA Testing

It took me awhile to try to wrap my brain around a new plan of attack. Mike and I had no matches that could connect to a paternal line in our DNA matches. Rick, however, had two promising leads, however both were in Canada. I decided this was my best effort to find at least one of the missing fathers.

By this time, Rick had two third cousins listed as matches. I sent messages to them through Ancestry.com on March 4, 2017. I received a very thorough reply on June 18th from Kim M. K_, and she was able to provide me with a wealth of information about her family. She tried to guess at which of her relatives might have fathered Rick. She had a few suspicions, but she needed to do more research. She did indicate that her great-aunt, Catherine, had moved to New York. Meanwhile, I contacted Rick's daughter, Christy, to follow up with Kim. While Christy and Kim did their research, I did mine.

My cousin, Helen, has been a huge help in my research. As a member of the Bedford, Ohio Historical Society, she had access to directories for the 1940's. I sent her a list of three last names based on the family tree Kim from Canada had provided. I was hopeful that one of the names would be a match as having lived in Bedford, Ohio in 1948. Helen very quickly responded with one of the names of the men. He had lived in Bedford, Ohio, during the time Rick would have been conceived. She also had an address which was very close to the house where my mother lived. My next job was to go through the 1940's census reports to find out the possible sons of the person. Not only did I find it, but Helen was able to locate a yearbook picture of this man who had attended Bedford High School in 1940. He was five years older than my mother, and lived very close to her. I continued researching and trying to expand this man's family tree. I was thrilled to be able to tell Rick that his father was a man named Nicholas Anthony R_. Rick's DNA matched with the 3rd cousins in Canada, and the creation of a backwards design family tree, was evidence that the Bedford, Ohio, Catherine who would have been a great aunt to Kim in Canada. Catherine had an only son, Nick, who was in the right place (Bedford) at the right time (1948) and lived very near Dorothy Clark. This trail made it biologically evident that Nick R_ was Rick's dad.

In my research I learned that Nick had eventually married a woman named Olga, and they had a daughter named after Nick's mother, Catherine. I learned that young Catherine had been sickly and passed away rather young. Both Nick and Olga passed away in DeLand, Florida in 1988 (Olga) and 1999 (Nick.) Nick and Olga had no other children, so Rick would be his only surviving child. I do not believe my mother ever told Nick that he had fathered her child. In fact, I can only guess that she honestly believed the college student she had identified in the intake papers as the father. Perhaps it was hopeful thinking on her part, but that young man's family history (located through various census reports and immigration forms) indicated he was not Italian, and Rick had a strong Italian DNA. Nick, however, was certainly from an Italian background.

In a strange turn of events, my cousin, Helen, told me that she found that a classmate of hers, Sandra F. S_, who had recently died the summer of 2017, was actually a cousin to Rick! Sandra was the grandaughter of Catherine, and the daughter to Rick's sister. I quickly did more research and found that Sandra left behind a sister, Marie F. W_, who lived within a few miles from Rick. When I shared this information with Rick and his daughter, Christy, she immediately recognized Sandra's name. She had just met her early summer when she went to the animal shelter to donate dog food after her dog had passed. Sandra was working at the pet shelter! How bizarre that Christy, unknowingly had met her dad's cousin! I must admit that I do believe that God has been on my side in my research. I find it amazing that Christy had this coincidental meeting with Sandra who unwittingly turned out to be a cousin to Rick!

My next step was to make arrangements with Marie to meet with Rick and his family so that Rick night be able to see any family photos and hear of any health history. What we know already is that Nick was on the Bowling Team in high school, served in the military during WW II. Both of Nick's parents had diabetes and heart issues, (important health history to know,) and his sister, Theresa, had a brain tumor. Theresa's daughter, Sandra, (who would be Rick's cousin,) had breast cancer, then was cancer free for fifteen years. She had recently been diagnosed with cancer throughout her body and she passed rather quickly. Rick now has some health history which will be useful to him and his daughter. Once we put together a visit with his cousin we are hoping Rick will see many similarities in physical features, and even interests. People who are adopted typically never know this individualized information from their bio families. When we looked at the picture of Nick we could see many similarities.

Ancestry.com provided a lot of information. Once you have a name you can do research through census reports, birth, marriage and death records, military records, some obituaries, and other resources. It is like a giant puzzle when putting together the secrets that DNA can reveal, so long as there are matches that are close to your DNA. Once you get 3rd cousins and more, it become increasingly difficult to uncover the secrets. For Rick, we solved his mystery, and Mike and I jokingly kicked him out of the "Who's Your Daddy?" Club.

Chapter 24: It's My Turn

Although I was thrilled that we uncovered Rick's mystery and identified his father, I was not very hopeful for Mike or me. Neither of us had any close paternal matches on our DNA that were closer than 3rd cousins. My husband has been a great partner throughout this research. His comment that, "You need to win, Barb. You deserve to break your mom's secrets," drove me to keep working to uncover the last of my mother's secrets.

My mother kept very few photographs from her younger years. Among them was a picture of my mother with a young man, Frank R. The picture was dated in 1950. I would have been conceived possibly in late October to mid-November, but the picture looked like it was a summer gathering. My husband, Michael, was playing detective and had determined the man in the picture with my mother looked like the two of them could be more than just acquaintances. The man in the picture was actually a brother-in-law to the sister of my mother's best friend, Josie. It made sense that he would have been visiting his family and extended family and my mother could have been at the gatherings. Problem was, he was married with children, and I couldn't bear the idea that my mother might have been with a married man. My husband reasoned that this could be why she named Edwin as the father, because Edwin was not married at the time. My husband spent months trying to find contact information for Frank's relations, convinced that I was Frank R_'s daughter. I was not convinced that he was on the right track. I also could not find enough close relations matched to my DNA from this family. Although Michael was convinced I looked like this man in the grainy black and white photo, I could not commit to accepting his logic. I did, however, try sending communications to several family members of this man, but none responded. I immediately felt gun-shy as I didn't want to repeat the mistake I had made with Edwin's family. I wanted more proof before I moved forward. I could not find that proof, so I did not move forward.

Michael was not to be put off. He checked my Ancestry account nearly every day to see if there were any additional matches on my DNA, hopefully pointing to Frank R's family. September 21, 2017, Michael asked me if I had seen a close match on my DNA. I immediately looked, and I found a Kim W_ listed as a first cousin. To those understanding matches on DNA, this was huge. Because I would be an only child with my mother and whoever my bio-father was, Kim could be either a first cousin, or possibly my niece! Kim had listed a small family tree including her father, and both sets of grandparents. There she listed a name that I had heard before. My heart started racing and I was hopeful that I had a very promising lead.

It did not take me long to contact Kim W_ via email on Ancestry. She responded the next day, and after several exchanged emails, I asked her to call me. In Kim's small family tree on her DNA site, the name that stood out to me was "Faith." That was the name my mother had mentioned to me after I was married in 1974 when I asked her about my bio-father. "Just remember to 'have faith,'" she had said. Later, in 1985 when I confronted her for some health information on my bio-father, I said, "All I know is his name was Faith." She responded, "Where did you get that name? His name was Edwin M__." I now had DNA proof that Edwin was not my father, but perhaps someone in Kim's family was my father.

Once again I contacted my cousin, Helen, and asked her to search the Bedford, Ohio directories found in the Bedford

Historical Society. Were there any Faith men listed in 1950? She responded there was a Bert Faith who lived in Bedford, but the records only showed him there in 1955. There was, however, a Frank Faith who lived in Garfield Heights, which was not far away. At least I had something to go on. Perhaps Bert lived nearby and only moved to Bedford in 1955. I needed to talk to Kim. I prepared some questions to ask her and waited for her to call me.

I was thrilled to speak to Kim, but as we talked she indicated there might be a possibility her grandfather was actually my father. I was alarmed that she would think such a thing. After all, her grandfather was married and had a seven year old daughter at home when I was conceived. It was when she revealed that her grandfather had been electrocuted in an industrial accident that I became very hopeful that I might have found the missing link. My mother had told me in 1965 that my father had died and he had been electrocuted. Problem was, Edwin M. had died in 1965, but not of electrocution. Frank Faith, however, had died, but in 1954 from being electrocuted in an industrial accident. It seemed my mother had mixed up information, perhaps intentionally. I tried to crawl into my mother's mind and figure out how she had put together her story to me, borrowing fragmented pieces of truth. Perhaps she really thought Edwin might be my father, so she revealed my adoption and death of my father in 1965, but used the story of Frank Faith's death when I asked how my bio-father had died. Or, perhaps it was all a lie and neither of these men where my bio-father, but Bert was. I was confused! The only way to solve this mystery was through DNA. Kim decided she would have her mother, Fran, Frank Faith's daughter, take a DNA test.

In the past it would take six weeks or more to get the results from the Ancestry DNA test. I was actually hopeful that the test would show that Fran was my cousin, not my sister, as this would mean that one of her uncles, possibly Bert, was my father. I couldn't bear the thought that my mother was with a married man who also had a small child. Waiting seemed like an eternity, however the test results came back in two weeks. It was official. Fran, Frank's daughter, was my sister, thus Frank Faith was also my father.

I had to come to terms with the idea that my mother had committed an even worse social taboo: adultery. I know that it takes two people to have an affair, but I was having a hard time understanding my mother's thinking. Adultery is so alien to me, and I feel badly that Fran would now know this reality. When I voiced this to Fran she dismissed it as she was thrilled to finally have a sister. She had grown up an only child, and now she had a sister. She was so happy, and, admittedly, so was I. The mystery of my lineage was now revealed. Fran's enthusiasm about our new relationship was truly contagious, and I couldn't wait to meet her.

I knew one of our first conversations would be my sharing with her the deceit my mother had in my birth, as well as the two other births which she hid. I would also share with Fran that my mother had named another man as my father. Trying to explain why she would do this would be difficult. No doubt she named Edwin as my father because at the time he was not married, owned an airplane (which I am certain made her feel like he was well-to-do and an exciting catch.) Perhaps she hoped he was my father. My childhood memory of my mother's dreamlike recollection of "my father" doing "loop-de-loops" in his plane as she looked on from below was told to a four-year-old child whom she probably thought would not remember the conversation. Little did she know that even as a little four-year-old, I would hold sacred any conversation she had with me as they were so very rare. Perhaps I was already preparing myself for my future "detective" self who would try to find out who my bio-father was.

To the readers of this memoir you have to understand that for someone who is adopted they always wonder who they are. When you know you are "different," you start looking at everything that makes you different. I was lucky as I was raised by my birth mother, so at least I could find some similarities with the Clark/Hahner sides of my family. However, I was missing information I needed. For over thirty years I believed Edwin was my father, and I tried to connect my personal traits to what I learned about him. When I learned that he was not my bio-father I was overwhelmed because I had always believed his health history was my health history.

Once it was proved Edwin was not my father I was once again left without knowing this vital information. As I am aging, it is important for me to know more about my father's family health history. Now that the mystery of my bio-father is solved, I need to investigate who he was and what was his family's health history. Do my personal traits reach back to his family? Do I look like him? Does my personality in some way match his or his family's? My looks? My health? So many questions and now I am in earnest to learn all I can. I am rising from the abyss of not knowing and believing I would never know the truth.

Within weeks of finding out this information, I had already seen pictures of my bio-father, who I do not look like. However, I do look a lot like his brothers and sisters. In fact, my youngest son looks a lot like Frank's oldest brother. It is funny how DNA gets mixed up and spits out a variety of concoctions which form each of us into unique individuals. I was excited to meet my new niece and one of my nephews prior to traveling to Florida to meet my new sister, Fran. I can see similarities in my looks with my newfound niece and nephew. When I went to Florida to meet Fran I was worried about how our meeting each other would go. I had absolutely no reason to worry! Fran was wonderful and the two of us hit it off immediately, and the three days we spent together were filled with conversation, and finding out about each other.

Since our discovery, I have already met Fran and her three children who are my niece and two nephews. Recently I hosted a picnic where Fran and two of her children and a grandchild attended, as well as a first cousin. I look forward to our continued discoveries about each other. Yes, I am blessed!

Barb and Fran

Chapter 25: Last Thoughts

I will never regret that I searched to uncover my mother's secrets. I am very blessed that I just happened to be in the Adult Psychology course and the National Writing Project at the time of my mother's health decline and death. The documents I created helped me analyze exactly why she could not bond with me. I do not believe she was hard-wired to not love. I believe the baggage she carried in her life shaped who she was. Her abandonment issues, and lack of attention and nurturing when she needed it most, left her a hardened woman. She continually searched for love, and being rather naive, fell into the trap that many young women do. She gave her heart and her body, but each time it backfired and she was left without the one thing she wanted: lasting love. Her carefree life with no accountability also became a reason for her downfall. When she became a married woman and a full time mother, the responsibility and lack of freedom became overwhelming. She didn't know how to love or show her love. She became selfish in wanting to escape and care only for herself. Her marriage was one of convenience, but with the large number of children and responsibility, she shut down. It had become her pattern to disassociate herself with stress, whether this was a survival tactic because of her skin disorder, her lack of attention from her mother, or non-fulfilling relationships, we will never know. Her relationship with my step-father, Stanley, was also tumultuous. Poverty played a part in this, but so did his own need for escape from the responsibilities of raising a large family. Short tempers were always a threat that Stanley would remind her of her past sins, and set her into a tailspin of depression. One can only imagine the self-loathing my mother felt and her constant fear that her secrets would be revealed.

I thought carefully of what I wanted for this book cover. The photo of my mother which I used was one that as a child I thought was beautiful. I could never understand why it was torn up. I learned she had torn it up herself. It was a declaration of her self-loathing which she could never escape. For a time, her unhappiness needed to be placed on something, or someone. Selfishly she placed the blame for her unhappiness on me as I was the manifestation of all her mistakes and a constant reminder of her failures of the past which she wanted to forget. My accomplishments became thorns to her as these accomplishments could have been hers if her life had taken a different turn. At no time, do I believe, was she able to place the blame firmly where it lay: on her. I willingly took that blame and never fought the injustice of it. I only wanted to see her happy and feel her love. As I finally came to realize, she was unable to do that.

I will always love my mother; however, there were certainly many things that caused me to not like her. I don't think she ever understood the impact of her negativity toward me. Her past experiences became the baggage which forever haunted her and blocked her from enjoying life and her family. She never allowed herself to fully envelop herself in loving her children. Her decision to quickly relinquish three children without even holding them set the standard for not attaching herself to someone she had helped create. The decision to take me out the adoption process in order to secure a marriage was probably not helpful, especially since I was at an age of separation anxiety and screamed and cried at being torn from the only stability I had known. She may have wanted to bond, but my inability to bond immediately with her further drove her feelings of inadequacy and abandonment. Living in poverty and having five children to care for was also cause for her depression and withdrawal of emotional support for her children. Her only role model was her mother, who had her own demons to deal with after the death of two children prior to Dorothy's birth. Having to deal with a skin condition which was on public display made my mother feel inadequate and persecuted. The only thing she owned and had full control over were the secrets she kept, and she carried these sacred, yet tortured secrets, to eternity.

For me, understanding and accepting my mother's emotional and physical make-up allowed me to continue to love her, despite her inability to truly love me as other mothers loved their children. When my mother was growing up and throughout her adult life, her personality disorder was never diagnosed, nor was treatment ever offered. People were not diagnosed with personality disorders and depression in the 1940's and '50's. Left untreated, it was no surprise that my mother was constantly depressed and could not connect with those she should most love. She became narcissistic and her focus was on her needs, rather than the needs of her children, who mostly just wanted her love and care. When talking about my mother today, I can state factually what life was like growing up with her as my mother. I do not get overly emotional about it, as I had learned to be made of sterner stuff. Although her inability to express love toward me, or my children, was hurtful, I made the excuse that "that is just who she is." I knew that I would never allow myself to have this kind of relationship with my own children.

My husband never spoke a word against my mother throughout our marriage until after her death. He allowed me to support my mother's needs without questioning my need to do this, even though he knew his mother-in-law was not like other mothers. After my mother's death, my husband became more outspoken about what he had witnessed my relationship with her. He was very protective of me. When I was researching and finding myself in numerous dead ends, my husband said, "She cannot win, Barb. You deserve to win." Sadly, for a long time I felt my mother did win when her secrets were taken to her grave. It was a long journey in trying to uncover the lies she made to cover her uncertainties and the shame she felt. She was certain I would make the same mistakes she did and I believe she waited with great expectations that I fail. When I did not, she openly showered me with negative commentary that I "thought I was better than her." At some point in my adult life I realized she was jealous of who I was becoming, feeling she had been robbed of that opportunity for herself. She never allowed herself to truly feel pride in what I was able to achieve, or encourage me to reach for the stars she was unable to touch. I am thankful that I developed a resilient personality and did not repeat the mistakes she had made, or worse.

My research saddened me when facing the reality of her promiscuity and the repercussion it caused her, as well as to my sisters and me. I have come to peace with who she was and why she could not love me. I just feel sad that she never opened up to love me, or my children. It was her loss.

When I told my sons I was going to write this book my youngest son, who also writes, asked me about a title. At the time I was thinking of calling it "Her Three Mistakes." My son said, "Mom! You, Uncle Mike and Uncle Rick are not mistakes!" He is right. We are so fortunate that abortion was not an option and that Mike and Rick were able to be adopted and brought up by good families. For me, I was able to turn my childhood experiences into shaping a resilient personality which helped me succeed in life. Perhaps some readers of this memoir will be able to find answers within the pages of this book to answer why some parents are incapable of loving their children.

I experienced both heartaches and joy in this journey. I am fortunate to have figured out why my mother became the mother she was. Her baggage was heavy and burdensome and her struggle to keep it hidden from view took its toll on her life and relationships with extended and immediate family, especially me. She knew she could not answer any questions as to which man fathered Mike, Rick or me. Such a revelation was testimony that she had broken the religious and social norms and expectations of her day. Such admission would have further destroyed her self-esteem. While her behavior was a shocking discovery to me, there is heartbreak that once her cycle of promiscuity began, it was hard to erase that reputation. Despite the setbacks discovered while writing this book, I still found great joy. My joy is that I have two wonderful brothers and their families who have made my life so much richer. I was always happy with my own family and my sisters and their families. Now I have Mike and Rick and their families, who have made my life so very blessed. With my recent discovery of who my bio-father was, I now have a new sister, as well as another niece and two nephews. I will enjoy getting to know my paternal family. I now celebrate my family: Stanley's (my stepfather); Dorothy's, and Frank Faith's. My blessings have been greatly multiplied.

I feel that science, through DNA testing, has the ability to provide the answers about paternity my mother was unable to provide. My only hope for a truly "happy ending" will be that one day someone directly linked to Mike's biological father will take a DNA test and we will finally find the answers we seek for him. So many television shows are now focusing on DNA testing and helping birth parents and children and siblings to meet each other. *Who Do You Think You Are?, Genealogy Roadshow; Long Lost Family;* and *Finding Your* Roots are all shows which address bio-families getting together, or learning about your heritage. The shows have become increasingly popular, which is testimony to the importance of the genealogical research being done through DNA. Such research is what my brothers and I were dependent upon to find the answers we sought. In an effort to make our questions reality, I have uploaded Mike's, Rick's and my Ancestry DNA results to both My *Heritage DNA* and *Family Tree DNA* in an effort to try to match with more DNA matches. We are hopeful that one day soon we will get a match for Mike, and he, too, will learn who his bio-father was and perhaps meet paternal family members.

To readers of this memoir, I hope that you have found my story educational, informative and interesting. For those who were adopted, I am hoping you found support in your own search for your bio-families. For those who grew up in homes of dysfunction, I hope that this book has provided some insights as to how the dysfunction takes root, and that you can chose to not let it drag you down to repeat history. Make your own "paper roses." For those who know me, perhaps this book will give you some insights as to why I am so passionate about my own family. For me, this book has allowed to give voice to years of searching for answers. I am forever grateful to those who helped me through this journey.

Part 4:
Poetry and Prose
and Research

A collection of poetry and prose written by
Barb about her relationship with her mother

Chapter 26 Understanding Our Dysfunction

I have included the two papers I wrote for a graduate level Adult Psychology course I was taking, coincidentally the same semester when my mother passed. The course requirement was to write two papers, using the various theories we studied in class to analyze relationships. I chose to analyze my mother's and my relationship as the subject of these papers. I will forever be thankful that I chose this topic as the papers were valuable to me as they finally let me lay to rest my frustration, and yes, anger, with my mother because she was unable to love me. What I learned was that while I am certain she did love me in her own way, she was unable to show that love and affection because of the psychological damage done in her own life.

My papers may be useful to others who suffer such a relationship with their mothers. For me, it allowed me to forgive my mother as I learned to better understand the baggage she carried. Not only did I better understand my mother, but I better understood myself and the person I had become. My Kent State University instructor, Dr. Linda Rogers, made a notation on both of my papers, "I hope you turn this into a future work."

At the time I had no desire to pursue this further. It wasn't until I began uncovering the many secrets my mother had that I decided to pull up these papers and begin writing this book. Keep in mind, these papers were written in 2000, which was long before I located my two brothers, and learned about my real bio-father. Nonetheless, the papers were instrumental in helping me better understand my mother and realize it was through no fault of my own that she was unable to love me.

I am also including several poetry and prose pieces which I wrote during this same time for the National Writing Project Fellowship which I competed in the summer and fall of 2000 at Kent State University. I truly believe these creative writings helped me in sorting out my emotions about my relationship with my mother.

The selected titles are:

My Muse, a piece that reflects on my childhood, specifically on the poverty. It shares my resilience theory in survival.

Clover Kingdom, a poem that reflects childhood memories. It shares a sense of escapism and imagination which are survival skills. It also shares the care and responsibilities of childhood and adulthood.

Mother and Child, a poem that reflects on my mother's and my relationship and my wish for a day of normalcy.

Wednesday's Clock, a poem that reflects on one day when I felt my mother and I had a normal day as mother and daughter, then my mother's unexpected death.

I believe God works in mysterious ways and I was meant to take both the Adult Psychology class and participate in the National Writing Project fellowship during this time of my life. Both classes helped me focus on the relationship with my mother, and my coming to terms with why she could not love me

My Muse: Rags to Riches

by Barb Baltrinic

June, 2000

Rags to riches—that's my life, my background, my heritage. The oldest daughter of five, I was often robbed of my childhood. Poor families have few frills in life and children become necessary helpmates to bring some sense of equality on the social ladder. Children became the maids, the shoppers, the nannies and the gardeners. I was often cast in these jobs and carried my duties seriously throughout my childhood. I still remember grocery shopping for seven people. I would tug the chrome cart to the local grocery store. My fear was that as it sat unattended in the front of the A&P someone would take it and I would be left carrying armloads of canned groceries home the mile stretch to my home. Canned milk, canned vegetables, bagged rice and beans, Rinso laundry soap (complete with free towel inside) and hamburger meat (three pounds for a dollar) were among the staples I'd haul home each week. Winter shopping was always more challenging as I tried to pull the overweight cart through the slush of the sidewalks.

322

Laundry was a duty I took over at a very young age. One of my scariest memories was running the wash through the wringer and swiftly pulling my hands back fearing they would be sucked into the pressing cylinders. Each load required one trip through the wringer into the rinse water, then another trip through the wringer before hanging the clothes. The relief I felt after escaping the wrath of the wringer was soon exhausted by my seven year old frame climbing up and down off a chair as I hung laundry to dry on the line, outside in the summer and in the basement in bad weather.

We had a coal furnace until I was twelve. Often I would have to fill the coal bucket from the bin, a dark, cold and frightening room whose only light was from the coal chute opening. I would open the furnace door and feed the hungry mouth shovelfuls of coal, careful not to drop any, and fearful that I would get burned from the hot door or from the flames which licked anything reaching inside its mouth.

Going out to dinner for us meant sitting in the family station wagon eating a fifteen cent McDonald's hamburger. What a magnificent treat this was. If Dad had worked overtime we could count on stopping for a dime cone at the custard stand.

Hand-me-down clothes were the norm, with only two new dresses to start the school year, and if money was available, one at Easter. There were advantages of being the oldest. Often I would get a "special occasion dress," for some event which of course meant that this artifact would be saved for that same event for each sister to follow. My tall and spindly form meant my special occasion dresses were usually bought larger than my size so that when my younger, but more substantial sisters inherited the frock it would be suitable for their bodies. The dress would be passed through the succession of G_ girls, and hanging in an odd array of angles dependent upon each girls' body shape. Five girls but none of us look alike or are built the same. This made it problematic when clothing was passed down.

I sound rather foolish when I tell anyone this, but I had no idea we were poor. It wasn't until Gloria, a fifth grade classmate was making a classroom presentation on a topic which I can't even remember. All I do remember is when she used me as an example of how poor people have very few nice things, like Barb. I could feel twenty four pairs of eyes all turning and looking at me as my face reddened while my mind tried to grasp how this newly announced for public information would change my life.

My poverty—this was my heritage. My parents were content with their lot in life and pushed for no more for their children. Their dream was that I would find a nice high school boy and immediately after graduation marry, start a family and continue living in the Cleveland ethnic neighborhood we called home. Despite my meekness as a child, I knew I wanted more. I wanted much more. I wanted a better life. Like the starving child of the Dickens's novel, I dared to say, "More, please!"

In life there are two kinds of gifts. While other children carried arms of beautiful bouquets of roses, I was handed toilet paper. Now those with the roses would find it quite amusing that some peers are stuck with toilet paper. I knew I was not going to allow the Glorias of this world sneer down their favored noses at me. Instead of sitting on the curb of life crying about my sorry lot, I carefully tore the tissue, folded, fanned, tied, and fluffed out each bundle, until I had created my own bouquet of paper roses. Those with the beautiful roses quickly found that the flowers withered and faded away. But my paper roses lasted a lifetime. My carefully crafted and created roses led me off to college and to waiting for the right man, a soul mate. They lead me to sacrifices which allowed me to get the home of my dreams. While others only held memories of once having beautiful roses, my paper roses continued to flourish and I had pride that I had made them from nothing.

My life is rich today. My bouquet of paper roses has given me a twenty six year marriage to a wonderful man. I have two healthy children who, occasionally, do admit they find me a tolerably ok mother, a fine home, and the means to give a better life to my children. I cherish a small photo album documenting this journey from rags to riches. It is my muse which inspires me to remember the life I had, and the life I now enjoy. Yes, I've gone from rags to riches, and I still make my paper roses.

The Clover Kingdom
by Barb Baltrinic

July 6, 2000

A castle made of clover chains
Harvested from strong neighborhood stock
Each clover carefully tied beneath the white flower
Chained, then strung to mark the perimeters
Of my dynasty, my kingdom
Only those permitted could enter
They bowed before me, the Clover Princess
My robes of clover chains flowing in the breeze
I had complete control of my small kingdom
Beneath the cool leaves of the sassafras tree
In the corner of our yard

But, an attack sometimes interrupted my peace
A wayward princess, angered that my kingdom
Was far more magnificent than hers
Would tear away the chains
As she attacked my floating walls

Maternal Failure

Laughing in delight as clover chains broke
Draping over her retreating form
Leaving me to stoop and restring
Reshape my kingdom into a grander fortress

Parents would also usurp my power from time to time
The Queen commands me to duties within the capital
Unprotected, my wilting castle walls collapsed
As lawn was mowed by roaring dragon
Driven forward by the strong and mighty King

Years later, the King and Queen are left powerless
I have complete reign now
My father rests hillside
Overlooking a pond
Where geese move to pluck away flowers I leave
On headstone proclaiming the dates of his domain
Beside him, my youngest sister lies
She lost her kingdom at too young an age
Clover chains are left above her marker
A reminder of those days gone by
My mother, no longer able to rule
Is now dependent upon me
I still perform the duties of the capital
This time, without command

I did not ask for complete power

I was happy in my corner of the kingdom

With clover chained castle walls

Beneath the sassafras tree

I would gladly relive just one day

Of independent bliss

Where the clover chains flowed in the summer breeze

With a younger princess laughing as she attacked

And the clover castle walls were once again rebuilt

Mother and Child

By Barb Baltrinic

July 29, 2000

We are mother and daughter
But too much baggage remains
Terms of endearment can never have full meaning
A childhood of little love and affection
Is the glue of this relationship
No bonding, cuddling, or I love yous
Snickers, impatience, jealousies of achievements
That's what I most recall
No encouragement, instead, stumbling blocks
Carefully, purposefully placed in my path
Accusations of misbehaviors
That, had she really known me, were laughable
Today I see those words were directed at a child
A child she could only see as herself
Someone she did not particularly like
I became the embodiment of a punishable her
Accusations directed toward repeated mistakes

Mistakes she assumed I would make

She did not know me

She did not want to know me

I was not the stuff she was made of

I became her excuse for unhappiness

My existence was a constant reminder

Of her youthful errors in her own search for love

Her attempt to capture love ended

In a reason for his escape

Her embarrassment, bitterness and anxiety

Was, in her mind, my fault

Thus, I became her indentured servant

My payment, scraps of attention

An occasional kind word

A hint of normalcy

With each overachievement, I looked for acceptance

Instead I found jealousy and neglect

My childhood gave me skills

Typical family relations do not provide

With each stumbling block placed in my path

I carefully worked to overstep each one

Each time seeking recognition for hurdle jumped

Yet, none received

Maternal Failure

Instead, my accomplishments became her achievements
A mother who provided the world with motivated citizen
Unknown, even to her, my motivation was for love
A price she was incapable of paying

A new generation arrived
And still, she shared no maternal instincts
A protective lioness I became
Refusing my children my experience
Instead, I provided gifts, cards
Words of pride, all penned from Grandma,
Santa Claus, Easter Bunny, Tooth Fairy
And Loving Grandmother were part of the mythology
Life continued, a fractured fairy tale
Fictionalized normalcy, yet nothing changed

Today she is dependent upon me
I am parent to my parent
I am trying to provide to her
The very normalcy she denied me
I attend her needs, provide encouragement
I remove stumbling blocks from her path
Understanding and accepting who she is
As the minutes click away in life's clock
I wonder if before the final chime

Barb Baltrinic

She will ever really know me
And more importantly, love me for who I am

Wednesday's Clock

by Barb Baltrinic

October 7, 2000

It was Wednesday

I had worked all day

I had a meeting on the west side

Afterward, I would stop and visit

Wrap up loose ends

Make arrangements

She was coming home Friday

I planned a short visit

Thirty minutes, nothing more

I was tired and needed rest

The clock was ticking

She was alert, awake and happy

Visibly happy to see me

That was a change

She said, "I thought you weren't coming!"

She was sincerely glad I was there

She was somehow animated

Her hair had been freshly permed
I had paid to have it done
"Your hair looks nice, Mom."
She fans her fingers out to show me
I fake a gasp! "Red?"
She laughs in delight and tells me
Not since childhood had she had red nails
She loved the manicure
"Thank you for letting me get them done!"
The clock ticks, but I don't notice

We talk. About my day. My day?
That's a bit unusual. We then talk about hers
She did well at therapy
I enjoy listening to her progress
We talk about arrangements for Friday
She was coming home
She's not been there for over a month
First it was the hospital
Frightful dancing against death's threats
Then here, to gain back strength
She looks great
I'm unaware of the clock ticking

We talk about her responsibilities
She must tell me if she can't cope

Maternal Failure

She must tell me if she is afraid
She must tell me if things don't work out
If she tells me, we will look at a move
The clock ticks slowly
We can both hear it

She cries. Why? I ask
Don't you like it here?
She answers she does. The room is nice
It is like a smaller apartment than her own
She likes the wallpaper border
The people are nice
She knows the names of the attendants
She even shares some insights about them
We laugh together in conspired glee
A man sang "Love Me Tender" to her
She's made a friend down the hall
They play bingo together
She shows me her winnings
Chips, trinket box and mirror tray
I laugh with her at the big prizes
The clock ticks
I do not notice

She talks about my boys
I didn't bring up the conversation

She laughs about my eldest's testing of me
She praises my youngest son's attentiveness
We joke about the trials of kids growing up
We are mother and daughter
Sharing the stories of tenured parenthood
I look at my clock
Shocked
Ninety minutes passed!
I'm disappointed the hour is late
I'd like to stay later, but I can't
We review the plans for Friday
I kiss her goodbye, and tell her I love her
She tells me the same
This time, I feel she means it

When I return home I talk to my husband
I casually say, "I don't know who took my mother,
but I like the woman that was there tonight."
We laugh.
I'm unaware of the clock.

Friday, I race out of work
I shop for last minute food to stock her fridge
I wait. I'm anxious to see her.
I want to continue Wednesday's chat
Phone calls reveal a problem.

Maternal Failure

I'm not worried.
She's weathered this same storm before
She'll probably come home tomorrow.
My Wednesday will just be delayed.

Saturday, sister calls after a morning visit
"Her color is not good"
She'll stay over the weekend
She'll be home Monday
I plan to see her later that day
I work on dishes, I work on floors
I work on laundry
The call comes
She's being sent to the hospital
Same problem as before
I'm not worried
She's weathered this same storm
She'll be home Monday, I'm sure

The clock moves, I am unaware
I finish household chores
I call the hospital twice
"Stable" they say. I'm content.
I casually arrive at emergency
The doctor meets me
"Critical but stable."

What exactly does that mean?

Problems are the same we faced before

The clock ticks, but I vaguely hear it

I reassure Mom that this is routine

Same problem we had before

She relaxes, eyes calming with my reassurance

She rolls over in bed. Not for comfort.

This time, to watch me

I chat aimlessly. I look over my books

She asks for water. She can't have any.

I deny her request.

Doctors enter and leave, I am not concerned.

Doctors enter and leave, I am not alarmed.

Doctors enter, and stay. I panic.

I'm told to call family. I do.

I cannot talk. I try to remain calm.

I don't want my voice to break.

Her eyes study mine. The clock ticks

Each second beating loudly in my ears

It ticks, and I cannot raise my voice above it

It ticks, and I cannot stop it

I cannot force my voice to speak

The clock is far too loud

Family arrives and quietly talk.

We recognize the end is inevitable.

I feel like I am talking about a movie

A novel, a dry plot of some neglected book

I cannot stop this clock.

Decisions must be made.

She had signed off help before

The papers are all on file

I ask her again. She hears the fear in my voice.

She panics. She says yes!

Yes to respirators

Yes to CPR

Yes to life support

My heart skips beats

She knows. I know. We all know.

That damn clock knows

But it won't stop ticking

Its deafening sound fills my brain

Shortly after she seemingly falls asleep

Sounds like a soft snore

I bravely speak now, coward that I am

My tears drop on her cheek

I tell her I love her

I tell her I'm sorry for any wrongs

I tell her....what do I tell her?

Do I tell her that Wednesday was my best day?
Do I tell her that Wednesday I was a daughter?
Do I tell her that Wednesday she was my mother?
Do I tell her I want more Wednesdays?
I ask her if she can hear me. Touch my fingers.
Nothing.
The clock is ticking, but she can no longer hear it
But I hear it. It ticks louder
Louder
Louder
And I cannot soften it

They move her to a new room
Quieter, softer lighting, less hurried and frenzied
They change her into a clean gown
Her hair is smoothed and tubes are removed
We talk quietly, gathered around her
We must voice our decision
Respirator? No
CPR? No
Life support? No
I said no. She had said yes.
I denied her again
My mind says I did right
My heart asks how could I?
The clock's ticking bangs in my brain

Maternal Failure

She has a short struggle
I think she is uncomfortable
I rearrange pillows
That's not it
I ask for more medication
I don't want her in pain
Then, slowly, without struggle,
Without pain, she
quietly
stopped
time

The air remained quiet
Even the clock stopped
We each kissed her goodbye
Each left, silently,
Caught in her own form of grief
I stayed, signing papers
Handling decisions
Dealing with my own grief
Knowing Wednesday would never come again

Barb's papers for Adult Psychology

Taken from:

A Personal Glimpse into Attachment Theory and Its Implications on My Life

by Barb Baltrinic

October 14, 2000 (some modification in 2016)

When Dorothy was sixteen, her father, a strict disciplinarian and military officer, died unexpectedly during World War II. Dorothy was left feeling abandoned by him. She had a photograph of him which she constantly carried with her throughout her life. Dorothy was left to be raised by her mother who was dealing with her own emotional grief. Her mother had lost two children to typhus from their contaminated well. Her oldest son was off to war, one daughter was married, and Dorothy and her younger brother, Joseph, were left in her care. Conditions were poor, and Dorothy's feelings of abandonment from her father made her want to escape this home. She left high school early, and shortly thereafter, she was pregnant without benefit of marriage. The male child was given up immediately for adoption.

Two years later, she had another pregnancy, a male child, also put up for adoption. A second pregnancy gave her the status of a girl with "no values." Dorothy never revealed to anyone, other than those who knew of it when it occurred, that she had born two sons, nor did she ever discuss this with anyone. It was a subject not discussed openly with anyone, including her sister and brother, who knew about the two boys. The subject remained taboo.

Dorothy's search for love and the abandonment she felt first by her father, then by two different young men, had to have left Dorothy emotionally and mentally scarred. She wanted to be loved by someone. She was twenty three when she became pregnant with her third child. Once again, the father of this child did not want her for a spouse, and once again, she was abandoned. She opted to put her daughter, Barbara, born August, 1951, up for adoption. It was post World War II, just in time for the baby boom, and babies, particularly girls, were not quickly adopted. Barbara's first nine months were in foster care.

Dorothy met Stanley a couple of months after having given up Barbara. The two quickly married, and Barbara was taken out of foster care at nine months of age (May, 1952.) Dorothy never signed the release papers until June, 1953, after having given birth to her first "legitimate" daughter. Barbara had cried often as a baby (separation anxiety from the foster home where she had lived for nine months.) The screaming and crying further alienated Dorothy and kept her from being able to immediately bond with the child. Thus, Barbara grew to be a quiet child, mindful that her mother was not patient or affectionate toward her.

Dorothy's perceived her sisters-in-law as not liking her, and she easily withdrew from their attention, preferring to sit in the car when her husband visited his family. Not stepping into her in-laws' homes allowed her to refrain from disciplining or mothering her children. Using the excuse that others didn't like her was not only her perception, but an excuse to step away from the demanding role of motherhood. Babies continued to arrive every two years until the family consisted of five children and two adults.

A support system would be beneficial for such a large family, however, there was no support system as even her own family resented Dorothy's actions as a reflection on their family reputation.

Dorothy's embarrassment of having an illegitimate child was evident as she tried to cover her secret by writing over the year of her marriage as 1950 to make it appear Barbara had been born legitimate. Many outside the family thought Barbara was both Dorothy and Stanley's child.

At age five Barbara was formally adopted by Stanley so Barbara would have the same surname as Stanley. Dorothy was on guard to protect her secret from being exposed to the public. It was in 1965 that Barbara was told she was adopted by Stanley, only out of fear that someone else would tell her that her natural father had died. Barbara was thirteen at the time and asked some questions; however, Dorothy was not very forthcoming and made it clear that the topic was not to be discussed again. Ever.

As the family expanded to five daughters, Dorothy's resentment of Barbara grew. She represented the reason for her unhappiness. As a result, Barbara became a very quiet child at home, and the child who worked especially hard to gain the love and affection she wanted. Barbara was an overachiever, eager to do everything and anything to get her mother to love her. Barbara grew up without being able to show her own mother outward affection for fear of further rejection. She was reserved and quiet around her mother, kissing her on the cheek, but not giving hugs or verbal outpourings of love, and she received none in return.

Dorothy's relationships with her other four daughters varied. Each was different; however, the displays of resentment and dislike was Barbara's alone. It was not unusual to be physically punished and emotionally abused. As Barbara looked for any way to gain her mother's affection, she took over numerous household tasks without complaint at a very young age. She was the main babysitter. She did family shopping, no matter what the season, by pulling a cart to the local grocery to pick up canned and boxed goods, and ground beef. She walked to banks and stores to make payments on the family bills, and doing laundry at the local Laundromat. Despite the vital role Barbara had in being her mother's helper at home, she still never received the affection she sought. Barbara therefore became very active in school, seeking the positive attention in substitution for the love she did not receive at home. She worked hard on grades. She joined numerous clubs and activities, both as a way to make her mother proud, and to glean the benefits of attention she would get from club advisors and peers. Many of the clubs Barbara sought membership in required a vote of acceptance. These were the clubs she most highly sought, then worked for leadership roles in each. These voted upon recognitions validated, in Barbara's mind, her self-worth and provided for her a sense of positive self-image and esteem that she was a worthwhile and cared for person. Such recognition was a substitution for validation typically provided by a parent. Barbara's acceptance into the voted membership, and the voted leadership roles, provided positive self-esteem and Barbara hoped would lead to acceptance and pride from her mother. However, Dorothy was unable to express this, and at times, made negative comments about Barbara's involvement and time commitments.

Barbara was frugal in dating, fearful to have too strong of relationships as she did not want to make the same mistake her mother had made, fearful that history would repeat itself. She pledged to live differently and love differently.

Barbara went to college, paying for it herself, and continued the same pattern there. Dean's List letters were sent home, and Barbara would ask if they arrived, hoping for some congratulatory remark, yet these were meaningless to Dorothy. They had been tossed away as worthless mail. Barbara's college graduation was totally ignored. There were no congratulations, no card, and no comment for having completed such a milestone. As Barbara looked back on all of this, she realized that her achievements were things Dorothy felt perhaps she could have accomplished had Barbara not entered her life and changed it.

As an adult, Barbara married and had two children. She worked very hard to make certain she did not repeat the negative comments her mother had used on her. Dorothy was never able to bond with Barbara's children. She couldn't. While Dorothy was never rude to them, she showed no sincere interest in them. Barb's children became an extension of Dorothy's relationship with Barbara. Barbara made certain that gifts were purchased in her mother's name for the children, and still shared pictures and stories about the boys with Dorothy, trying to bridge the chasm which was their relationship. Despite Barbara's attempt to bridge this chasm, Dorothy missed the opportunity to learn how to bond, first with her own children, then with her grandchildren.

As time went on, Stanley passed away, and Barbara took over responsibility for Dorothy. Barbara moved her into an apartment near her and decorated it very nicely. As Dorothy's health began to fail, Barbara took over more and more responsibilities for her care. Dorothy recently told one of

Barbara's sisters that she realized that she lived as long as she had because of Barbara's care of her, yet she was never able to tell this to Barbara.

Two weeks ago Dorothy passed away. She was never able to tell Barbara how much she loved her. Barbara knows she did, but Dorothy had spent a lifetime not allowing herself to be close to the very people who will miss her most now that she is gone. Barbara firmly believes that her having surrendered two illegitimate children prior to Barbara's birth, and the lack of initial bonding time with her, combined with the guilt she felt of her many secrets, caused the lack of attachment Dorothy had with Barbara.

Looking at Attachment Theory: When looking over the above scenario it becomes obvious that had Dorothy received adequate counseling, her life would have been very much enriched through positive parenthood experiences. Such counseling was either not affordable, or practiced in the 1940's through 1950's when the majority of the damage had been done. If this same scenario were to happen today, numerous indicators would be recognized and identified. The client could receive counseling and assistance to make certain positive relationships were established with the children and an entire lifetime of regrets, misguided anger and resentment would be avoided. Dorothy's relationship with Barbara would have signaled problems even before Barbara's birth.

Problems in Prenatal Stage: John Bowlby is credited with the term "attachment" whereas, "people who are securely attached take pleasure in their interactions and feel comforted by their partner's presence in time of stress or uncertainty" (Shaffer 40). When looking at attachment with parent and children, he also stressed that this needs to be a reciprocal relationship as the child need to attach to the parent, and the parent needs to attach to the child. This bonding begins even before the birth process. If the pregnancy is unwanted, the alienation begins prior to birth. Other researchers (Sameroff & Chandler 1975 and Vaugh et al, 1987) found that babies of highly stressed mothers tend to be highly active, irritable, and irregular in their feeding, sleeping and bowel habits. If indeed Dorothy was feeling stressed, as would be expected with an unwanted pregnancy in the 1940's and 1950's, a time era where such behavior was socially unacceptable and a social disgrace, the child may well have developed these traits of irritability which are viewed as negative, particularly to a new parent trying to achieve bonding with a child already nine months old. Another researcher (Brockington 1996) determined that mothers who "have no friends or other basis of social support to turn to for comfort (138) are indeed stressed and are more likely to have babies who have the above mentioned behaviors, which could add additional stress to the bonding process.

Problems in synchronized routines: Barbara was in foster care (unknown as to consistency of foster care, or in how many homes Barbara was placed) for the first nine months of her life. When she was paced in Dorothy's home there was a break in the synchronized routines which caregivers and infants establish over the first months of life, as described by Stern, 1977, and Tronick, 1989. A break in such synchronized routines would create an irritable child, thus creating more stress in the bonding process once the child was placed in the permanent home.

Additionally, Dorothy and Stanley's synchronized routines were broken. They went from newlyweds to parents in seven months' time. One can only imagine the decision process and anxiety as Dorothy and Stanley determined whether or not to bring a child from a previous relationship into their home, a home already riddled with poverty, and lack of family support. Their first apartment was not much more than what could be described as a studio apartment by today's standards. The letter from the social worker indicates a suggestion is made to find a larger place where the new family could spread out a bit. One can also speculate that Dorothy was not totally convinced that this arrangement and marriage would work. Although Barbara was taken out of foster care in May 1952, it was not until June 1953, after the birth of Stanley and Dorothy's first child together, that the adoption files for Barbara fully negated.

Problems in Primary Attachments: According to Rudolph Schaffer and Peggy Emerson (1964) there are specific phases of attachments in infants. There is the asocial phase (0-6 weeks) where the infant makes little protest, and the infant begins recognizing familiar faces. There is the indiscriminate attachment of week 6 to 7. During this time the infant enjoys any and all companionship. Finally, specific attachment phase is 7 to 9 months. At this time the infant protests if separated from one particular individual. They become wary of strangers. It is at this time that Barbara was removed from foster care and placed in what appeared to be a stranger's home. The crying behavior would be typical of a child subjected to this trauma. Bonding, especially with a mother who had no contact with the child for nine months, would be very difficult.

Problems in Stranger Anxiety: There are numerous steps which are used to combat stranger anxiety.

1. Keep familiar companions available
2. Arrange for companions to respond positively to the stranger
3. Make the setting more familiar
4. Be a sensitive unobtrusive stranger
5. Try looking a little less strange to the child (410)

While these are excellent suggestions for helping a child overcome stranger anxiety, not only were these procedures not necessarily practiced in the 1950's, they were not practical for the situation between Dorothy and Stanley's removal of Barbara from foster care. The process was immediate. Once the adoption papers were placed in a holding file, the child was turned over to the natural mother. There was no counseling, there was no guided trial period, and there was no slow acclimation process.

The resulting crying and struggling of Barbara was a natural consequence of stranger anxiety. With a mother unfamiliar with bonding and motherhood, such behaviors could be further reinforcement of lower self-esteem and unworthiness as those felt during the pregnancy. Bonding would be difficult at best.

Recognizing the At Risk Traits for Insensitive Parenting: Depression can be a major risk factor in the primary caregiver becoming an insensitive parent. Rake-Yarrow (1985) and Teat (1995) researched and found that an identified diagnosis of clinical depression of the primary caregiver will most certainly produce an insecure attachment with the child. In the 1950's such diagnosis were not done, or even recognized, let alone provision of intervention. Insecure attachments make the caregiver not recognize the baby's social signals, and cause a failure to establish "satisfying and synchronous relationships" (416) with their infants. This was witnessed Barbara's inability to show overt affection to her mother.

Dorothy would no doubt have been diagnosed today as clinically depressed. She had a third unwanted pregnancy, she was hiding the knowledge of two other births prior to Barbara from everyone, and she was lacking support from her family as well as her in-laws. She had low self-esteem issues, which were inherent in the 1950's as her behavior was a major social taboo. Her child had not been adopted, this providing the image that she had not produced a child who was wanted or lovable by anyone else. Once the child was taken into her own residence, the child had separation anxiety, which could have been further interpreted by Dorothy as her unworthiness as a parent. Barbara was quiet and non-aggressive in showing affection to Dorothy. This was a learned behavior, as described by Campbell, Cohn and Meyer (1995) and Field (1988) as her inability to show outward displays of love and affection were reflected of the treatment she received from her own mother.

Another factor in being at risk for becoming an insensitive parent is if the primary caregiver felt unloved, neglected or abused as a child. Dorothy's own father had died when she was sixteen. He had been a strict disciplinarian. His sudden death at such an early age left Dorothy feeling abandoned. She carried his picture with her throughout her life. He may have abandoned her, but she never abandoned him.

Dorothy's mother was left with the task of dealing with two of her four children on her own under financial difficulties. Dorothy's own childhood home was also riddled with problems, thus Dorothy inherited problems from her own childhood, which she carried into her own role as a parent. She had few examples of positive role modeling of parenting from her own childhood.

Dorothy also had the difficult task of dealing with three men who rejected her as a spouse when she became pregnant with their children. Such rejection would leave her feeling unloved, neglected and abused as she was left to deal with the pregnancies on her own.

Stelele and Polack (1974) discovered that when such adults are faced with irritable, inattentive and fussy infants, the adult feels rejected again. Biringen (1990) and Crowell and Feldman (1991) also identified that such parents withdraw their own affection, and at times can also become neglectful and even abusive. Such behavior became a norm in Dorothy's household.

Ecological Constraints: Primary caregivers who face health and financial problems often become insensitive parents. Murray (1996) identified insecure attachments were highest among poverty-stricken families. Dorothy and Stanley were in this category. Stanley was a high school dropout, and had a minimum wage paying job. He also never sought to gain additional training which could have improved his position or wages. He preferred his free time to be spent enjoying his interests of fishing and hunting. Bettering his position for the sake of family obligations was never a consideration. Having a family of five children and working on his income alone, which had limited benefits, made life very difficult. Children were not taken to the doctor for check-ups, let alone for ailments, unless life threatening. Caring for sick children without the benefit of medical attention can add to the stress in the home, further enhancing depression and insensitivity as a parent.

The quality of spousal relationships can also have an effect on parent-infant relationships. Cox (1989) and Howes & Markman (1989) identified factors in unhappily married couples prior to the birth of the child as being indicators for problems with attachment after the child is born. Barbara was born prior to the marriage, but the marriage was not with the natural father, and Barbara was not brought into the home until she was nine months old. The marriage was in many ways flawed as the couple did not know each other well, Stanley's family did not accept Dorothy, Dorothy's family was not supportive, there was a six year difference in age which was substantial at ages 24 (Dorothy) and 18 (Stanley) in maturity and in recognizing societal reaction to their situation. Stanley would also use Dorothy's prior relationships as a tool to hurt her when arguments arose, thus furthering her fragile self-esteem.

Still, the research by the two studies mentioned above indicates that many of the same problems occurred: unhappiness in marriage causes insensitivity in care giving, there are less favorable attitudes toward the child and the role of parenting, and less secure ties with the child are established. It would appear that many of the now recognized risk factors of the home environment were well established by the time Barbara was placed in the home.

There was little, if any, intervention available in the 1950's to such at-risk parents, especially if they were plagued with financial restraints. Today there is support monetarily, with medical and utility and food needs, and there is adequate counseling available. There are also people who identify these at-risk problems prior to the birth of the child. Pre-natal service typically identifies at-risk parents and recommends assistance. Today school counselors are trained to identify and act as advocates of children identified in at-risk families, whereas in the past little interference was made.

Effects of Social Deprivation in Infancy and Childhood: The obvious question would be how Barbara survived such interaction with Dorothy, her primary caregiver? All studies indicate the children who lived under deprived conditions in early infancy tend to have many problems as they mature. Barbara has records of all well-baby visits while in foster care the first nine months. In the records a notation is made that Barbara is a "happy" baby. It would be assumed that she was in one foster care home where she had been able to estab-lish attachment, thus the obvious display of separation anxiety when placed in Dorothy's home at nine months. Because she had established bonding with someone in the early months of development, she did not suffer the recognized symptoms of children who are deprived of all early bonding.

According to research by DeAngelis (1997) and Hodges & Tzard (1989) children who are deprived of bonding experiences for up to the first two years of life can overcome this if placed with highly educated, affluent parents who foster adaptive de-velopment. This, too, did not happen to Barbara. Other studies show that children in this situation who receive individualized attention from responsive caregivers flourish. This did not happen either. It would have to be assumed that because of the care given to Barbara in those first nine months she understood what bonding was and sought to achieve it. She also found sub-stitutes to provide attention and affection. Such substitutes in-cluded aunts and uncles and cousins, who were kind to her, and later to teachers and peers. Barbara's substitution of affection further drove a wedge between Barbara and Dorothy. Dorothy did not want anyone else to love her daughter (as witnessed in the principal interview example cited in the reflective writing)

Through Barbara's search for attention and affection and her over-achievement, she was able to build her own self-esteem. This allowed her to break the cycle of inability to bond.

Barbara also vowed not to make the same mistakes her mother made (illegitimate parenting) as she did not want to repeat that pattern and have children left feeling unwanted and unloved. Later, Barbara made certain her own marriage was secure and financially stable prior to having children, thereby bypassing all the problems she had witnessed Dorothy and Stanley's relationship and struggles in raising their family. While Dorothy was unable to express pride in Barbara (i.e. Dean's List example) Barbara received recognition from countless other sources. She created her owns self-concept, realizing she had value, despite her mother's inability to verbalize or show this. Barbara had social acceptance, task/scholastic competence, behavioral conduct and some physical/athletic competence, which all attributed to a positive global self-esteem (Susan Harter 1982, 1990). While very quiet at home, Barbara became a leader in school activities and activities which required voted membership (National Honor Society, Student Council, girls' service sorority). The acceptance by these groups provided her the acceptance she sought. This pattern continued throughout Barbara's life, as did Dorothy's inability to express pride in these accomplishments.

Conclusions To Be Drawn: In conclusion Dorothy was bound to be an insensitive caregiver. She had all the at-risk signs from pre-natal stage throughout birth. She lived with guilt and remorse and never learned to bond with her child from infancy through childhood. This pattern never changed.

Barbara had to have had some boding experience from her very early months of development, thus allowing her personality to explore ways to achieve bonding with her mother. She sought recognition, which she thought would bring bonding. Instead, the offshoot was she built a positive global self-esteem which allowed her to achieve stability and bypass repeating the cycle of becoming an insensitive caregiver. She sought resilience in an environment which offered little support.

Works Cited

David R. Shaffer. *Developmental Psychology: Childhood & Adolescence, fifth edition.* Brooks/Cole Publishing Company 1999.

Creating a New Life Agenda for the Protean Self to Survive a New Reality: A Study in Resilience in Children

by Barb Baltrinic

November 12, 2000

Overcoming Stress and Trauma in Childhood and Adolescence: Why do some children not survive after childhood trauma? Some children cannot cope. Yet others have some ability to withstand the horrors of their youth and seemingly adjust well. Researchers refer to this ability as a child's resilience. Resilience is the term used "to describe a set of qualities that foster a process of successful adaptation and transformation despite risk and adversity" (Benard 1). Benard suggests there are strategies and personality traits which allow a person to succeed and function despite problems, trauma and dysfunction introduced in their lives. It is interesting that many adults need therapy to teach such strategies to them Studies indicate that between "half and two-thirds of children growing up in families with mentally ill, alcoholic, abusive or criminally involved parents or in poverty-stricken or war-torn communities do overcome the odds and turn a life trajectory of risk into one that manifests 'resilience'" (1). Benard also states that "we are all born with an innate capacity of resilience, by which we are able to develop social competence, problem-solving skills, a critical consciousness, autonomy, and a sense of purpose" (1).

Werner and Smith (1977) studied children at risk and asked, "Why are there, among the children and youth in this community, ...some who learned to cope, unaided, with great biological and environmental handicaps? Are they anomalies or invincible?" (Dugan & Coles 111). These children appear to have invulnerability, resiliency, and stress resistance.

This entire concept of resilience in children is something observed in numerous case-studies. Sometimes it is identified as resilience, sometimes as hardiness. Still others view it as an ability of the child to be "gifted" and able to overcome the obstacles. Others describe children with this ability as being "tricksters."

For adults there is always therapy and psychoanalysis to assist the adult who has lost sight of resilience strategies. There are also a host of self-help books, like Carol Orsborn's *Art of Resilience*, which offers a hundred strategies for those needing help in overcoming stress and obstacles. Such strategies include regrouping, spiritual guidance, relaxation, positive escapism techniques, and other such strategies. Adults have the advantage of approaching therapists and obtaining such self-help books as Orsborn's, but what about children? How do they cope?

Robert Lifton believes that all of us, whether adults or children, are fluid and many sided. He calls us the "protean self." He took this term from the Greek sea god, Proteus, who was able to take on many shapes with his fluid form." The protean self emerges from confusion, from the widespread feeling that we are losing our psychological moorings...But rather than collapse under these threats and pulls, the self turns out to be surprisingly resilient. We find ourselves evolving a self of many possibilities" (Lifton 1). He goes on to say that our resiliency strategies allows us to evolve and change into a new self which can better withstand the trauma, dysfunction and new realities we must face. While Lifton examined how man, as a being, has always adapted to the new realities he was forced to face, the same concept can be seen in children who face new realities in their life structure. These new realities are often the realization that their interacting with parents, family structure, and environment are not the realities of the norm. Instead their lives are filled with new realities which force them to do one of two things. The child will either remain fixed, unable to adapt or survive this new reality, or create a protean self, a fluid self, which relies on finding resiliency strategies which help him survive the new realities of life.

Identifying the Strategies of Resiliency in Children:
According to E. Virginia Demos, the child must be able to persist and continue trying to find a way to improve things or to return to a positive state. The child takes an active stance to overcome the obstacle. The child develops a collection of strategies to identify the obstacles, and what strategy he will use to overcome it (Dugan & Coles 4). Those children who chose to move forward and create a protean self, are those who identify resilience strategies which will help them deal with the new realities of their lives. Unlike adults who can consult therapists, or read self-help books, the majority of children pull from within to identify the very strategies necessary to help them in overcoming the obstacles in their new realities.

The Blessings of Being "Gifted": Alice Miller uses the term "gifted" when describing certain children with specific traits. She does not mean "gifted" as in owning talents in various multi-intelligence areas. She means some children are gifted in their resilience to overcome obstacles and trauma in their lives. Miller acknowledges that "every child has a legitimate need to e noticed, understood, taken seriously, and respected by his mother" (Miller 52). Yet in reality, this does not always happen. Some children do not bond with their parents and "the crucial significance of bonding has only recently been proved scientifically" (54). So, for those children who have not bonded with their parents, how do they develop healthy relationships when their initial and most important relationship, that with a parent, has been interrupted or is dysfunctional? These children tend to look for strategies available to them to make life bearable and tolerable. In order to survive, the typical family hierarchy is abandoned, and the child creates a new life agenda.

One such strategy is to look for ways of making life better for the adults. The child typically looks to "bring honor, glory, prestige to family, to help family gain social status" (59). Examples of such would be for the child to overachieve and be recognized for success which will bring happiness to the adults who are seemingly unhappy with the child. The child may believe that by bringing such honor and glory to the family, love will follow. In a family where the parent is incapable to bonding or showing affection to the child, the child will continue to feel he/she is never good enough as the achievements did not bring the desired love. A typical behavior to follow would be for the child to continue with looking for bigger and greater forms of glory and honor. This creates a personality trait called "grandiose." In this example, the grandiose personality of the child actually is a new life agenda. The child becomes a role model for the parent in hopes that the wanted affection and respect from the parent can be achieved. The child enlists the protean self to morph into a high achieving person which he/she believes will achieve the desired love of the parent

The Grandiose Personality Resiliency Strategy:
"The grandiose person is never really free, first because he is excessively dependent on admiration from others, and second, because his self-respect is dependent on qualities, functions, and achievements that can suddenly fail" (60). Some children with grandiose personalities face depression because they can never achieve the desired love and attention from their primary caregivers. This new life agenda is a way the child wants to improve his new reality, a household where the parent is incapable of bonding or loving the child. It becomes the child's reality which he tries to alter via a new agenda. Sometimes if the parent is still unable to bond or love, another new agenda is created, that which finds substitutes to give love and attention.

Sometimes the love and recognition earned from peers and other role models is enough to give the child the self-esteem necessary to be content. These children overcome the feeling of loss from the non-bonding with primary caregivers. "Our access to the true self is possible only when we no longer have to be afraid of the intense emotional world of early childhood: (81). The grandiose personality child who is capable of accepting his/her self-worth from the recognition of those other than primary caregivers, will be able to find his/her true self. He has put aside that intense emotional world of longing for parental acceptance. Thus, he develops a resiliency strategy which will allow him to be successful and happy in life. Miller goes on to say that the child must find support within himself in order to avoid becoming victimized by feelings of neglect (83).

One of the results of the resilient child developing a grandiose personality is that the child typically denies his childhood reality by living as though the availability of the parent could still be salvaged through the illusion of achievement (85). This means the child will continue his grandiose behavior always in hopes that someday a change will occur in the parent's attitude. The personality trait becomes a life-long resiliency strategy ingrained permanently in the child, thus his protean self is one of grandiose nature.

Opposing Values as a Resiliency Strategy: Another resiliency strategy is when older children attract themselves to new values, often opposed to those of the parents. Often this is done to get love and admiration from other groups since the parents are unable to provide the emotion desired by the child (83-4). By opposing the value system of the parent, the child is outwardly seeking approval from substitute figures who can provide the wanted affection, attention and recognition the parent figure is unable to provide. This protean self creates a new reality, a reality he can live in and survive in, and not repeat the patterns of the parents.

Confronting the Parent About Injuries Felt as a Resiliency Strategy: Another strategy, typically not seen until a child is old enough to communicate clearly to the parent without fear of physical repercussions, is that of the personal confrontation. When children are older they can confront parents about injuries felt. Parents can acknowledge what was done and apologize. Thus, the chains of "neglect, discrimination, scorn, and misuse of power (91) can be cast off and healing can begin. Unfortunately, if a child tries this strategy when the parent is still able to wield power over the child, it can further damage the self-esteem of the child. "Disrespect is the weapon of the weak and a defense against one's own despised and unwanted feelings, which could trigger memories of events in one's repressed history" (91). Thus a parent confronted by their child who is trying to relate his need for building self-esteem, and the need for the parent to acknowledge his or her part in damaging that self-esteem, may not e able to accept yet another confrontation. The resilient child tries to express what he views as abuses with hopes that the parent's acknowledgment will break the cycle of abuse and neglect. Unless the parent is willing to accept this confrontation as an opportunity to break the cycle of abuse and neglect, it will only provide an opportunity for further deepening the dysfunction.

Personality Traits of the Resilient Child: Cognitive skills and styles are consistent with stress-resistant outcomes. Werbner and Smith (1982) found resilient adolescents to have better verbal communications skills, were reflective, and had impulse control. Garmezy (1981) found that intelligence and competence were necessary for resiliency. Werner and Smith (1982) found resilient adolescents scored higher on California Personality Inventory in responsibility, socialization, achievement via conformance and communality than those who were not resilient(Dugan & Coles 111). Resilient children could regulate impulsive drives and delay gratification and maintain future orientation and were viewed as cooperative, participatory and emotionally stable children as found by Garmezy in his 1981 study.

Relating the Resiliency in Children Theories to Barbara: Barbara's survival and positive adult life was because Barbara ha resiliency traits which allowed her to develop positive self-esteem. Barbara's personality and resilience strategies allowed her to survive. She had to create new agendas in order to live in the new reality she was given. In traditional families children were loved by parent and valued. Their self-esteem was enhanced through a supportive family structure. Barbara's reality was different. In order to survive, per protean self had to emerge and change, creating a new life agenda which would provide for her the necessary love, attention and recognition she needed in order to survive and become a successful person.

E. Virginia Demos' definition of resilience states that a child takes an active stance to overcome obstacles. Barbara did this. She developed a grandiose personality in an attempt to take on challenges in order to bring honor and glory home in an effort of earning positive recognition from her mother. Barbara did this first by taking over home responsibilities including shopping, cleaning, and child care chores. When Dorothy was unable to provide the feedback Barbara needed, Barbara was flexible enough to find substitutes who would provide positive assurances of her self-value and worth. By seeking acceptance in clubs which had voted membership, Barbara earned the affirmations that she had value as a person. This building of Barbara's self-esteem provided her the opportunity and confidence to continue seeking recognition.

In a situation which appeared hopeless and where the child was destined to grow up set to continue the cycle of dysfunction, Barbara was able to overcome the odds and find resiliency strategies and not use the escaping route through chemical abuse, suicide, or other negative escapism channels. As an adult, she created a "mythology" (as seen in the poem "Mother and Child) where she purposely tried to break the cycle of dysfunction

Barbara would fit Alice Miller's description of "gifted" as she was able make a better life for her mother as witnessed by moving obstacles from her mother's path ("Mother and Child") and decorated her mother's home and cared for her after Stanley's death. Barbara also brought home honor and glory from school awards and later as a motivated citizen, which allowed Dorothy to feel she had "achieved" by having a daughter with accomplishments. The grandiose personality traits developed by Barbara as a child have continued throughout life, thus giving her resiliency skills which she continued to use throughout her life. Barbara also fit Werbner and Smith's profile of a resilient child who has good verbal communication skills, is reflective, has impulse control, and could score well on the California Personality Inventory. She is responsible, social, regulates impulsive drives and delays gratification and is future goal oriented. She is cooperative, participatory and emotionally stable. It is the accumulation of these skills which allowed Barbara to develop the grandiose personality which became her major resiliency strategy in battling the dysfunctional relationship she had with her mother. She had a new agenda in her new reality.

Another resiliency strategy Barbara developed was that of adopting values different than her mother's. Barbara was determined not to make the same mistakes as her mother. Thus, she recognized the mistakes at a young age and resolved to practice and nurture values which would avoid mistakes made by her mother. By practicing delayed gratification and impulse control, responsibility and emotional stability, Barbara was able to create a new agenda which would not repeat Dorothy's choices When Dorothy was abandoned first by her father, then by three different men who left her pregnant and unmarried, Dorothy made choices which left her unable to bond with own child. Barbara was able to recognize that the cycle of being an inattentive parent could and would continue with her own children if she did not actively remove the obstacles which had caused her own mother to not bond with her child.

As witnessed in the research, resilient children continually try to salvage their relationship with their parents and long for normalcy. Barbara did this right up to her mother's death ("Wednesday's Clock.) Barbara continued to hope for a change in her mother's attitude.

One resiliency strategy which Barbara was never able to perform was that of confronting her mother. If Barbara had been strong enough to confront her mother with all the truths of their relationship, could their relationship have been salvaged years ago? Barbara was never able to confront her mother (Wednesday's Clock) as the years of fear of further rejection kept her from communicating her feelings. Barbara's fear that Dorothy was so overwhelmed with her own self-loathing she would only see the confrontation as yet another abandonment and withdrawal of love and support, albeit from the very child she had long since abandoned emotionally, thus furthering deepening the chasm which was ever present between her and her daughter.

In Conclusion: Children do not always have the advantage of receiving counseling and therapy at a young age, nor reading self-help books to identify and put into effect resiliency strategies. Yet somehow, internally, they figure out these strategies on their own. Research tells us that between half and two-thirds of children have some inherent strategies they can call upon to help them survive when their new realities of a dysfunctional home, non-attentive parents, trauma or stress enters into their live. Some researchers believe it is our nature to use our protean self to adapt and survive the changes life sends us. It is known that specific personality types are more readily able to call upon these resiliency strategies in order to make a new agenda to make life more bearable, and to build a positive self-esteem needed to feel value as a human being. From where this comes and how children learn to use these skills is still under investigation. Typically, once children master these strategies they can carry them into their adult lives. These strategies continue to help them survive all new realities they face as they know who to create new agendas for themselves and how to survive.

Resilience theory is, no doubt, that part of our human makeup which falls into the category of survival techniques. Without the ability to use our protean self, the ability to create new life agendas, and the ability to identify the new realities we face, we could not survive.

Works Cited

Bonnie Benard. "Fostering Resilience in Children. <u>Parenthood Web.</u>. EDO-PS-95-9 August 95.

Timothy F. Dugan, M.D. and Robert Coles, M.D., editors. <u>The Child in our Times: Studies in the Development of Resiliency.</u> Brunner/Mazel, Inc. New York, 1989.

Robert Jay Lifton. <u>The Protean Self: Hujan , Resilience in an Age of Fragmentation.</u> Basic Books, a Division of Harper Collins Publishers, New York, 1993.

Alice Miller, translated by Ruth Ward. <u>The Drama of the Gifted Child: The Search for the True Self.</u> Basic Books, Division of Harper Collins Publishers, 1994.

Carol Orsborn. <u>The Art of Resilience: 100 Paths to Wisdom and Strength in an Uncertain World</u>. Three Rivers Press, New York. 1997.

Elaine Shaw Sorenson. <u>Children's Stress and Coping: A Family Perspective.</u> The Guilford Press, New York, 1993.

Acknowledgements

I give Dale Pease, of Walking-Stick.com, my heartfelt thanks. His continued support and professionalism in cover design and formatting my books is greatly appreciated.

To Dr. Linda Rogers, my instructor for an Adult Psychology class in 2000, prompted me to consider turning my papers for her class into a larger work. Linda, it took eighteen years, but I finally got there.

I am so very thankful of Michael Baltrinic, my husband, who was not only my first proofreader, but unbelievable partner in my research. To Christy Shula, Jennifer Caldwell and Sarah Hamlin, thank you for the hours spent on proofreading and editing my book and providing positive feedback throughout the process.

Of course, I would be amiss if I did not thank my two brothers, Mike and Rick, who I only met in late 2013, and my sister, Fran, who I only met in November, 2017. It was my brothers who encouraged me to write my story. You, and your families, have all enriched my life and brought joy to my family and me. Even if we were not related I would find your friendship a valuable asset to my life.